The London Years

The London Years

by Rudolf Rocker

Translated by
Joseph Leftwich

F. ROCKER

AK PRESS
EDINBURGH · OAKLAND · WEST VIRGINIA

www.fiveleaves.co.uk
www.akpress.org

The London Years
Rudolf Rocker

Translated by Joseph Leftwich

This edition published in 2005
by Five Leaves Publications,
PO Box 81, Nottingham NG5 4ER
www.fiveleaves.co.uk, info@fiveleaves.co.uk

and by
AK Press, 674a 23rd St, Oakland,
California 94612-1163
www.akpress.org

First published by Robert Anscombe & Co. Ltd.
for the Rudolf Rocker Book Committee in 1956

(c) Fermin Rocker
Introduction (c) Colin Ward

ISBN: 0 907123 30 9 (UK)
1 904859 22 4 (US)

Five Leaves acknowledge financial support from
Arts Council England

Typeset by Four Sheets Design and Print
Printed in Canada

This book is an abridgement from the memoirs of Rudolf Rocker and
translated by Joseph Leftwich. Despite every effort we have been unable to
trace the estate of Joseph Leftwich to acknowledge copyright for the
translation. If notified, the publisher will be pleased to rectify this in
subsequent editions.

This new edition of Rudolf Rocker's *The London Years* is published by
permission, and in memory, of Fermin Rocker, who died as it was in press.

Contents

Introduction

Rudolf Rocker was born at Mainz on the Rhine on March 25th 1875. His parents died during his childhood and he was brought up in a Catholic orphanage. Influenced by his uncle, Rudolf Naumann, he was drawn towards the underground socialist movement but was repelled by the rigidity and authoritarianism of the German Social Democratic Party. "It was clear to me," he wrote of this period,

> "that socialism was not a simple question of a full belly, but a question of culture that would have to enlist the sense of personality and the free initiative of the individual; without freedom it would lead only to a dismal state capitalism which would sacrifice all individual thought and feeling to a fictitious collective interest."

It was this perception that determined his lifetime adherence to the anarchist movement. After his apprenticeship to the craft of bookbinding, he wandered as a journeyman in the old German custom through several countries, making contact everywhere with the anarchists, settling in Paris in 1893, but coming to London two years later in order to unite and print anarchist propaganda intended for smuggling into Germany. In 1898 he was asked to take over the editorship of the Yiddish paper *Der Arbeter Fraint* in London, having learnt the language in order to start *Dos Fraye Vort* in Liverpool.

Two years later he began a further Yiddish monthly *Germinal* which sought "to acquaint its readers with all libertarian tendencies in modern literature and contemporary thought." How he managed, he reflected later, "to write both papers and to set one of them as well is still a mystery to me." From that time until 1914 Rocker was busy, not only with the weekly and monthly journals, but on the platform, both in the effort to organise the workers in the tailoring and baking trades, and in lecturing on literary topics to audiences at the Sugar Loaf public house in Hanbury Street.

On the outbreak of the First World War, Rocker and his partner Milly Witcop, were arrested and, as related in this book, she was imprisoned without trial while he was interned. For four years he was the spokesman of his fellow prisoners and the implacable defender of their human rights, fostering solidarity between them, educating them, making use of the miserable situation in which they found themselves to open their eyes to the worlds of literature and of social thought.

Deported to Holland at the end of that war, (for although for the British government he was an enemy alien, he had also been deprived of his citizenship by the German government), he returned to Germany during the brief revolution of 1919. He drew up the declaration of principles of the German syndicalist union FAUD. In a period of intense activity, after the murder of Gustav Landaur and the imprisonment of Erich Mühsam, Rocker

1

with Fritz Kater and Augustin Souchy, strove to rescue German socialism from the authoritarianism of the SPD and the KPD.

With the advent of the Nazi regime in 1933, Rocker left Germany with little more than the manuscript of the book he had been working on for years, *Nationalism and Culture*. In the United States, where he and his family settled, some of the Jewish immigrants who had heard Rocker's lectures in Berlin and London, introduced a small group of people on the West Coast to his manuscript, which finally appeared in 1937. His work had never attracted commercial publishers in English, but the Spanish revolution of 1936 led the London publisher Secker and Warburg to seek an introduction to anarcho-syndicalism, and the dutiful Rocker obliged. His small advance from the publisher was swallowed up by the translator's fee. His book made a permanent impression on the young Noam Chomsky, who as a boy used to take the train to New York to sit around in the office and bookshop of the Yiddish-language anarchist newspaper *Fraye Arbeter Shtimme* where it was serialised, and later found it "on the dusty shelves of a university library, unknown and unread, a few years later."

Rocker and his partner Milly Witcop (1877–1953) settled at the Mohegan Colony (an anarchist settlement forty-five miles from New York), where he gathered up the threads of his work and produced a stream of anarchist journalism in the Yiddish press, much of which was instantly translated for the anarchist journals of Mexico and Argentina. During the second world war he was designated an 'enemy alien' by the United States authorities and restrictions were placed on his movements. Even after the war, in his old age, he and Milly were 'investigated' and it was rumoured that they would be deported. Happily this did not happen, but the threat of it symbolises the whole course of Rocker's life. Obliged to leave imperial Germany in his youth, and deprived of his citizenship under the Bismarkian anti-socialist laws, deported from Britain after four years behind barbed wire, placed 'under protection' by the Weimar Republic in Germany, fleeing from Germany one step ahead of the Nazi security police, this mildest of anarchists was indeed a man without a country.

Some key events of London labour history are recalled in this volume. One is of the strike that broke out among the tailoring workers of the West End in 1912. Theirs was a completely different world from that of the "mass-produced sub-divisional sweatshop tailoring of the East End Jewish workers," but it became clear that strike-breaking work was being done in their area. So Rocker and his colleagues called a meeting in the Assembly Hall in the Mile End Road, to demand a strike. Over eight thousand attended and another three thousand gathered outside. The strike grew from a sympathy strike with the West End tailors into a demand for the ending of the whole sweatshop system.

During the tailoring strike the London dockers were also on strike. Joint meetings had been held and when the dock strike dragged on after the victory of the tailoring workers, and the dockers' families were suffering rank want, Jewish families offered to take in the dockers' children. They came "in a terribly undernourished state, barefoot, in rags", and over three hundred of them were clothed, fed and housed by Jewish families, themselves poor, in Stepney and Whitechapel. This was the real triumph of Rocker and his associates.

In twenty years of Yiddish propaganda and education, they had welded the friendless and unorganised Jewish immigrants into a proud and culturally active community, able despite a hostile environment to take their own place in the society around them.

Rocker died, aged 85, in 1958. I remember speaking at meetings both at the Workers' Circle in Alie Street to celebrate the original publication of this book in English, and at Toynbee Hall in Whitechapel to commemorate his eightieth birthday and his centenary, and being told by people with tears in their eyes, "Everything I am, I owe to Rocker."

If the fascinating story before you arouses further interest or curiosity, I should advise readers that the fourth edition of his massive book *Nationalism and Culture* and the 1989 edition of his *Anarcho-Syndicalism* are still available from Freedom Bookshop in London, while his son Fermin Rocker the artist, celebrated his own ninetieth birthday in 1998 with a London exhibition of his paintings, and with the publication by Freedom Press of his delightful memoir *The East End Years: A Stepney Childhood*.

But Rudolf Rocker's own story, that of an immigrant, deprived of citizenship in his country of origin, and deported from Britain after years of internment, has its own message for another generation struggling with the dilemmas of a multi-cultural Britain.

Colin Ward

Author's Acknowledgement

My friend Max Nettlau was always urging me to write this book. When I returned to Germany in November 1918 after an absence of 26 years Nettlau was living in Vienna. But he often came to Berlin, so that we not only corresponded regularly, but also met quite frequently. He started urging me already then to write my memories. How could I? We were living in the midst of a revolution. I was on the go all the time. I never had time to write. The present kept me too much occupied to be able to set down what I had experienced in the past. Nettlau realised that. Yet he kept urging me to write down my memories, at least the rough material for a book that I would do later on. At the beginning of 1923 he wrote to me:

"Collect your material. Put it in writing. All the important things you remember in your life. You can write it up later, when you get more time. You have had such close contacts with the leading people in our movement. Your long activity in the Jewish Labour movement is an important piece of history, about which little has been written. That alone should be enough to persuade you to start work on the book at once."

My friend Nettlau was an historian. As the author of *The History of Anarchism*, the *Life of Bakunin*, and other works he knew the importance of not letting historical material get lost. He knew how easy it is for people to pass from the stage without leaving any records of what they had known about the events in which they played their part. I knew he was right. Yet I could not find time to write down even the notes for a later work. I doubt if I had remained active in Europe whether I would have found any opportunity to write this book. But when Germany opened her doors to Hitler's Third Reich a phase of my life came to an end. I started a new exile. I went out into the future with no idea of what it would be like.

Milly and I were fortunate to have been able to escape from Germany. We spent about six months in Switzerland, France and England; then we went to the United States of America. We came to New York in September 1933. I hadn't been in America more than a fortnight when I received a letter from Nettlau. He urged me again to start work on my memories. He wrote:

"No one knows when you will be able to go back to Germany. From all I can see it will be a very long time before the present system in Germany is overthrown. How it will come about it is impossible now to foresee. This is the time to write your memories. If you don't do it now you may never get the chance. You are no longer a youngster, my dear Rocker. You are now at the age best fitted for such a task. Don't let the opportunity slip. It may never come again."

I wrote to Nettlau that I would do it. He was delighted. But I couldn't get down to it. I spent the first six years of my stay in America travelling from coast to coast, lecturing, from the Atlantic shore to the Pacific, from Mexico to Canada. It left me no time for writing a book. But I started work on it at

4

last. There were many interruptions; I kept being called away to do other things. But I had begun; and I went on. The work gave me great joy. Now I could no longer leave it alone. I was sorry each time I had to put it aside to do something else. But I kept adding page after page. The first seven chapters were completed in Towanda, a small town in Pennsylvania, where Milly's sister Fanny and her family lived. It was a quiet little place, which gave me more time for writing than I had in the rush of New York. I got into the full swing of writing it when I found I was getting too old to undertake more long lecture tours. In 1937 I went to live in Mohegan Colony, a small international settlement forty miles from New York. There I was able to complete this book.

Author's Foreword

The history of the Jewish Labour movement in Britain is an integral and an important part of libertarian socialist history. It should be better known. The reason so few people know about it is without doubt the fact that it conducted its activities, its meetings and its publications in Yiddish, a language that was hardly understood outside its own circles, especially as its alphabet is Hebrew, and even the characters are therefore strange. But the movement did a great work for decades. It was not only the most powerful immigrant movement that had developed in Britain; its membership was larger than that of the native libertarian movement in Britain, and it was able to do things beyond the possibilities of the English comrades. The mass meetings of the Federation of Jewish Anarchists in the Great Assembly Hall in Mile End and in the Wonderland in Whitechapel were attended by thousands of people, five, six, seven thousand.

My first contacts with this movement, which was at first a completely foreign world to me, were in Paris, where I saw for the first time the *Freie Arbeter Shtimme*, which appeared in New York under David Edelshat's editorship, and the *Arbeter Fraint*, edited in London by Yanovsky. Of course, I was not able to read these Yiddish papers at that time. Their Hebrew characters were as unintelligible to me as Egyptian hieroglyphics. If anyone had told me then that I would a few years later be the Editor of the *Arbeter Fraint* I would have laughed at him. I would have said it was impossible.

When I arrived in London on January 1st, 1895, my first thought was to find employment, to earn my living. Several months passed before I succeeded. It was not till then that I could find time to pay my first visit to the Jewish comrades in the East End ghetto. It was a Friday night. The Jewish comrades held their weekly meetings at that time in the Sugar Loaf public house in Hanbury Street. I repeated my visits quite frequently. I joined in the discussions, as I had done in Paris, and soon made a number of friends among them, David Isaacovitch, Kaplan, Frumkin, William Wess, Doris Zhook, and Baron. There were many thousands of Jews living in this great London ghetto; they had left their old homes in Russia, Poland and Romania because of the oppression and the pogroms. In London they found entirely new conditions, to which they had to adapt themselves. They had to learn new trades. Large numbers went into tailoring, and built up the big tailoring industry in the East End. But they were immigrants; they did not know the language of the country and its ways; they were poor, and ready to work under any conditions, for as little pay as they got, so as not to starve. They had no experience of trades unions, and no knowledge of an organised struggle for economic betterment. They were an easy prey to exploitation. The result was the sweatshop system.

That gave rise to the libertarian movement among the East End Jewish workers, and determined its unique character. It had to be more than an

6

ideological movement. It was born out of desperate needs. The Jewish comrades had to combine ideological discussions with an effort to organise the Jewish working masses. They started Jewish trades unions. They built contacts with the general trades union movement in the country; they joined in the general economic struggle, and very often they took steps to initiate the struggle. Besides that they tried to provide for the cultural needs of the Jewish workers. Most of the immigrants from Eastern Europe had grown up in the old Jewish religious traditions, and had no idea of the modern trends of culture in Western Europe. Modern Yiddish literature was still in its beginnings. New horizons had to be opened for the Jewish working class. The movement took upon itself this educational task. The work was not easy. But it opened the doors for the movement to enter into a great many activities. It was the many-sided character of its work, and the self-sacrificing devotion of its followers that gave the movement its strength and enabled it to exercise such a powerful moral and cultural influence on the Jewish masses over a period of years. The movement was not limited to London. It had adherents and groups in Leeds, Manchester, Glasgow, Edinburgh, Liverpool, Birmingham, Hull, Cardiff and Swansea. They took our publications, the *Arbeter Fraint*, *Germinal*, and all the other literature we issued. More than that. Many of the immigrants went further afield afterwards, to the United States, Canada, Argentina, South Africa, Australia. Those who had been in our movement maintained their contact with London, continued to take our publications, and used them for their activity in the new places. I have met many old comrades during my later lecture tours all over the United States and Canada, in every place I visited, people I had known in England. It showed me how fruitful our activity in London had been in those early years.

There were few movements whose periodical and other literature was so widely spread in different countries as ours. It circulated in Paris, Berlin, Vienna, Lemberg, Bucharest, Sofia, Constantinople, Cairo, Alexandria, and it circulated illegally, through the Jewish Labour underground, in the Russian Czarist Empire, in Warsaw, Vilna, Grodno, Bialystock, Odessa. Our movement in London was a hub, from which spokes went out in all directions, to a great number of people, in all countries.

Only faint traces have been left in England of that movement which once, for decades, carried on such a useful and productive work, and achieved so much. The libertarian movement among the Jewish workers in Britain died not because its forces were spent, as with other immigrant movements, which developed abroad, and vanished, leaving no sign. It fell a victim of the First World War, when it had reached its peak. The *Arbeter Fraint* was stopped by the British government in the second year of the war, its printing press and administrative office were closed and sealed by the police, and those in charge were imprisoned. An attempt was made to revive it after the war, but without success. The conditions in the interval had completely changed. Many active members of the movement went back to Russia after the Revolution. Others, like myself, were deported to Germany straight from the internment camp. The movement had lost most of its best people.

There was little fresh immigration after the war, so that no new forces took their place.

Every immigrant movement depends on immigration; the Jewish movement in Britain more than others, because the great majority of the immigrants remained only for a while, and then went on to America and elsewhere, so that the movement could only be kept alive by fresh immigrants. Without immigration it was doomed.

But for the two world wars I believe the movement would still exist, for it had shown no sign of internal decay. It was killed by outside forces and events.

For two whole decades I gave the best years of my life to this fine and fruitful movement. I have never regretted it. They were unforgettable years for me. Some of my non-Jewish friends in London could never understand how I, who was not a Jew, could exercise so much influence over these Jewish workers. The explanation is simple. For twenty years I lived with them, lived as they did, shared their life, their troubles and their anxieties, their struggles, their dreams and their hopes for a better future. I took part with them in the fight for their daily bread. And I was able to pass on to them certain spiritual riches which brought some rays of light into their hard, drab, harassed lives. I gave them all I had to give, and I gave it to them gladly, for there is no greater joy than to see the seed one has planted sprout. They were devoted to me because they saw that I was honestly devoted to them, that I was working with them, at their side, as one of them.

Social ideas are not something only to dream about for the future. If they are to mean anything at all they must be translated into our daily life, here and now; they must shape our relations with our fellow-man. It was this kind of human relationship that placed its seal on all the strivings and aspirations of the libertarian movement of the Jewish workers in Britain, and made it such a fine and blessed thing. The comrades in the inner circle of the movement were like one big family, all friends and neighbours, bound together in one close common bond. This comradely relationship between them radiated further, and linked together the whole movement. It was only in that way that the movement could have attained that great influence which it had upon the entire Jewish working class in Britain.

People like to talk about the importance and the significance of certain persons in a movement, about their special gifts and abilities, and the way they were able to win the support of their followers. We must not exaggerate these things. We must never forget that the most important people in any movement are the ordinary rank and file, the men and women whose names are rarely mentioned, but without whom, without their tireless day to day work there would be no movement. I convinced myself of that during the many years I spent in the Jewish working class movement. I gave it everything I had, all my abilities as a speaker and as a writer, but without the loyal support of the mass of the ordinary workers I could never have achieved anything. I did all I could; but so did others. That must never be forgotten.

That this movement finally fell a victim to circumstances over which it could have had no influence is a saddening thought; but what it accomplished, culturally and spiritually, will always remain unforgotten. Not only individuals are subject to the risks and chances of life; movements are too. The important thing about a movement is not how long it existed, but what it did in the course of its existence, its creative work, the ideas it spread, the spirit with which it filled its followers. It is a great satisfaction to me that I have been privileged at the end of my life to produce this history of a wonderful movement, so that those who have no knowledge of it can learn about it. It may be symbolic that the task has fallen to me, who comes from a people which for twelve years endured the hell of the so-called Third Reich. The barbaric representatives of this political cannibalism not only hurled the greater part of the globe into an abyss of blood and destruction, but cold-bloodedly sacrificed six million Jews to their mad racialism, and so took upon themselves a guilt that can never be forgiven.

I hope the younger generation will learn something from my book. The veterans of the movement will re-live the old struggle, will recall their youth. I send them my greetings across lands and seas. I feel as closely bound to them now as in the days of our great aspirations, the golden dreams of our youth. Nothing is ever lost that is done for the great ideal of social justice, freedom, human brotherhood, and the liberation of all peoples.

Rudolf Rocker
Crompond, New York

Chapter 1

My First Jewish Encounters

I was walking along the Paris Boulevards with a friend one lovely Spring evening in 1893 when he asked me if I would like to go with him to a meeting of Jewish anarchists.

"Jewish anarchists?" I said. "Are there such? Are there Catholic anarchists? Protestant anarchists?"

"These are not Jews by religion," he explained. "They have as little to do with religion as we have."

"Then they are not Jews," I insisted. "Just as we are not Christians."

He told me that these were so-called East European Jews, from Russia, Poland and Romania, belonging to a certain ethnic group, who speak their own language, which has similarities with German.

I became interested. I had never heard of such people. I knew there were German Jews, who were like other Germans, except for their religion. I had no Jewish acquaintances myself. That was probably because in my native town, Mayence, all my friends and acquaintances were workers, and the Jews in Mayence were businessmen and shopkeepers and professional people. There was no antisemitic movement in Mayence. Any friction there was rather between Catholics and Protestants.

But there was antisemitism in the villages, especially in Upper-Hessen, which was at that time the centre of the antisemitic movement in Germany. There were large numbers of poor peasants in Upper-Hessen; the cattle trade in the area was for generations largely in the hands of Jewish families. The peasants grumbled about the Jewish cattle-dealers. It was thereabouts that the German antisemitic movement started.

Our whole socialist activity among the village population was to explain to the peasants the real cause of their poverty. It was not easy to do that, and it was often dangerous. The infuriated peasants, incited by the antisemites, often chased us out of the villages with sticks and cudgels. They were more ready to accept the stories of the antisemitic agitators about the Jews being to blame for their poverty. They wanted the Jews as a scapegoat. We were accused of being in the pay of the Jews. Socialism was of course branded as a Jewish movement. There was an anti-semitic song of that time, which went something like this:

Those who would all things overthrow,
Into the Jewish trap must fall.
The leaders of the socialists
Are Karl Marx and Lasalle.

So I had been denounced as a slave of the Jews before I knew any Jews. I wanted to meet these East European Jews, who were anarchists, like myself.

I went along with my friend to their meeting. It was held on the first floor of a cafe, that had been hired for the evening. We found there fifty or sixty people, men and women. I wouldn't have known them as Jews if I had met them casually in the street. I would have thought they were Frenchmen, Italians or Spaniards. Many of them could easily have passed as Germans or Scandinavians. A few looked definitely Mongolian.

I saw no one who looked like the Jews of the antisemitic caricatures, with big hooked noses. I had not yet made my study of the race problem then, but it was clear to me already that the Jews were no more a pure race than any other group of people.

I was interested in their language. It sounded to me like a German dialect which I couldn't follow, because every now and again they used words which were completely unintelligible to me. Yet after a while, listening carefully, I managed to get the sense of what they were saying. Then I discovered that I could understand some of the speakers better than others. I realised that their language was not uniform, but like other languages had dialects. There was one speaker whom I understood easily for a time; then came a flow of words and phrases that were absolutely strange to me. But my friend, who was Czech, understood him. The speaker was using a lot of Russian in his Yiddish, and Russian and Czech are both Slav languages.

Later, when I knew my Jewish comrades better, I learned that the group had been formed by some Russian-Jewish students in Paris, and that in its first years they had used only Russian at their meetings. As the group had grown, and had won more members among the Jewish workers, it was compelled to change over to Yiddish. That was difficult for the original members, who knew Russian better than they knew Yiddish. But their Yiddish gradually improved.

I became a frequent visitor at their meetings. They invited me to lecture to them, in German. I tried to speak a simple language, and they understood me. I got to know them also in their homes. It opened a new world to me, of which I had known nothing before.

I was struck by the fact that unlike the Jews in Germany, who were mostly businessmen and shopkeepers, doctors and lawyers and journalists, these East European Jews were workers: tailors, shoemakers, carpenters, printers, watchmakers and suchlike. Even those who had been at a University had learned a trade in Paris, and were earning their living in the workshop. Another thing that struck me was the large attendance of women at these meetings. They took an active part in the discussions, just like the men. It was taken for granted, as natural. I hadn't seen it in Germany.

One could talk with these women, and forget that they were women. Yet they were no blue-stockings, nor were they the kind of feminists who aped manliness. They were womanly, and 'motherly', but they were conscious of their own equality, and of their human self-respect. It added to their charm. Some of them, who had taken part in the underground movement in Russia, showed a certain puritanism, which reminded me of Stepniak's women in his *Underground Russia*.

11

My first Jewish friends were the Silbermans. They had a small tailoring workshop, where they two alone did all the work, because they considered it wrong, according to their principles, to use employed labour. They were simple, honest work-people. They had wandered in many countries. They had come from Jerusalem, and had lived in Egypt and Turkey and Greece, and for a time in America, before they had settled in Paris.

Rodinson and his wife Tanya were an altogether different type. They had both been students in Russia, and spoke Russian among themselves. Rodinson had been at school with Chaim Jitlovsky, the famous Yiddish socialist writer and theoretician. He was active afterwards in the Jewish nationalist movement. He had had to escape from Russia because of his revolutionary connections. When he came to Paris he had to learn a trade. When I knew him he was making raincoats. He had a nice home, where he had fixed up one of the rooms as a workshop. His wife worked with him. He was an intellectual, a fine man, absolutely honest, kindly and warmhearted. He was everyone's friend. The comrades had complete trust in him, and nothing ever disturbed it.

His home was a meeting place for the Russian emigres. On a Sunday afternoon you would always find there a dozen or so Russian comrades, Jews and non-Jews. The walls were hung with pictures of Russian revolutionaries, a big portrait of Bakunin among them. The comrades sat round the table talking, and drinking Russian tea. The Samovar which stood in the middle of the table was on the boil all the time.

Many of those I met there had spent some time in Siberia, some for years. Gordon had been exiled in Irkutsk for five years. He was an intelligent and likable man. His wife and he were very poor, and had a hard struggle to make a living in Paris, but he never complained. He had a brother in Paris, David Gordon, who was a Marxist, a Social Democrat, a good speaker, and an active socialist propagandist. Gordon and his wife were anarchists. But we were all good friends together. I had many fierce arguments with David, and often clashed at public meetings, but it never disturbed our personal relations. There was a great deal of tolerance in that circle, more tolerance than I had known in Germany.

Another man I knew among the Jewish revolutionaries in Paris was Solomon Rappaport, who became famous as Sh. An-ski; he wrote *The Dybbuk*. He was a life-long friend of Jitlovsky's. I first met him at the Rodinsons. This lank, lean man, with his pinched face, and sad, dreamy eyes rarely joined in our discussion. He sat listening to us quietly.

One day Rodinson told me that Rappaport was a bookbinder by trade, like myself. So I talked to him about our work. I told him I had a lot of difficulties, because my workshop was small and cramped, and I hadn't any good tools. He suggested that I should share his workshop. He said it would probably be no better than mine, but it would be helpful to work together. We could assist each other, and that would make things easier. I liked the idea. It would be something to have a colleague to talk to as we worked.

Rappaport was living in a poor attic, his workshop and living room combined. His tools were no better than mine, and neglected, not properly looked after. I found that he was not a good book-binder. He told me he had just picked up the craft, while he was living in Russia with a friend who was a bookbinder. He could do a plain linen binding, but he had no idea at all of the finer type of work.

I cleaned and repaired his tools, and I brought my own tools. We worked together for three or four months, till I got a job.

My friend Rappaport An-ski was a man of great talent, but extremely humble and modest. He was living in utter privation; you could not help seeing it in his appearance. He often lived on dry bread and tea. He never spoke to anyone about it. In company he was silent and retiring. But while we worked together in his room he lost a little of his shyness, and spoke to me about lots of things, mostly of course about the social problems in which we were both interested. He told me about the Russian Narodny movement (going to the masses) in which he had taken part, about his life among the Russian peasants and workers, with whom he had lived, to try to win them for the cause.

I was enthralled by his stories. He told them simply, with a natural gift of story-telling, and a natural love of the simple folk.

He longed to go back to Russia; when the Revolution broke out in 1905, and the Czarist government proclaimed an amnesty, he returned to Russia. He remained there till the Bolshevik Revolution. Then he left, and went to Warsaw. He died in Warsaw.

I also got to know Yanovsky in Paris. He was then editor of the Yiddish anarchist paper *Arbeter Fraint* in London. The comrades in Paris had brought him over to speak at a Yom Kippur meeting. He was an able journalist, and his paper had a great influence at that time on the radical groups among the Jewish workers.

I made many friends among the Jewish workers in those years. When the Nazi movement in Germany raised the Jewish question I felt that I must oppose my knowledge and experience of the Jews against that terrible barbarity. I lived and worked with Jews for a great many years. I never found them any different from other people. I never held that the Jews are the salt of the earth. But certainly they are none of the terrible things of which the Nazis, in their search for a scapegoat, accused them. Antisemitism has always been a weapon of the reactionary forces. A country is judged by its attitude and its behaviour to the Jews.

Chapter 2

London

It was a bleak, foggy morning when I arrived in London. It was like coming into a world of ghosts. Even the roar of the traffic was muffled. People flitted through the murk like shadows. There was a thick, clammy yellow mist over everything that damped my spirit, and depressed me. I have never shaken off the impression of my first meeting with King Fog in London.

I hadn't notified my friends when I would be arriving, so nobody met me at the station. As I had a good deal of luggage I took a hansom, a two-wheeler cab much in use at that time in England, and in half an hour it brought me to Wardour Street, where my friend Gundersen lived.

I had not been expected; but they made me very welcome. After we had chatted for a bit we went to see Wilhelm Werner, who lived in Cleveland Street, also in Soho, not far away. We found the whole family at home. Of course, they hadn't expected me either; their joy at our reunion was all the greater. We had such a lot to tell each other since we had last been together in Berlin.

Werner's family had joined him in London only a few months before, and he had not yet got used to the new conditions. He was a first-class workman at his trade, and had from the end of his apprenticeship been a member of the German Book Printers' Union; but so far he had not succeeded in getting employment in London, because the conservative-minded Trade Union made it almost impossible for a foreigner to be admitted as a member. Werner was eventually compelled to take a job in the Provinces, in Nottingham, till the Trade Union finally accepted him as a member. After that he got a good job in London.

Luckily he had a little money to get along with. His wife had with the help of friends in Berlin sold the small printing plant he had left there; so he was able to manage for a while.

After lunch we went to look for a small room where I could live. We found one almost immediately, in Carburton Street, near the Werners. The same evening we visited Grafton Hall, a spacious, comfortable club house of the German movement in London. At this first visit I met a number of old acquaintances, and I made many new contacts among the comrades.

It was not the first time I had been in London. I had spent a few days there two years before, in 1893, on an invitation from the Autonomie group. They had wanted to discuss with me what we could do to resume smuggling our literature over the German-Belgian frontier. Some of our comrades who had been engaged in this work had been caught and arrested. My impression of London at that time had not been a good one. It looked dirty and grimy, and the whole city had a forlorn and melancholy look. I missed the gaiety of Paris, the bustling boulevards and the open-air cafes. The people I saw in the streets seemed to be in a dreadful hurry, grimly intent on their own affairs.

I had come grateful for the trust which my comrades had in me, especially when I discovered that they wanted me to take charge of the whole work. The risk of it appealed to my youthful adventurous spirit.

But after several meetings with the comrades in London I discovered that they were by no means agreed about the whole plan. I found there was a good deal of weariness among most of the group responsible for publishing *Autonomie*. They had been issuing the periodical and a lot of pamphlets for about seven years; they hadn't received a penny from Germany, so that the whole cost, including that of smuggling the literature into Germany fell on the shoulders of a few people. At the same time it was clear that *Autonomie* was no longer able to satisfy the needs of our German movement. It wasn't worth the effort.

I stayed a whole week that first time in London. The weather turned out to be wonderfully good. It was a spring-like February. I remember an excursion we made to Greenwich Park. I went from end to end of the huge city, trying to get to know as much of it as I could in those few days. I paid a number of visits to the Autonomie Club in Windmill Street. It was a very small place, just two rooms, which served the comrades as a meeting centre.

Nothing came of the idea for which I had been called to London, and I returned to Paris with a certain sense of relief that I was back there. Soon after, *Autonomie* stopped publication.

On my second London visit I found the German movement flourishing. The persecution on the continent made many comrades fly to London from Switzerland, France, Belgium and other countries, with the result that they strengthened the London movement. The Grafton Hall club had over 500 paying members, and it was also visited by comrades from abroad.

The group that had been publishing *Autonomie* had, since the paper was stopped, given up their club in Windmill Street, and were homeless. Social life at that period depended entirely on the clubs. At the same time the members of the First Section of the Communist Workers' Educational Union, which consisted mainly of old followers of Johann Most, Social Revolutionaries, and a few adherents of the young movement in Germany were looking for a new club; they found suitable premises and excellent conditions in Grafton Street. The long conflict which had split the German movement in London for years had gradually come to an end; the two hostile sections got together, and the rest of the old Autonomists joined the Grafton Hall club.

The Communist Workers' Educational Union was the oldest of all the organisations of German socialists abroad. It was started in the middle of the 1840s by German refugees belonging to the Secret Society of the Communist League, and it continued to be the centre of socialist propaganda among the Germans in England till the First World War put an end to its existence. It counted among its members the most important people in the German movement, Joseph Moll, Heinrich Bauer, Karl Pfaender, Wilhelm Weitling, August Willich, Karl Schapper, all socialist leaders before Karl Marx's appearance; Karl Marx, Friedrich Engels and Wilhelm Liebknecht were also members at this time.

When the Communist League split in 1850, the great majority, the Communist Workers' Educational Union, the Willich-Schapper faction, expelled Marx, Engels and Liebknecht. In later years the Union sided strongly with the Young Social Democratic movement in Germany, till Johann Most came to London after the anti-socialist Laws were enforced in Germany, and was asked by the Union to publish *Freiheit*.

The paper, which was started in January 1879, was at first a social democratic organ, and described itself as such. But it soon plunged deeper into the revolutionary waters, a process considerably hastened by the intolerance of the old party leaders in Germany. Then when the secret Congress of the German Social Democrats held in Switzerland in 1880 expelled Most from the party, the Communist Workers' Educational Union split. The great majority took their stand with Most, and held the Union's property, including its valuable library. The seceding members started a new organisation under the old name, but calling itself the Second Section. The First Section were the majority.

The First Section underwent all the changes that Most himself went through on his road to anarchism, and remained devoted to its libertarian concepts, till the outbreak of the First World War, when most of its members were arrested, and its activity was stopped.

The new Grafton Hall Club was the finest meeting place the foreign revolutionaries in London ever had. There was a large room on the ground floor, where the comrades who lived in the neighbourhood came every evening, for company, and for their evening meal. On Saturdays and Sundays it was packed with comrades from other parts of the huge city, who could come only on those days. The big, bright, comfortable library was at the back.

The entire first floor was taken up by a spacious hall, which easily seated 500 people, and was often hired for meetings by groups of French, Italian and other foreign comrades. The office rooms and committee rooms were on the second floor.

There wasn't much contact in those days between the foreign colonies in London and the native English population. They lived for the most part their own separate lives, segregated in their own streets, speaking their own language, following their own occupations, and they had little need of contact with the native English population. Many remained foreigners in London all their lives, without ever being able to speak or read English. I knew French people who had fled to London after the collapse of the Paris Commune, who had in all the years they lived in London not learned more than a dozen English words, and they could not pronounce even these properly. They lived all the time among French people, worked with French people, bought only in French shops. It was like that till the First World War, which broke down the barriers; the children who were born in England became completely anglicised.

16

When I came to London the whole district from Oxford Street to Euston Road, and from Tottenham Court Road to Cleveland Street was almost exclusively inhabited by Germans, French, Austrians and Swiss. The language spoken in the streets was more often German or French than English.

It was only gradually I came to understand that though the German movement in London was large and active, even the most successful emigrant movement could never reach more than a limited circle. Furthermore, such movements were exposed to all kinds of outside influences, and flowed and ebbed according to conditions outside.

The club life too had certain unpleasant features, which I discovered later. A place like Grafton Hall was expensive to run, and those who were responsible for its upkeep could not be selective in their admission of members. They also hired the hall to all sorts of bodies; it was not always pleasant. Most of the revenue came from the bar, from selling beer, wine and other intoxicants.

Most of the people who frequented Grafton Hall were sympathisers with the movement; they had radical ideas, but were not much interested in the movement as such; they contributed to the funds, but only when they were pressed by the comrades. They rarely came to the discussion evenings. We could count on their attendance only when the discussion concerned one of the conflicts that so often occurred in the life of the emigre population. One of the important activities of the club was to raise funds to send regular contributions to the comrades in the homeland, for their work there.

My most difficult problem was to find employment. The bookbinders' union in London was one of the best organised trade unions, and had already then secured an eight-hour day for its members. But a foreigner had little chance of acceptance as a member. There was one possibility. The Zehnsdorf firm gave its workers an eight-hour day, but paid beginners only 28 shillings a week, instead of the union's minimum wage of 36 shillings. If one could get a job with Zehnsdorf one could advance in time to the minimum wage of 36 shillings a week, and then the union could no longer refuse membership. My friend Albin Rohmann and a handful of others had in that way become members of the union. But they were exceptions.

I tried Zehnsdorf, but without success. I was told there were no vacancies; that I should try again later. So I decided to start work on my own for the time being. As I still hoped to go back to Germany before long I was not much worried about the future. Luckily I had brought my tools with me. There was a German bookseller in the club who had something for me to do every week. Also two French booksellers promised me work. And I could count on a few private customers.

Soon after I was, on Werner's and Rohmann's proposal, elected Librarian of the Workers' Educational Union. I found its old and valuable collection of books terribly neglected. My predecessor, a man named Milo, had been going through the books, making an index of them. The first thing he did was to put aside about 300 French books, which he said were useless, and should be got rid of. Luckily they were still there, because in the midst of his

17

work he got another job in Paris, and went off, leaving everything in the library as it was. The first book I picked out of this heap that he had flung aside as useless was the *Histoire de la conspiration pour l'égalité, dite de Babeuf*, by Buonarroti, which had appeared in Brussels in 1828, and had soon after the July 1830 revolution been out of print and unobtainable. The book had a tremendous influence on the movement and had a scarcity value. I could hardly believe my eyes. There wasn't a single book in the whole heap that could be described as valueless. On the contrary, there were a number of rare and valuable books among them, including works by Bazard, d'Argenson, Leroux and other early socialists, and a collection of propaganda works by French communists of the 30s and 40s that were practically unobtainable.

I found my work in the library absorbing and a great joy. I discovered an almost complete collection of the old German socialist literature, all the first editions of Wilhelm Weitling, August Becker, Sebastian Seiler, Andreas Dietsch, Ernst Dronke, Moses Hess and others. Early French and English socialist literature was equally well represented. There were all the first editions of Marx and Engels, except *The Holy Family*. The minutes of the Union, which were kept till the first half of the 40s, and had not been continued beyond that date, were valuable material. The library showed signs of the very definite swing there had been in the Union since the split following Johann Most's appearance. From this time on the libertarian movement was appropriately represented among the books in the library though much was missing, especially French and English books and periodicals, so that one found little of the rich literature of French anarchism. The reason seemed to be that the Communist Workers' Educational Union had often had to move its premises, and the books were packed in cases and left for some time in a cellar belonging to one of the comrades, or in a furniture depository, and some of the books were lost. During my period of office as Librarian I succeeded in filling some of the gaps, though the task was not easy, as there was not much money for buying books.

Chapter 3

Louise Michel and
Errico Malatesta

The Grafton Hall Club, as I said before, was also used by comrades of French, Italian and other nationalities. I met there for the first time Louise Michel, one of the heroines of the Paris Commune. It was at an international gathering called to commemorate the Commune, where I was to translate her speech into German. I saw a good deal of her after that. She lived in Whitfield Street, a stone's throw from my new lodgings in Charlotte Street, with her friend Charlotte Vauwelle. When I first visited her I found the two old ladies in a small, dark room, which was their home. Louise was 66 then. Her hair was grey, and she was a little bowed with age. But her mind was astonishingly fresh, and though she suffered much illness her vitality never left her till she died.

This extraordinary woman, whose character was so distorted and misrepresented in the reactionary press that it became unrecognisable, and was branded everywhere as an incendiary, was really a kindly, warm-hearted person, with a clear mind and a noble soul. That is the feeling of all who had the good fortune to know her. Her inborn fearlessness, which made her shrink from no danger, risking her life and liberty for her beliefs, was not the result of hardness of character, but came from her intense love of humanity.

Louise Michel had the character of an apostle, who is so convinced of the justice of her cause that she cannot make the slightest concession to the unjust. When she faced the Versailles Court in December 1871 she flung these words at her judges: "Since it seems that each heart that beats for freedom has the right only to a bit of lead, I demand my bit. If you let me live I shall never cease to call for vengeance, and to put the cowardly murderers of my brothers in the pillory." She kept her word. When she returned to France after the general amnesty after ten years detention in the penal colony New Caledonia, she threw herself passionately into the revolutionary movement. She was an anarchist now. "I came to recognise," she said, "that power, of whatever kind, must work out to be a curse. That is why I avow anarchism."

When the Hunger Demonstration took place in 1883 at the Invalides Esplanade in Paris, and baker shops in the streets round about were looted by the unemployed, Louise was there with Emile Pouget. Though neither had anything to do with the looting, which was done by people whom the police had prevented from making their way to the Esplanade, Pouget was sent to prison for eight years and Louise for six. While Louise was in prison her old mother, to whom she was devoted died.

Louise left prison unbroken, and continued her activity. In January 1888, while she was addressing a big meeting in Havre, a poor fanatic, incited by a priest, fired at her and wounded her in the throat and behind the ear. She did everything possible to save her would-be-assassin from the law.

She had hardly recovered when she was again on the war-path. The authorities, seeing that nothing could stop her, and fearing her popularity with the people, laid a plan to shut her up in a lunatic asylum. A high official, named Roger, whose conscience revolted against this plan warned Louise; she fled to England.

When I got to know Louise she lived in great poverty, as she did all her life. Yet she was always ready to share the little she had with others who she thought were poorer still. She always wore the same black faded dress, and the same shapeless hat; but she was so frugal that she was content. Friends sometimes sent her clothes, but she gave them away to others. A French comrade gave her a coat he had himself made for her, because the coat she wore had rubbed so thin that it gave her no protection against the cold and wet of the London winter. She wore it for a few weeks. Then she appeared again in her old coat. She had been stopped one night in the street on her way home by a woman in rags, who asked for a few pence. Louise took off her new coat and gave it to her.

That was Louise Michel, who was known in the outlying parts of Paris as "la bonne Louise", "the good Louise", for her kindheartedness and selflessness had become proverbial. Had she lived in an earlier century she might have been venerated as a saint. There burned in the great soul of this rare woman the flame of an inextinguishable faith, that could move mountains. I would not therefore describe her as an idealist, for the word has become so banal that it no longer explains what Louise was. She always did what she felt was right. It was her nature. Though she was a woman not only of great spirit but also of great intellect, the compass of her life was always her great and noble heart. She was often misused by flatterers and people who were unworthy of her, but this was something she could not avoid; it was part of her character. Her bitterest experiences could not destroy her absolute faith in people.

It was always a joy to me to hear her speak about her experiences in New Caledonia, where during the ten years of her banishment she had been a teacher among the natives. They were devoted to her. They had never before known such a representative of the white race. When she left to return to France, after the amnesty to the Communards, hundreds of natives came to the ship, weeping, as they said farewell to her. Her eyes lighted up when she spoke about the Kanaks of New Caledonia. She sang their praises, their simplicity, their natural intelligence, their complete readiness to help others. She did not overlook the gradual disappearance of these fine native qualities through the inroads of white civilisation.

Louise had a collection of small objects that she had brought away from New Caledonia, including photographs of her school and her pupils. She never parted from these. She remembered all her friends there, and she loved to tell stories about each of them. She once showed me a picture of a native girl whom she had nursed through a dreadful illness. It was hopeless; the child died. Before she died Louise found her sobbing bitterly. She tried to comfort her. The child said that she was crying because she had been knitting a cover for Louise, and she wouldn't be able to finish it. "My sister is not old enough to finish it."

Louise Michel wrote a great deal. Besides her memoirs, of which unfortunately only the first volume appeared, and a book about the Commune, she wrote novels and plays. Most of them appeared in serial form in newspapers and periodicals. Some were afterwards published in book form, like *Les microbes humains, Le monde nouveau, La misère, Nadine, Legendes canaques*, etc. I am sure if she had devoted herself completely to writing she would have been an important figure in literature. But she was a fighter by nature, and literature to her was only a means to an end. Art for art's sake meant nothing to her. Her novels and her plays — and *Nadine* was a considerable success when it was produced on the stage — were intended to call attention to the great injustices and the social misunderstandings of the time, and to inspire people to fight. Yet they contain powerful pictures of life, such as George Sand might have written. Some of her poems too are beautiful, like *La Frégate*, where she almost foretold her own future fate.

The sculptor Derré made a statue of her after her death, which conveys an idea of the nature of this great and very simple woman. It shows her in a long flowing dress, with an expression of maternal tenderness on her face, and a little girl looking up at her lovingly. Her love of animals and birds is symbolised by a small dog and by some birds on the low base of the statue. The inscription reads: *Louise Michel, 1836–1905. Fut la bonté même, ne connut que la misère et la prison.* (She was kindness itself, and knew only misery and prison.) She never knew the joy of motherhood, but her heart was full of motherliness for all who were unfortunate and in need.

I saw her last at a commemoration of the Commune in the club of the Jewish anarchists in the East End of London. It was in March 1904. She took leave of us, and soon after returned to France; she died there in January 1905.

At Grafton Hall I also met for the first time Errico Malatesta, with whom I afterwards worked for many years in the International Bureau of the Anarchist International; I remained closely connected with him till he died. I had heard a great deal about him, first in Germany and then in France, about his amazing spirit and his adventurous life. I don't know why, but I had always imagined him a man of giant physique, like Bakunin. I was therefore astonished to find him a slight, little man, nothing like what I had expected.

Yet Malatesta's splendid head, pitch-black hair, expressive face, finely-chiselled features, and clever, flashing eyes, which radiated so much warmth of heart and untameable will-power, made an unforgettable impression. He was a personality.

When I got to know Malatesta he was about 42, in the full power of maturity. Except for Bakunin no man had such an enduring influence as

Malatesta on the libertarian movement in the Latin countries, especially in Spain and Italy.

He was born in 1853 in Santa Maria di Capus Vetere, near Naples. He was a youngster when he joined the Republican movement, which found expression in the Young Italy of Garibaldi and Mazzini. The long, hard struggle for Italian national unity did not produce the republic their movement had sought, but had established a dynasty which reaped the harvest for which thousands had given their lives. Mazzini's motto, "The voice of the people is the voice of God", did not win the decision for the "political theology", which was Bakunin's description of Mazzini's theories, but for the House of Savoy, which took over the legacy of Mazzini and Garibaldi.

Young Italy was not content with this result; new movements sprang up, which went far beyond the narrow confines of national unity. In 1870 Malatesta, who was then 17, and studying medicine at Naples University, was arrested during a students' demonstration, and expelled from the University. That set him on the revolutionary road, which he followed for the rest of his life.

The Paris Commune rising had a powerful influence on the young movement. The Federalist efforts of the Commune roused an echo, especially in Spain and Italy. In Spain federalism found an outstanding representative in Pi y Margall. In Italy, in Carlo Pisacane, the great antagonist of political centralism who fell in 1859, fighting at Sapri. When Mazzini dared to vilify the Paris Commune at a time when 36,000 men, women and children were being slaughtered cold-bloodedly by their victorious opponents, the breach between him and the best part of the Italian youth became unavoidable. Bakunin who had after his escape from Siberia settled in Italy, had an incalculable influence on this development. He succeeded in winning some of the best of the youth away from Mazzini, for the cause of the social revolution.

Malatesta, whom Bakunin later described as the Benjamin of the movement, was one of these young people. Bakunin had good reason to be proud of his Benjamin, for there have not been many who have given up their lives so completely to the cause, till the day he died.

The Italian government feared Malatesta, for his courageous, uncompromising, unflinching spirit, his clean and incorruptible character, and the irresistible influence he exerted upon the masses of the people. When the Italian government proclaimed an amnesty after the First World War, under revolutionary pressure, Malatesta was the only one it excluded from the amnesty. Of course, that only poured oil on the flames, and in the end the government, very much against its wish, had to let its relentless enemy return. It had only shown what great significance it attached to Malatesta's person. Not without cause; for though Malatesta was forced to spend long years in exile, he was always in intimate contact with his native land.

For this reason too, the British government kept a watchful eye on him during all the many years he lived in London. His home in Islington was shadowed by Scotland Yard men, who followed every movement he made. It never stopped Malatesta disappearing from London without trace every time the waves of wrath and resentment rose high in Italy. The old rebel always found a way to send the watchdogs on a false trail. I could never understand why the British government spent so much money and time to spy on Malatesta's movements and plans. He certainly never disturbed the peace and security of the British State. England served him only as a place of exile, because no other country in Europe would let him stay there. He knew well enough that no foreigner could have any influence on the shaping of English affairs. His public activity was confined to propaganda, the spoken and the written word. But as he found it hard to express his thoughts in English, he rarely spoke in that language. It was always an effort for him to accept an invitation from the English comrades to speak to them. His contributions to English publications like *Freedom, Liberty, The Torch* were hardly ever written originally for them. Most of his articles that appeared in English and his few English pamphlets were translated from Italian and French papers. We must therefore assume that the strict watch kept on Malatesta in England was inspired and required by the Italian government.

Chapter 4

The East End

My plan, which brought me from Paris, to settle my position with the German Consulate in London and to go back to Germany, came to nothing. At the Consulate they told me brusquely that I could not have the usual medical examination; I must go back to Germany for that. I asked why they refused me the ordinary procedure of a medical examination. They said I ought to know that myself.

Now it was clear. I hadn't expected the officials in the London Consulate would know about me. They did. At that time it was no doubt the practice of the German government to keep its Consulates posted about people like me.

I realised that the road back to my native land was closed to me forever, unless there was a revolution there, and that was too much to expect even of my youthful enthusiasm. Germany seemed to me at that time the one state in Europe that was most firmly and most solidly established. There was nothing to do but make the best of it, and to adjust myself to the conditions in London. Even so, I had no idea then that London would be my home for so many years.

As I was remaining in London for the time being I thought I should know more about this vast city. I had heard and read much about "Darkest London", a lot of it in the writings of John Henry Mackay. I wanted to see these places of poverty and misery for myself. Otto Schreiber had lived in London for years and also moved by Mackay, had made a number of excursions through the slum areas. I asked him to show me round.

We chose Saturday afternoons for our expeditions. England was at that time the only country in Europe where work stopped on Saturdays around 1pm or 2pm. The whole picture of the town changed. Factories, workshops, offices, banks were closed. The city which, on all other days was alive with people and traffic, full of their roar and bustle, was dead on a Saturday afternoon and Sunday. The businessmen and the clerks stayed at home or went out on pleasure. Few people lived in the city except caretakers. The residential parts of London, on the other hand, were more alive than ever, especially in the neighbourhood of the big market places, where people came to do their week-end shopping.

We had arranged to meet every Saturday afternoon, if the weather were at all favourable, and to make our way into the districts where the London poor lived, Bethnal Green and Hackney, Shoreditch and Whitechapel, Shadwell and Limehouse, the grim streets of Dockland, and across the river, Deptford, Rotherhithe, and Lambeth. It was worse than my reading and what I had been told had led me to expect. I came back from our excursions physically and spiritually exhausted. It was an abyss of human suffering, an inferno of misery.

Like many others I had believed in my youth that as social conditions became worse, those who suffered so much would come to realise the deeper causes of their poverty and suffering. I have since been convinced that such a belief is a dangerous illusion, like many beliefs and slogans we had taken over from the older generation. My wanderings through the distressed parts of London shook this early faith of mine, and finally destroyed it. There is a pitch of material and spiritual degradation from which a man can no longer rise. Those who have been born into misery and never knew a better state are rarely able to resist and revolt.

There were at that time thousands of people in London who had never slept in a bed, who just crept into some filthy hole where the police would not disturb them. I saw with my own eyes thousands of human beings who could hardly be still considered such, people who were no longer capable of any kind of work. They went about in foul rags, through which their skin showed, dirty and lousy, never free from hunger, starving, scavenging their food out of dustbins and the refuse heaps that were left behind after the markets closed.

There were squalid courts and alleyways, with dreary, tumbledown hovels, whose stark despair it is impossible to describe. And in these cesspools of poverty children were born and people lived, struggling all their lives with poverty and pain, shunned like lepers by all decent members of society.

Could anything spiritual grow on these dung-heaps? These were the dregs of a society whose champions still claimed that man was made in God's image, but who evaded meeting the image face to face in the slums of London. I have seen pictures of social misery in other countries, but nowhere was the contrast so vast between assertive wealth and indescribable poverty as in the great cities of Britain. Riches and poverty lived almost on top of each other, separated by a street or two. You need only leave the fine main road and plunge into a side-street to find yourself in the most horrible slum.

It seemed to me that people took less notice of such things in England than elsewhere. Even the leaders of the trade union movement took them for granted. I remember a talk I had with Ben Tillet, who was not only one of the most prominent trade union leaders, but also one of the best known figures in the Social Democratic Federation, the only purely Marxist body in Great Britain at the time. His view was that an improvement of social conditions was possible only where the urge to work and the hope of a better future had not been completely extinguished. He thought many of those who lived in the black spots of misery had been so demoralised by want that they no longer had any desire for anything better. In times of revolution, he said, it was from these quagmires of degeneration that the hyenas of the revolution emerged. A socialist government would therefore have to think of ways and means to get rid of this scum; false pity for them would harm the socialist cause.

Certainly the old slogan, "The worse the better", was based on an erroneous assumption. Like that other slogan, "All or nothing", which made many radicals oppose any improvement in the lot of the workers, even when the workers demanded it, on the ground that it would distract the mind of the proletariat, and turn it away from the road which leads to social emancipation. It is contrary to all the experience of history and of psychology; people who are not prepared to fight for the betterment of their living conditions are not likely to fight for social emancipation. Slogans of this kind are like a cancer in the revolutionary movement.

My expeditions in darkest London brought me again in touch with the Jewish comrades. Since I left Paris I had rarely found the opportunity to visit them, in the East End. I was busy with my own affairs and with my German comrades. I had met a few of the Jewish comrades in Grafton Hall, William Wess, his sister Doris, A. Frumkin and L. Baron. Frumkin, who was then editing the *Arbeter Fraint,* had asked me in 1896 to contribute an article to his *Commune Number*. It was my first contribution to the Jewish press.

One day coming back from an expedition to Poplar, Schreiber and I met Baron in Commercial Road. He asked us into his house. Several Jewish comrades were there, and we spent an interesting evening with them. I learned a good deal about the Jewish Labour movement in the East End of London. And when the comrades asked me to come to their meetings sometimes, I was glad, and went there quite often, with some of the other German comrades.

The meetings were held every Friday evening in a public house in Hanbury Street; they were always attended by about a hundred people. I took part, in the discussions, and I was invited to deliver lectures, so that I soon became a frequent guest of the Jewish workers.

Hanbury Street is a long, narrow, winding street, leading from Spitalfields to Whitechapel. It looked a drab, miserable place. The Spitalfields and Whitechapel area had been a notorious criminal quarter. The influx of Jewish immigrants from Russia and Poland had gradually displaced the old inhabitants, and this unsavoury part of London had become the home of the Jewish working class. It was now possible to walk through these streets at night without being molested. But it was still a slum district. There was a church at the corner of Commercial Street, at the Spitalfields end, where at any time of the day you would see a crowd of dirty, lousy men and women, looking like scarecrows, in filthy rags, with dull hopeless faces, scratching themselves. That was why it was called Itchy Park.

At the Whitechapel end of Hanbury Street was the public house, the Sugar Loaf, where the Jewish comrades held their weekly meetings in a back room. There was no separate entrance, so we had to go through the pub, which was not pleasant, because there were always several drunks there, men and women, who used foul language and became abusive when they saw a foreigner.

But it was hard to find other accommodation; so we made the best of it. The meetings themselves were good, and I enjoyed them. I was struck by the difference between the meetings of the Jewish anarchists in Paris and in the London ghetto. In Paris they were held in a pleasant cafe in the Boulevard Barbis, where the proprietor went out of his way to make us comfortable. The people too were different. The Jewish workers in Paris were mostly skilled artisans. Many had received a higher education in Russia, and when they came to France they spent years learning their trade. They were usually well-dressed, and had adopted the jaunty Parisian manner. The Londoners looked sad and worn; they were sweatshop workers, badly paid, and half-starved. They sat crowded together on hard benches, and the badly lighted room made them seem paler than they really were.

But they followed the speaker with rapt attention, and as the discussion afterwards showed, with understanding. There were a good many women at the meetings, who showed the same intelligent interest in the proceedings as the men. It was an intellectual elite, who met every week in this common public house room, and in time brought into existence a movement that contributed an interesting chapter to the history of libertarian socialism.

Chapter 5

The International Socialist Congress in London

In July 1806 the International Socialist Labour Congress met in London. It was the fourth congress of the kind since the two Paris Congresses of July 1889. As at both the previous Congresses (Brussels 1891 and Zurich 1893), the question of admitting the anarchists and other trends played an important part in the discussions and gave rise to fierce arguments. The young people of today may find it strange that the anarchists at that time placed so much weight on being represented at these Congresses, for they could never have hoped to have any appreciable influence in the decisions. The fact is that from the time of the First International till 1889, no general socialist Congresses had been held. The so-called World Congress in Ghent in 1877 was no more than the echo of a period that had passed and had no practical significance for the future. It was only with the two congresses in Paris that a new chapter was opened. A new International was born, which had little in common however with the original aspirations of the First International.

The Second International was an association of political Labour parties, whose practical activity was mostly confined to co-operation in the bourgeois parliaments, and of trades unions which were largely under the influence of those parties. Had the Congresses of the Second International not concealed their true nature and acknowledged themselves for what they were, international conferences of Parliamentary socialism and of social democratic parties, the anarchists would have been the last to want to be represented. But as long as they called themselves International Socialist Labour Congresses it would be wrong to deny them admission. For the anarchists too were after all socialists, for they opposed economic monopoly, and worked for a co-operative form of human labour, aiming to satisfy the needs of all and not the profits of the few. Nor could it be disputed that the great majority of the anarchists in the different countries belonged to the working class.

True, the Zurich Congress had decided that only trades unions and those socialist movements that recognised the necessity of political action should be admitted to all future international congresses. But the anarchists were never opponents of political action as such. They only rejected a specific form of it, parliamentary activity. The anarchists had never repudiated the defence of political rights and liberties; they had often joined in the struggle for them against reaction.

The fact that the Zurich Resolution admitted the trades unions as such complicated the matter still more. The English trades unions had no connections at that time with any political party. Their members voted for whichever party they wished. The British Labour Party came into existence

28

only three years after the London Congress. The great majority of the Spanish trades unions were anarchist. The Spanish Socialist Party embraced only a small minority of the Spanish labour movement. In Italy, Portugal, Holland and other countries there were definite movements in the trades unions which rejected parliamentary activity in principle. There was at that time, largely under anarchist influence, a growing powerful anti-parliamentary tendency in the French trades unions, which a few years later led to the formation of the Confederation Generale du Travail; it was soon the strongest organisation of the French working class, and because it was working for a socialist transformation of society, it rejected all co-operation with the socialist parties. Some of the most influential representatives of the French trade union movement were avowed anarchists.

At the same time there was a split in the socialist parliamentary parties in the different countries, the beginnings on the one, hand of the revisionist movement started by Eduard Bernstein and, on the other, a definite swing away from belief in the value of parliamentary action. In Holland the great mass of the socialists had formed a new organisation with a clear anti-parliamentary line. The Socialist Labour Party of Holland launched in 1894 and generously assisted by funds from the German social democrats, represented then only a small minority of the Dutch labour movement. In France the socialist movement was split in half a dozen different parties, and the Allmanists had completely abandoned parliamentary activity, and concentrated on propaganda in the trades unions. In Italy, especially in Romagna and the south there were powerful revolutionary tendencies which were often very troublesome to the parliamentary leaders. In Belgium, Switzerland and Denmark too there were similar smaller socialist trends.

The 1891 International Congress in Brussels had already given me occasion for losing some of my youthful illusions. But what I now saw in London outdid it all in petty spite and brutal trampling down on all freedom of opinion. The Germans surpassed themselves in London with their unashamed intolerance, their refusal to see any point of view but their own.

The 750 delegates included a considerable number of anarchists and representatives of other libertarian movements in Great Britain, France, Italy, Spain, Holland, Switzerland, Denmark and Germany, whose position the Congress had to consider before it could proceed to business. Malatesta, for instance, was entrusted with mandates from a number of trades unions in Spain, Italy and France, including one from the Catalonian railway workers, who had a larger membership than the entire Socialist Party of Spain. Of the thirteen delegates from Holland only two or three belonged to the Social Democratic Labour Party; the rest represented the Socialist Bond and the trades unions in the National Labour Secretariat. The twenty Italian delegates were equally divided, ten representatives of the Socialist Party of Italy, and ten anarchists, including Malatesta and Pietro Gori who also represented trades unions. There were over a hundred delegates from France, most of them representatives of trades unions and of different trends of the socialist movement, who almost invariably voted against the Congress' majority. The French delegation in particular gave the Germans a real headache. They couldn't understand how any socialists should refuse to follow the line set by the German social democrats.

Britain had of course the largest representation, though it remained a mystery how all those mandates had been filled. For example, the Social Democratic Federation (SDF) which at that time had barely 4,000 members in the whole country had over a hundred delegates, while the Independent Labour Party (ILP) with a membership of over 40,000 had less mandates than the SDF. In the other countries there were no large socialist parties then except in Austria, Belgium and Switzerland. Elsewhere the movement was still in its beginnings. It was represented by only a few delegates from each of these other countries. Yet these delegates turned the scales at every vote.

The Congress began on Sunday, July 26th, with a peace demonstration, followed by a mass meeting in Hyde Park. As the first marchers entered the park there was a cloudburst, and most of them fled for shelter. There were twelve speakers' platforms, but very few people round them. The downpour persisted, till even those few melted away. Only the anarchists, who had gathered under Reformers' Tree, went on with their meeting, till the end. We were soaked to the skin.

The Congress proper was opened the next day in Queen's Hall. Over the platform hung solitary a huge flower-garlanded oil portrait of Karl Marx. It was the symbol of the narrow-minded attitude of those who had arranged the Congress. For one might have expected at least one more portrait, that of Robert Owen, who was the great pioneer of British socialism; he had influenced the whole movement in Britain, while Marx, though he had lived in England for many years, never had any influence on the British labour movement, and after the Hague Congress of 1872, which had split the First International, he was at daggers drawn with all the prominent leaders of the British trades union movement.

The first important question before the Congress was that of admitting the anarchists and representatives of other anti-parliamentary groups. The resolution adopted by the Zurich Congress on this question was worded so vaguely that everybody could interpret it differently. True, the anarchists had been excluded from the Zurich Congress on the grounds of this resolution, but feeling among the French, Belgians, Dutch and others rose so high against it that a rider had to be added to the resolution. Its text, introduced by Bebel, Kautsky, Adler and others, and adopted by the majority of the Zurich Congress, said that it was not intended to mean "that everyone who comes to the Congress is bound in consequence to engage in political action under all circumstances and in every detail in accordance with our definition. It asks only for the recognition of the right of the workers to use all the political powers of their countries, according to their own judgment, for promoting the interests of the working classes, and to constitute themselves as an independent labour party."

It was, quite clear that the rider had been added at the time only to secure the future participation of the trades unions, without which the congresses could never have claimed to be labour congresses. All the socialist parties, without exception, included socialists who did not belong to the working class. But only workers could belong to the trades unions. No anarchist, as Gustav Landauer said at the London Congress, defending his right to his mandate, had ever thought of denying to other socialists the right to engage in parliamentary activity. What they asked was the right to hold a different opinion about the value of parliamentary action.

The Germans tried to steamroller the Congress on this question so ruthlessly that it infuriated a great many delegates. The English trade unionist leader Ted Legatt, who belonged to the anarchist wing, thundered against it. "Proletarians of all countries unite!" he cried, in his powerful voice that the chairman's bell could not drown.

The conduct of the majority on the second day was even worse. Examination of the mandates had shown that three members of the French Parliament, Jaures, Viviani and Millerand, had no mandates and took the attitude that their mandates in the French Parliament were sufficient. The French majority, which was entirely anti-parliamentary, had agreed to admit these three, thereby showing a tolerance that was totally absent from the Congress majority. Some of the leading British delegates, including Bernard Shaw of the Fabians, protested that being a Member of Parliament did not itself confer the right to attend the Congress as a delegate. The Congress majority ignored them.

Germany had sent 46 social democrats and five anarchists. Switzerland with 12 delegates had two anarchists among them. Denmark with seven delegates had one anarchist. The Dutch delegation consisted of two social democrats and 13 anarchists. Bohemia sent one social democrat and one anarchist. The Italian delegation was also equally divided, ten social democrats and ten anarchists.

The Chairman on the second day was Paul Singer, a member of the German Parliament (Reichstag). He tried to stop the discussion, and said he would take the vote on the question.

Pandemonium broke loose. The Chairman's gong, which sounded, like a big church bell, was drowned in it. The Germans, the Austrians and their supporters in other delegations backed Paul Singer's ruling. But Keir Hardie, of the ILP, who was deputy chairman of the session, got up and making himself heard above the uproar, told Singer that people didn't conduct meetings like that in England. Before the vote was taken both sides must be given a hearing. So Malatesta and Landauer were allowed to speak.

The reports about the Congress in the London press were very sarcastic about Singer's behaviour in the chair. Of course, Malatesta and Landauer and other speakers made no impression at all on the Congress majority. Damela Nieuwenhuis, who had at that time not yet joined the anarchists, said: "We do not contest the right of any movement to hold congresses and to decide who is to attend to fit in with their programme. But then it must be made absolutely clear what sort of a congress it is. This congress has been called as a general socialist congress. The invitations said nothing about anarchists and social democrats. They spoke only of socialists and trades unions. No one can deny that people like Kropotkin, and Reclus and the whole anarchist-communist movement stand on the socialist basis. If they are excluded, the purpose of the Congress has been misrepresented."

On the third day, Millerand, in the name of the French minority, said that as the French majority had spoken for admitting the anarchists the minority refused to continue to work with the majority. He asked that the Congress should recognise two separate French delegations, each with its own vote.

There was an outburst of protest. The English delegates lost their temper. Vandervelde, one of the moderates of Belgian socialism, opposed the idea of splitting the French delegation. If that were agreed to, he said, the same right would have to be given to the Dutch and the Italians. Karl Marx's son-in-law denounced Vandervelde as a traitor to the cause.

Bernard Shaw rose on Millerand's proposal, to move next business. The Chairman informed him that the French Marxists would then leave the Congress. Shaw's answer was that if that were so he really insisted on moving next business.

Delegates who tried to speak on the motion were shouted down. It went on for hours, and most of the third day was simply wasted. At last the Chairman succeeded in putting Millerand's proposal to the vote. Britain, France, Holland, Belgium and Italy voted against it. The Germans were supported by Austria, Switzerland, and fourteen other delegations like Portugal, Poland, Romania, Bulgaria, etc., most of which had only two delegates each. But it gave them a majority. So France was split into two delegations.

The fourth day saw the expulsion of the anarchists. I often asked myself during this London Congress what would happen if people so intolerant and despotic as these German social democrats ever came to power in a country. I began to fear that socialism without liberty must lead to an even worse tyranny than the conditions against which we were fighting. What has since happened in Russia has proved my fears to have been more than justified. The anarchists held an international protest demonstration in the Holborn Town Hall. A great many messages of support were received and were read from the platform, including messages from William Morris, Walter Crane and Robert Blatchford of the *Clarion*. They roundly condemned the intolerance which had manifested itself at the Congress. William Morris said that if he were well enough he would have come to express his condemnation from the platform.

Keir Hardie and Tom Mann came and spoke. Keir Hardie said he was no anarchist, but no one could prophesy whether the socialism of the future would shape itself in the image of the social democrats or of the anarchists. The crime of the anarchists in the eyes of the Congress' majority appeared to be that they were a minority. If they agreed with that attitude then the socialist movement as a whole had no right to exist, because it represented a minority. The other speakers at the meeting included Kropotkin, Elisée Reclus, Malatesta, Louise Michel, Kenworthy and Landauer.

During the term of the London Congress the anarchist delegates and others met in the Italian Club in Soho. I first met Kropotkin there. I also met Gustav Landauer there. This tall, lank, narrow-chested man made the impression outwardly of a poor, helpless, ineffectual creature. But he was a spiritual giant. He had fine features and thoughtful eyes which seemed to look beyond all around him. One felt when he spoke that every word came from his soul, bore the stamp of absolute integrity. I hadn't much opportunity to get to know him during the London Congress, but I had another occasion later, when he lived for a time in London; I learned to know him well.

Landauer was a mild-natured man, with a deep sense of justice. It did not prevent him being sometimes harsh in his judgments and even unjust. But he was always ready to admit that he had made a mistake. He demanded the highest standards from himself; he was always searching for the truth, and therefore kept far away from all dogmas. As he expected the same from others he often found himself in conflict with his closest comrades. Though he was all his life actively engaged in social movements he was never a man in a movement. His influence extended therefore only to a small elite who could understand his thoughts and were devoted to him. His close friend Fritz Mauthner, the philosopher, said of him after his tragic death: "Gustav Landauer failed because he was no politician, and was yet driven by his passionate compassion for the people to be active politically, too proud to join a party, not narrow enough to form a party round his own name. Thrown upon himself, a leader without an army. An eternal anarchist, who rejected all rule, and therefore above all party rule. That was one thing he was sure about."

When the Kaiser fled after the First World War, and the Weimar Republic was established, Landauer saw an opportunity of carrying out his humane socialist ideas. He was brutally murdered by German officers and soldiers. Ernst Toller, who witnessed it, being himself in the same prison, described it. "They dragged him into the prison courtyard. An officer struck him in the face. The men shouted 'Dirty Bolshie! Let's finish him off!' A rain of blows from rifle-butts descended on him. They trampled on him till he was dead."

When Landauer came to London that first time he was in conflict with many of the comrades in Germany. He was at the time editor of the *Socialist* in Berlin. On taking over the paper he had ranged it on the side of the anarchists, and had made it a highly intellectual paper. The result was that it lost its old propaganda value. It was a magazine for discussing theoretical questions. It made big demands on the minds of its readers. Most of the comrades were dissatisfied with it. They wanted a propaganda sheet, which the ordinary working man could understand, and which would bring adherents to the movement.

If the movement could have run both Landauer's paper and a propaganda sheet there might have been no trouble. But there were not enough funds for that. So there was constant friction. Landauer and his friends refused to bind the paper, refused to make concessions to intellectual poverty. Landauer put his faith in the intellectuals. He discovered in time that his faith was misplaced. Many who had worked with him in those days afterwards deserted him, and took very, strange roads. Some made a big name in German literature. But they had no further connections with their previous beliefs.

Landauer's opponents were mostly good, honest comrades, who were as convinced they were right as Landauer was about himself. He must have felt it himself, for in the end he agreed to publish also a small propaganda sheet, *Der Arme Konrad* (Poor Conrad), edited by Albert Weidner. Weidner did his best with it, but it was too small to have a great influence, and it did not satisfy Landauer's opponents. They started a new, larger paper, and Landauer's *Socialist* slowly died. Its death was a severe blow to the intellectual German movement. The new paper was poorly edited and badly written, and it was little consolation to plead that it was produced entirely by ordinary working men. For Landauer it was a tragedy. It deprived him of a valuable activity, for which he was supremely fitted, and in which he rendered splendid service. It made him feel isolated and solitary.

It was during the London Congress that I first met Max Nettlau, the historian of libertarian socialism. He was still little known at that time. Only a few of the older comrades like Kropotkin, Elisée Reclus, Malatesta, James Guillaume and Victor Dave knew his early studies. Even the German comrades hardly knew him then. His first historical writings appeared anonymously, and as he was no public speaker and took no active part in the movement few were aware of his existence.

Nettlau used to come to London for a few months every year regularly at that time, to work at the British Museum Library. He had little contact with the German comrades in London. The reason for this was that there had been continual quarrelling in the earlier movement, and it had left an unpleasant memory with Nettlau; he couldn't rid himself of it afterwards. He maintained active relations with Malatesta and the Freedom Group, the only association of which he was a member, except for William Morris's Socialist League, which he had joined at Victor Dave's urging. He remained with the Freedom group till Tom Keel's death.

I met Nettlau in the Italian Club in Dean Street, which the comrades frequented during the London Congress. He was then about 30. He was tall and well-built, with fair hair and beard, blue eyes and fine features, the real type of the Nordic; the later representatives of the Third Reich would have envied him.

Nettlau was born on April 30th, 1865, in Neuwaldegg, near Vienna. His father belonged to an old Prussian family in Potsdam, who settled in Austria, but never abandoned his German citizenship; so that Nettlau himself was a German all his life. He received an excellent education. At 23 he got his Doctorate of Philosophy for a thesis on the grammar of the Celtic languages. He once showed it to me and remarked that he had always been attracted to unpopular causes; for few people bothered at that time about the Celtic languages. Later he chose for his subject Bakunin, the memory of whose powerful activity had paled in most countries or had been distorted and caricatured by the Marxist historians.

He came into the Austrian radical movement as a young student, and soon found himself in the ranks of libertarian socialism, to which he afterwards gave invaluable service. He contributed a number of historical essays to Johann Most's *Freiheit*. His first essays on Bakunin's life also appeared as a series of articles in *Freiheit* in 1891, as well as his first study on *The History of Anarchism*.

When I first met Nettlau in London in 1896 I could not have foreseen how much I would come to owe him. He was already engaged at that time in collecting his materials for his monumental biography of Bakunin, which he never considered finished. There was hardly a person who had been connected with Bakunin whom Nettlau did not talk to or correspond with. He made long journeys, collected enormous quantities of letters and unpublished documents and manuscripts, before he started to write the actual biography. He discovered many first-hand sources which are invaluable to any future historian. Everything that has since been written about Bakunin and his circle and the First International is derived from Nettlau's material, and would probably have disappeared but for Nettlau.

It was a tragedy that he never had the satisfaction of seeing his great work printed. Only fifty copies were multigraphed by Nettlau himself between 1896–1900 and distributed among a few friends, and in the big libraries in London, Paris, Berlin, Vienna, Madrid. It is in German, in three volumes, and runs to 1,281 pages. Between 1903–1905 Nettlau wrote four more volumes.

Elisée Reclus persuaded Nettlau to write his *Bibliographie de l'Anarchie*, which appeared in 1897 in Brussels. It contains in about 300 pages a list of everything printed till then on this subject, books, pamphlets, newspapers, arranged according to languages and countries. No-one but Nettlau could have done such a work. Elisée Reclus said in his foreword that he had never realised before "how rich we are." This was the first work which had Nettlau's name on it; it was his introduction to those outside his own small circle of friends.

It is impossible to speak here of all his other immense contributions to our literature. Except Proudhon there is no-one in the whole libertarian movement who has left so much monumental work behind him. Nor is it propaganda work. It is valuable historical work. Nettlau was an absolutely honest historian.

In spite of his great knowledge and his immense industry and the historical value of his work Nettlau never earned a living by his writing. Until the First War he was in the fortunate position of being financially independent, and so able to devote his whole time to his studies. He had a small legacy from his father which he found enough for his needs. Much of his time was spent in travelling and visiting the great libraries of Europe. The war changed all this. Robbed of his income he lived in a tiny room in Vienna, with no comforts or conveniences, in real poverty, often in bitter want. But he went on working hard, and most of his important works were written in that period.

Nettlau and I became friends. I was intensely interested in his work, and I tried to help him by collecting for him over a period of years all the anarchist publications in Yiddish that appeared in England and America, periodicals, pamphlets and books.

We kept up a regular correspondence over the years. Unhappily most of his letters fell into the hands of the Hitler barbarians and are probably lost.

Nettlau had an individual place in the libertarian movement. He was in the anarchist movement, but he belonged to no particular school. Neither Tucker's individualist anarchism nor Kropotkin's communist anarchism could quite satisfy him. He believed that the proposed economic system must first be tested and tried out by the practical realities of life because, he said, things that appear logical in theory are often quite the opposite when they encounter difficulties in real life that no one could have foreseen. Economic forms must serve a purpose, must not be made a purpose in themselves. Their value could be judged only by the way in which they proved useful or harmful to the development of a free human society. Free experiment was to him the only criterion of a really free society; only experience could show what was right in the theory and what was wrong.

Nettlau was therefore the first to stand up for the rights of minorities in socialism. Without that, he said, the new society would be only a tyranny. He saw that the endless differences that existed in the socialist movement of his time made it impossible that the social revolution could develop in only one special direction, and that to impose one particular trend by brute force must lead to the suppression of all the other trends, as the Russian Revolution has demonstrated so terribly.

Nettlau's ideas had their roots in the liberal thought of the 19th century, which does not mean that he was behind his times, or had no understanding for later developments. He had a wide vision, and he realised that not all development is progress. He felt that the great technical achievements of our day were not keeping in step with our ethical development, and that there was a decline of social conscience. He was afraid that the increasing mechanisation in economic life and the centralisation of the modern state also mechanised our thoughts and feelings and weakened our moral sense. He considered this the gravest danger of our time, which he said could only lead to terrible social disasters.

Nettlau was the sworn enemy of dogmas and slogans, which hamper thought and fetter reason. He hated the despotism of ideas as much as he hated political and economic despotism. He called himself a heretic, and that was indeed what he was. He never hid his opinions, and he often told some uncomfortable truths to his own comrades, only they never paid enough attention to them. He knew that, and it made him sad. He once wrote to me: "To think for yourself is the hardest task of all. Yet one single new idea is worth more than a whole stock of mouldy musty theories."

Among those I met in London in the early days was Hermann Jung, who had been the Secretary of the First International. He had a small watchmaker's shop off the Gray's Inn Road. He was a Swiss, born in the Bernese Juras, but he had lived for many years in England, and spoke English as well as he spoke German and French. He told me a lot about the differences and clashes which had led to the split in the First International. According to him they had existed from the start, from its formation. He did not see how it could have been otherwise. The great service of the International Working Men's Association, which became known as the First International, he said, was that by the principles laid down in the Inaugural Address, and by the federalist nature of its statutes it had allowed complete liberty of movement to each national association, requiring only that its members in all countries should work for the common aim of the Association, the economic, political and social emancipation of the working class. As long as each of the different trends could work for this aim in its own way there was no danger of a split.

The trouble started when the attempt was made at the London Conference in 1871 to impose the political methods of one special school of thought on all the national associations. Even the Juras Federation, which Marx and Engels and their followers always blamed for the split had, according to Jung, never contemplated anything like it. Jung said he had never shared the socialist conceptions of the Jurassiennes, and he still believed that socialist ideas and endeavours had been most clearly formulated by Marx. Yet he had to admit that the Internationalists of the Juras were absolutely right in their defence of the principles of the International, and Marx and Engels were wrong, because they had arbitrarily tried to alter the old principles which, according to the statutes could be done only by a congress.

Jung put the blame for what happened in London on Engels who, on leaving Manchester in 1871 to settle in London, had become a member of the General Council. His domineering attitude got everybody's back up. Jung who had no good word to say for Germans generally, considered Engels a thorough German, even though he had lived in England for almost 50 years. He was never able to understand anyone else's point of view. As it happens, Max Beer expressed the same feeling about Engels in his book *Fifty Years of International Socialism*. According to Jung the members of the General Council had always got on well together, till Engels appeared. Marx had always consulted his close colleagues, and had considered their opinions. As soon as Engels opened his mouth there was trouble. With him it was bend or break. He knew no middle way. He refused to yield on any question, as people must do in a body like the International, which was composed of divergent trends, if it is to exist at all. Engels behaved in the General Council like a bull in a china shop, Jung said. When Engels was appointed corresponding secretary for Italy and Spain the clashes became inevitable. There was no longer any chance of co-operating in the General Council. Marx fell increasingly under the influence of Engels, and so became estranged from most of his old friends. Jung thought that Marx could not oppose Engels because Marx's family depended for years on the financial help they received from Engels. But this was a subject Jung was most reluctant to talk about.

Jung said the clashes in the General Council continued until he, Georg Eccarius and most of the English members of the Council became convinced that the International must collapse, unless the General Council was transferred to Belgium or Switzerland. Marx and Engels opposed any such idea; it ended with the split in the International. What is important about Jung's story is that he remained a life-long Marxist, and stood at all the congresses of the International for the theoretical principles laid down by Marx.

Chapter 6

Milly:
How We Went to New York
and Came Back

I continued my visits to the Jewish comrades in Whitechapel. I was working at the time in Lambeth, and I found the journey easier from the East End. So I rented a room in Shoreditch, in the house of a Jewish comrade, Aaron Atkin. He kept a small shop. Some comrades in the Jewish movement used to meet in his shop parlour. I spent many pleasant hours with them, talking and discussing.

It was in that circle I really got to know Milly Witcop, who afterwards became my life's partner. She was one of the most devoted members of the *Arbeter Fraint* group. I had met her before in the West End, among the German comrades. She used to go there to sell papers and pamphlets, and to collect funds for the activities of her movement. She was 18 or 19, a slim young girl, simple and unaffected, with thick black hair and deep, large eyes, earnest and eager and zealous for our cause. Everybody held her in high regard. But it was only when I came to live in the ghetto that I got to know her rare and beautiful character. We became close friends.

I had met a girl at home in Germany, who followed me to Paris. We had a child, my son Rudolf. We lived together in Paris, and afterwards in London, but without ever discovering any spiritual bond between us. We parted. She insisted on keeping the child. Later, when she married another man, the child was in his way, and Milly and I took him. He was six at the time. Milly and I had meanwhile found our way to each other. She was a good mother to my son. Milly and I have been together for a very long time now. Our union has withstood all the blows and buffettings of fate. We have been happy together. We have never regretted our choice. Our companionship has brought out certain qualities in me that could never have developed under less favourable conditions. A man who has stood as I have from his earliest youth in the crush and throng of a movement must have a place where he can find inner peace, and another human being who is not only his wife, but his friend and comrade, to whom he can open his heart and trust her with everything.

Not even the freest and most emancipated ideas about the relationship of the sexes can alter this fact. I know there is no golden rule in these matters, that human beings are very different in their nature, and that one can't lay down any general principle that will apply to everybody. I realise that I have been a very lucky man in this regard. We have gathered no wordly treasures on our life's road. We have been richly acquainted with hardships and dangers. But we have carried the burden together; we have lived and worked and fought as good comrades; we never had reason to reproach each other, for our cause was the same for both of us. But in return we have had much joy, such as is given only to people for whom the struggle for a great cause has become a vital need. We did not have to go searching for the blue bird. He was always with us.

Milly was born in Zlatapol, a small town in the Ukraine. She had a hard childhood. Her parents were very poor. Her father was a tailor, who made and repaired clothes for the estate owners round about. However hard he worked there was always want in the house.

Her mother was a deeply religious Jewess, a fine woman, who in spite of her own poverty was always helping others poorer than herself. She did the same afterwards in London. She devoted herself to the relief of the poorest of her Jewish fellow-beings. Her reward was that she was venerated in her own circle as almost a saint. She was always looking for something to do for others. And she was so modest and unassuming about it that everybody had to respect her.

Milly had been very religious as a child. The family was proud of her piety. She came to London in 1894 hardly more than a child. She went to work in the tailoring sweatshops of the East End, and for years grudged herself a bite of bread to save up the fare to bring her parents and sisters to London and provide a home for them.

But meanwhile she had undergone a change. At home, in the small town in the Ukraine, her world had been one of simple folk, who held strictly to the traditions of their Jewish faith and practice. In London she found people for whom religion had become a dead ritual. The conditions under which she lived and worked forced her to draw conclusions which she could not reconcile with her old beliefs. Her young spirit was tormented by doubts. Milly was one of those natures who cannot accept anything by halves. She always looked for a whole. It must have been agony to her to be a divided being.

She came upon a strike meeting of Jewish bakery workers in the East End. The speeches made a tremendous impression on her. She felt that she must join the fight against injustice. She had started on the road that led her to the meetings of the Jewish anarchists at the Sugar Loaf public house. The rest followed. Milly read our literature, attended our meetings regularly. She had lost her old religion, but she had replaced it with a new faith.

When her parents at last arrived in London with the other children they no longer found the daughter they had known before. She was a grown, mature person, standing on her own feet. She was still devoted to them, helpful, affectionate.

But one could hardly expect these old people, completely untouched by modern ideas, to understand the inner transformation in their daughter. They showed the same love to her as always, but they felt they had lost her. The father could not help reproaching her sometimes. The mother never did. She kept her grief hidden in her heart. To her, utterly absorbed in her religion, the calamity that had struck her was God-ordained, something against which man must not complain, but must accept and make the best of it. The three other daughters, Polly, Fanny and Rose later went the same road as Milly. It was a heavy blow for their parents.

When I first got to know her Milly was living with her parents and her three sisters. There is no doubt that she felt and was moved by the grief of her parents, but what could she do? Should she hide her real beliefs, and play a game of pretence? That her nature would not allow. She had to be completely, wholly herself. She could give her parents everything in her power, but she could no longer think as they thought.

In December 1897 I had a letter from an old friend in New York, proposing that I should come to America. He said I was sure to find a good job there. He offered to send me the tickets for the passage as soon as I would be ready to come.

But I felt I belonged to Europe. To go to the New World seemed to me an act of desertion. Therefore I wrote to my friend that I couldn't think of it.

Yet four months later the idea came back to me. There was a strike where I worked, against a reduction of wages. We lost the strike. I lost my job; and it didn't look as if I could find another for a long time. So I thought of America as a way out of my difficulty. I wrote to my friend and he sent me the ticket.

Of course I spoke about it to Milly. We were not living together yet. We had no relationship as man and wife. But we had now been close and intimate friends for over a year. She agreed at once to go to America with me.

We had arranged to go in the middle of April; but war broke out between the United States and Spain, and the American government requisitioned all the big passenger ships for war service. The shipping companies could offer us accommodation only on a small boat leaving Southampton on May 15th. We had registered for the passenger list as married, which meant we would have a small cabin to ourselves. I mention this private matter only because it became the subject of a big state action against us, which occupied the attention of the American Press for weeks.

The "Chester" was an old tub, that had been hastily got ready for the purpose. Our cabin, which was between-decks, was tiny and gloomy, without any comfort at all. Yet we did not mind, for we were two young people about to step over the threshold into our new life together. The voyage took two whole weeks, but the weather was favourable, and we had few other passengers on board, which was just what we wanted. We were due to arrive in New York on the morning of May 29th. But we were delayed outside New York harbour by a sudden thick fog. The engines had to be stopped, and we lay there all that morning. The fog signals were kept going all the time. The fog began to lift about noon. Soon we saw the blue sky again and the sun shining on the sea. New York lay before us, and in the distance the Statue of Liberty, holding the torch.

We stood on deck the whole time, feeling almost sorry that the voyage was over, for it had sealed our union. It was not till late in the afternoon that we reached the landing pier. After the first formalities were over we were driven like a herd of cattle on to a small boat that took us to an island. That was the place where the immigrants were put through their examination. The old building where the immigrants had to wait till they were given permission to go ashore had been burned down a short while before. A temporary building had been hastily erected.

Sometimes immigrants had to wait several days before a decision was reached about them, and as there was no sleeping accommodation there the immigrants were put at night on an old ship, where the men had a dormitory between-decks, and the women slept on the upper deck. Next morning we were all brought back to the island, where we had our meals, in a vast hall. It was empty and ugly, making us feel very unhappy and dejected. We didn't expect comfort, but this place was filthy and verminous.

When we first entered it the hall was packed with immigrants, who had arrived on two other boats the day before. We were divided by the alphabet into small groups, to the accompaniment of a continuous shouting and bellowing in every language under the sun, so that it sounded like a madhouse. Sometimes the officials poked their sticks into those of us who did not understand, to show us where they wanted us to go. We noticed that it was those who looked shabby or less intelligent who were mostly subjected to this treatment. When it came to our turn we were taken, a group of us, into a smaller room, where a great many officials sat at their desks, which were heaped with papers. The official who dealt with us asked me several questions. I answered briefly. Then he asked for our marriage papers.

We hadn't any. He noted this down, and told us to go. The next day we were taken to another room, where four high officials and an elderly lady sat round a table. We were offered two chairs. One of the officials addressed me in German: "You say you have forgotten your marriage certificate. People don't forget such things when they come on a journey like this."

"I didn't say that," I answered. "I said we have no marriage certificate. Our bond is one of free agreement between my wife and myself. It is a purely private matter that concerns only ourselves, and it needs no confirmation from the law."

The old lady looked straight at Milly, and said to her: "But you can't as a woman agree with that. Don't you see the danger you are in? Your husband can leave you whenever he pleases, and you have no legal hold on him."

"Do you suggest," Milly answered, "that I would consider it dignified as a woman and a human being to want to keep a husband who doesn't want me, only by using the powers of the law? How can the law keep a man's love?"

"This is the first time I have heard a woman speak like that," the old lady said reproachfully. "If everyone ignored the law in respect of marriage, we should have free love."

"Love is always free," Milly answered. "When love ceases to be free it is prostitution."

The old lady bit her lip, and said no more. Then the official who had addressed me before asked if I would swear that I was not legally married to another woman. He said I need not answer the question, if I didn't wish

42

to. I said I could answer it, and would. I was not married to any other woman. He handed me a Bible, and asked me to swear on it. I said my word would have to do, because neither of us belonged to any church.

Next morning a number of people came to question us. We assumed they were police agents. They were very polite to us, and the officials too treated us very courteously. Some were most friendly. One of the officials, who was born in France, to whom I had mentioned that I had lived in Paris for a few years, remarked that people looked at these things differently in France; America was a puritan country, and he was afraid that unless we agreed to get married we would both be sent back. He told us he had held his post on the island for ten years, and had never come across a case like ours before.

My friend who had sent me the ticket for the journey came to see me. He knew what had happened. Those people who had questioned us were newspaper reporters. The papers were full of us. He brought a batch of papers with him for me to see. Most of the reports in the big dailies were sensational and unfriendly. The reporter of the Yiddish social democratic paper *Arbeter Zeitung* brought us a copy of his paper, which headed its report: "Love without marriage, rather than marriage without love."

Then an old gentleman came to see us. We were taken to a very comfortable room, and offered coffee and cakes. The old gentleman assured us that he had no doubt about the purity of our intentions, but society could not exist if everybody thought and behaved as we did. "You are young people," he said, "trying to break through a brick wall with your heads. One day you will discover that it is impossible."

He told us there would be a proposal made to us, which would solve our difficulty, and he advised us to accept it. We found afterwards that the old gentleman was T.V. Powderly, who had been President of the Knights of Labour, once a great trade union organisation; he was the Commissioner-General of Immigration.

Two days later the proposal was made to us. It was that we would be admitted if we first got legally married. We might have agreed, for there seemed no other way. But we could not see why we were being ordered to do something for which there was no law in the United States to justify such intervention in our private life. The only people who were excluded by the immigration laws were criminals, the feeble-minded and those with incurable diseases. We were none of these. The law against the admission of foreign anarchists, which has not been properly tested juridically even now, came into force five years later. Therefore our case was unique. We said we would prefer the journey back to Europe, as we considered the decision taken with regard to us contrary to the law, and we did not believe that we had done anything wrong, for which we ought to reproach ourselves. Honest people had sometimes to sacrifice material advantages for the sake of their self-respect.

The day before we left I had another unpleasant experience. My friend had promised to come again, to say goodbye to us. We were sitting in our usual places when an official came to say that there was a letter for us. It was from my friend, who had written that he found it impossible to get away in time. But I did not know that. They did not give me the letter. They took me to a room, where an official I had never seen before asked my name. I told him. He then produced a letter, and instead of giving it to me slit it open, and started to read it. That made me furious. After all, we were not criminals in prison, but passengers who had paid our fares.

So I snatched the letter away from him, and put it in my pocket. That made him mad. He stormed and raged at me, and said I must give him back my letter. I refused. Our voices rose higher and higher, till two officials came running in from the next room to see what the row was about. When I explained, one of them, who behaved very decently, assured me that this was the procedure with all letters for immigrants; it was a precaution they had to take to prevent immigrants who came without money, as required by the immigration regulations, getting it sent to them by friends outside.

"Then I should have been told that," I answered. "I would have opened my letter, and I would have let you see that there was no money there. But I will not have you open my letters." Next morning we were taken back on board the Chester, where everyone, of course, knew our story. But we were treated there with the utmost consideration. It was a beautiful, bright summer's day when we started our journey back to England. We stood on deck, and watched the green banks of the Hudson glide past. When we saw the Statue of Liberty again she looked to me as though she wore the dress of a nun.

There were few passengers on board, and as the weather continued good all the way the voyage on this old tub turned out to be more of a pleasure trip for us than a punishment. The first morning out from New York we were approached on deck by one of the ship's officers, with a steward carrying a great bowl of fruit, which he handed us very politely. He introduced himself as the first engineer. He said he had come to express his personal sympathy at the way we had been treated in New York. He said he shared our views, and respected us because we had stood up for them. He asked if we knew Benjamin Tucker. I said we did not know him personally, but we knew of him, and we knew his views, and we knew his paper *Liberty*. He said he was a follower of Tucker's, and a regular reader of *Liberty*. He came to see us every day, each time bringing gifts of fruit, chocolate and cigarettes. We spent many hours together, talking.

Then the purser asked to see us. He wanted to know why we had been sent back. We told him. "Yes," he said, "that is what the newspapers reported. But that isn't what the immigration authorities told the company." We asked him what the company had been told. He said it was that we hadn't the minimum amount of money required for entry under the immigration laws. I took out my wallet and showed him my money. "Thank you," he said, "that is all I wanted to know."

Now why did the immigration authorities tell the shipping company this untruth? I can only suggest it was because the real reason gave them no legal ground for sending us back.

Our little adventure caused more stir than we had thought. Friends in America sent us batches of newspapers and periodicals from all parts of the

States, with reports and articles about us. C.E. Walker had a long article in the Chicago *Lucifer* telling our story, and condemning the behaviour of the immigration authorities. It completely supported our attitude, But there were points of detail that were misreported; they had been copied from the reports in the daily press. I wrote to Walker, explaining the facts, and dealing with the whole general question of the way the immigrants were treated. My letter appeared in *Lucifer* as an article running to two whole pages, and with a note on the front page directing special attention to it.

When we reached Southampton, and were landed without any questions being asked, without any examination, we felt doubly welcome after our experiences in New York.

Chapter 7

How I Became a Yiddish Editor

We did not stay long in London. I was not hopeful about finding work there. I made up my mind to try my luck in Brussels. But as the summer was a bad time there we postponed our departure till the autumn. Meanwhile we decided to try the provinces. We went to Liverpool. Walking along the street there, near the station, we were stopped by a young man, who turned out to be one of the Jewish workers who had attended our meetings in London. He told us that Moritz Jeger, whom we both knew from London, had a small printing shop quite near. The young man offered to take us there.

Jeger and his wife were glad to see us. When they heard we intended staying in Liverpool for a few months they suggested that we should take a room in their house. The rent was very little; two shillings a week. But the room was quite bare; not a stick of furniture in it. Jeger had two long, wide benches, which we could use as beds. The big case in which we had brought our belongings became our table. We added a couple of broken chairs. That was all our furniture.

We learned from Jeger that there were a number of Jewish comrades in Liverpool. But no activity. This was strange for Jewish anarchists, who were usually very active. It was due to internal disagreements for which, I learned later even from my own experience, Jeger was chiefly responsible. I had known Jeger in London only slightly, just from seeing him at meetings. I got to know him much better in the three months we lived under his roof. He was a man afflicted by a morbid ambition, far beyond his ability. His egoism was such that it was impossible for him to have any comradely relationship with the other comrades, they had gradually withdrawn from all activity, and had left him isolated.

The cause of the trouble was a small sheet, *The Rebel*, which Jeger had started about six months before we arrived, with another man we also knew from London, Albert Levey, who was cut from the same cloth as Jeger. There had been only two issues of the paper, because Jeger and Levey had soon found themselves at loggerheads. Each wanted all the laurels for himself. Their conflict monopolised the whole business of the group, with the result that the comrades gradually stopped coming to the meetings.

When we arrived Albert Levey had left Liverpool for Hull. Jeger was feeling his isolation. Few of the comrades came to see him, and he had no one to whom to show off. He was having a hard struggle to make a living. He was a poor devil, with an exaggerated sense of his own importance, whose unfortunate character made it impossible for him to have real friends. Like all unrecognised "geniuses", he never, of course, thought the fault might be his own. He blamed everybody else.

Our arrival gave him another chance to get in touch with the comrades. He sent a message to some of them who lived near, and that same evening we met Schaffler, Goodstone, Radutzky and Schatz, four good men, who had been in the movement for years. Then we had a meeting with all the comrades of the old group. There were about a dozen of them, including Silverstone and his wife, two very old comrades, who had been among the pioneers of the Jewish labour movement. They had been very active previously in Leeds. These plain, straightforward, active and thinking working class men and women were all excellent people. One could begin to do something with them. They were mostly middle-aged, older than I was. But except Jeger there was no one there who could speak for the cause on a public platform, And as the *Arbeter Fraint* had stopped publication they had no way of activity open to them. Some had for that reason joined the English group, which was really active at that time in Liverpool. The English group had three good, popular speakers, Kavanagh, O'Shea and Despres, who spoke every Sunday morning at the Monument, in the heart of Liverpool. Our English papers and pamphlets sold well there.

We decided that evening to revive the old group. We rented a small hall in Brownlow Hill for our meetings, which were quite well attended. I spoke there most Sunday evenings. It looked as if things were moving. Then suddenly, a few weeks later, Jeger got up at one of our meetings and, without having consulted any of us, not even me who lived under his own roof, proposed starting a small publication in Liverpool. He said a paper was essential in Liverpool, and as the London comrades were not able to do anything like that now, Liverpool must take the initiative. He offered to subscribe thirty shillings a week for the paper. He was sure it would also sell outside Liverpool, all over the country.

The comrades received his proposal very coolly, thinking that he was suggesting a revival of his own *Rebel*. But his next words made us all sit up. "Rocker will of course be the editor," he said.

It hit me like a bolt from the blue. I objected that I could neither write nor read Yiddish. I had learned the Hebrew alphabet while I was in London. I could decipher the heavy-type headings in the Yiddish papers, but that was all.

Jeger said I could write everything for the paper in German; he would translate it into Yiddish. But, I pointed out, I was not intending to remain in Liverpool. Jeger's answer was that if I left Liverpool, Frumkin would take over. He said he had corresponded with Frumkin, who was then in Paris, and Frumkin had agreed that if the paper was put on its feet he would come to Liverpool to carry on.

Frumkin afterwards assured me that there was not a word of truth in the story. Jeger had never been in touch with him about it. He had invented it all. But we didn't know that at the time. So Jeger won us over for his plan. Silverstone was the only one who remained doubtful about it. He thought we should at least consult the comrades in London and Leeds. It was no use starting a paper, and having to stop after the first two or three issues.

I shared his view; but the other comrades crowded round me, and finally persuaded me to take on the editorial duties for the first three months. If the paper was still going by then Frumkin would come from Paris to continue, The comrades had a whip round for the paper that evening, and we collected about £5. They promised to make the same contributions every week, till the paper paid its way.

If I could have had any idea then of what I was letting myself in for I should never have agreed. I didn't know my Jeger yet. He was what we call an intellectual. In Galicia, where he was born, he had gone to a good school, and he knew German and Polish fluently. He had even published in Lemberg in 1896 a few numbers of a Polish sheet called *Trybun Ludowy*. It was said that he had assisted Frumkin in editing the *Arbeter Fraint*. Of course I couldn't judge his literary and journalistic abilities. I knew neither Polish nor Yiddish. I had no reason to think that he couldn't translate what I would write into Yiddish.

That episode in Liverpool shaped the rest of my life. By such pure chance I found my way into the Jewish labour movement. If that young man who saw us near the railway station in Liverpool had not recognised us we should probably not have looked up the Jewish comrades, and all the rest would not have followed. I never thought when we went to Liverpool that it was to be the beginning of my career as a Yiddish editor.

Our first issue, four pages, appeared on July 29th, 1898. We called it *Dos Freie Vort* (The Free Word). Silverstone, a good, dependable man, was a reliable business manager. But I soon found Jeger impossible. He took liberties with my articles. Not only were his translations poor; he kept adding a lot of inflated phraseology of his own, so that I didn't recognise what I had written when it was read out to me. He also put stupid reports in the paper, which made us look silly. For instance, he printed a story about a boatload of shipwrecked sailors who were devoured by sharks. "This is what we get as a result of capitalism," was the strange comment he printed at the end of this report. I couldn't understand what the sharks had to do with capitalism. As I couldn't read the Yiddish proofs, I was at his mercy.

So every time the paper appeared I had to have a row with Jeger. In the end it was decided that nothing must be put in print that I hadn't been told about before. It didn't help me very much, because I still depended on Jeger's translations, and he made an unholy mess of everything I wrote. I felt like chucking the whole thing, but that would have been desertion. The comrades were so selflessly devoted, so dedicated to the cause that I couldn't leave them in the lurch. The only thing to do was to learn Yiddish. I made fairly rapid progress, particularly as Yiddish was much closer at that time to German than it is now.

Dos Freie Vort was still a poor paper. It hadn't room enough for me to deal adequately with theoretical questions; and so far as propaganda was concerned I knew neither my readers nor their language well enough. So I was surprised at the warm reception the paper got from comrades all over the country. Congratulations, subscriptions and donations arrived from Leeds, Manchester, Glasgow, from London itself; and after the first few issues the paper paid its way. Of course, our only expenditure was for printing and despatch. Everything else was voluntary. After four or five issues had appeared I received a letter from Eyges, the Secretary of the *Arbeter Fraint* group in London, telling me that the London comrades had decided to revive the *Arbeter Fraint*, if I would agree to be the editor. He thought London was a more suitable place for a paper, and an eight-page publication would serve our purpose better than a small provincial sheet. He was right, of course. Eyges added that David Isakovitz would take over the administration, and Frumkin in Paris had agreed to be a regular contributor. Everything depended on my decision.

I put the whole thing to the Liverpool comrades. They said they would of course have preferred me to remain with them, but they recognised that it was more important for the movement to have a paper like the *Arbeter Fraint*, which before it was suspended had existed for twelve whole years. Also Jeger was giving us all a lot of trouble. The decision was to keep our paper going till the London comrades would have completed all their arrangements for the reappearance of the *Arbeter Fraint*. I communicated this decision to Eyges, and the London group expressed its complete satisfaction with this decision.

The eighth and final issue of our paper appeared on September 17th, 1898. Immediately after Milly and I returned to London. Four weeks later the first number of the renewed *Arbeter Fraint* came out, beginning its thirteenth year.

Chapter 8

Aaron Lieberman

I ought to say something at this point about the beginnings and the background of the Jewish socialist labour movement working in Yiddish among the East European Jewish immigrants, into which I had now entered. It was started in London about the middle 70s. Its immediate initiator was Aaron Lieberman, who is rightly called the "father" of Jewish socialism. He was one of the most remarkable men in the socialist movement of that period. It is only recently that some light has been thrown on his life and tragic death, notably in a valuable study, *Lieberman and Russian Socialism* by Boris Sapir, which appeared in 1938 in the *International Review of Social History*, published by the International Institute for Social History in Amsterdam. The author drew mainly for his material on previously unpublished letters in the archives of the Russian revolutionary Valerian Smirnov, which are now in the possession of the Institute in Amsterdam. Smirnov was a close associate of Peter Lavrov.

Lieberman was born in 1849, of a Jewish bourgeois family in the Grodno district in Russia. He was given a strictly religious Jewish education and upbringing. He became a student at the Technological School in St. Petersburg, but could not complete his course. In Petersburg he got to know a group of young Russian socialists. He read the socialist literature which was circulated by the underground movement, and broke away from his religious traditions. He was greatly influenced by the ideas of Peter Lavrov, in his periodical *Vperiod* (Forward), started in Zurich in 1872. He became one of its contributors. In the early 70s he went to Vilna, where Sundelewitch introduced him into a secret group, which seems to have consisted entirely of Jewish intellectuals. Vilna, "Jerusalem in Lithuania", had a famous Rabbinical Seminary, where socialist ideas were becoming widespread among the students. It was the same sort of thing that was going on at that time in the Russian priesthood seminaries, which produced a great many socialists. This subterranean activity could not be concealed for long from the teachers and directors of the Rabbinical Seminary. They naturally tried to cover it up, so that it should not come to the attention of the government, which might have endangered the existence of the seminary. But there was a traitor among the students, a man named Steinberg, who informed the police. The government closed the Rabbinical Seminaries in Vilna and in Jitomir. It did not stop the revolutionary movement among the students. They went to the Russian high schools or they went to study at the universities abroad, and were caught up more than ever in the revolutionary activity.

But the Jewish students who were won in this way for socialism carried on their activity in the general Russian movement. While they were in the

Jewish Seminaries they had spread their ideas in their own Jewish circles. Now they worked with their Russian comrades. Many of them went "to the people", like the others; they lived with the Russian poor, shared their life, with the idea of influencing them. It didn't occur to them that they could also work among the Jewish masses of Poland and Lithuania, to win them for the new ideas, and to help them to improve their social and spiritual condition.

One could find several explanations for this strange fact. The intellectually progressive Jewish youth in Russia considered religion and religious ritual the great obstacle to the development of free thought, and when they had emancipated themselves from the Jewish traditional ways of life they felt as though they had escaped from a prison. They were out of the ghetto. They saw the great world open before them. They had no wish to keep up their contact with the Jewish masses, who were completely under the influence of Jewish tradition. Even their language, Yiddish, was still undeveloped; the Jewish intellectuals despised it as a "jargon", and used Hebrew, which the Jewish masses did not understand.

The young Jewish socialists of that period consequently had no connections with the Jewish masses. They were content to gain new adherents among the Jewish intellectuals, but they devoted themselves to Russian propaganda. Vladimir Jochelson, a close comrade of Lieberman's in Vilna, described this state of affairs later in his memoirs published in the Russian periodical *Byloe*.

"It may be asked why we wanted to work among the Russian people, and not among the Jewish population. The explanation is that we had broken away and become estranged from the culture of the Russian Jews of that period; we had a negative attitude to the bourgeois and orthodox sections, whom we had left when we became acquainted with the new teachings. As for the Jewish working masses, we believed that the liberation of the Russian nation would also liberate all the other nationalities in Russia. I must admit that the treatment of the Jewish world in Russian literature had impressed us with the idea that the Jews were not a nation, but a parasite class. This was the view put forward even by progressive Russian writers."

The group which Lieberman joined in Vilna had been started in 1872, by a Jewish student named Finkelstein. Sundelewitch, whom I knew afterwards in London, was the leading figure in that group. It maintained contacts with a revolutionary circle in Petersburg, including Anna Epstein, Rosa Idelson, who became Smirnov's wife, and Dr Leo Ginsberg, a follower of Lavrov. Anna Epstein, who came from Vilna herself, and was studying at Petersburg, kept the group supplied with illegal literature, for study by its members. The group as such, Sundelewitch told me, belonged to no definite socialist trend, but studied everything it could get in the way of socialist literature. Russian youth was at that time very much under Bakunin's influence. Lavrov's followers were also very much to the fore with their ideas, which were not much different from Bakunin's. Lavrov also wanted political decentralisation and the exclusion of the state from the life of society. They differed only in their methods.

51

Jochelson writes about Lieberman at that period: "He had obtained a European education. He had a command of several European languages, and he was an orator. He was thoroughly conversant with the Talmud, and he had a great love of the Hebrew literature. He was a talented Yiddish publicist. He was a free-thinker, but he was no less occupied in our circle with questions of nationalist conscience with regard to the Jewish people. He worked in our group to get socialist literature published in the Yiddish language."

Yet Lieberman was not a Jewish nationalist. He was far from holding nationalist ideas. That is clear from his writings. In the first issue of his periodical *Haemeth* (The Truth), he wrote: "It is not national love that moves us to publish this periodical. We do not consider our nation superior to any other. A nation should not be superior to another, any more than one man should be superior to another. Only love for mankind in general and the oppression of the people moves us to tell the truth in the language the people understands."

Lieberman was the first man who recognised the importance of socialist propaganda among the East European Jews. To understand what that meant we must have an idea of the social life of the Jews in Russia at that time. There is an excellent description of it, called "The Development of Socialist Thought in the Hebrew Press of Eastern Europe", which appeared in the Year Book for Social Science and Social Politics (*Jahrbuch fuer Sozialwissenschaft und Sozialpolitik*) published by Dr Ludwig Richer in 1881 in Zurich.

It begins: "Russian Jewry is in no way to be compared with that of Western Europe. The one is thoroughly demoralised, sunk in usury. The other is a factor with which the future revolution must reckon."

I interrupt the quotation to point out that this wholesale condemnation of West European Jewry must, like all sweeping generalisations about any collective body be taken with a grain of salt. Though most Jews native in the countries of Western Europe belonged to the middle class, and some were engaged in high finance, a very considerable number took a prominent part in general cultural life as artists, writers, doctors and scientists, and must not be lumped together with the socially harmful elements who exist in all nations. Nevertheless, this contrast drawn by a socialist East European Jew between the East European and the Western Jews deserves to be noted.

The article proceeds: "Cramped in a comparatively narrow strip of the vast Russian Empire, three million Jews live almost entirely in the towns, where they form the majority of the population. They are workers and artisans. They are land workers and factory workers, carriers and cart drivers; they are the urban proletariat. Only a minority are merchants and bankers and factory owners. The reactionary educational policy of the Russian autocracy, and the lack of schools has led to this proletariat being brought up in ignorance of the Russian language. There was need of an independent agitation among them, but there were no agitators, because all who are of Jewish origin preferred to work in the Russian field. That was the time when everybody thought the work must be concentrated on the

Russian agitation. When this centralisation was abandoned, and each nationality began to organise its own work, the Hebrew Press came to life."

Lieberman was not only the first man who recognised the need of a socialist activity among the East European Jews. He also knew that each national group has certain qualities and historic traditions, of which the socialist movement must take account, if it is to find any contact with the people. Liberman believed he had found these points of contact in ancient Jewish history. Thus he wrote in *Vperiod*:

"The community has always been the basis of our whole existence. The revolution itself created our tradition. The community was the basis of our legislation, which in unmistakable words forbade the sale of the land, and in the sense of equality and brotherhood required a redistribution of the soil every seven years. Our most ancient social system is anarchy; our true federation over the entire earth — the International. The great prophets of our time, Marx, Lassalle and the others, based themselves on the spirit of our people, and thus attained inner ripeness."

It was because Lieberman believed that he had found in the ancient traditions the true socialist core of Judaism that he hated the rich upper class of his people with all the passion of the prophets of old. Thus he wrote in his *Call to the Jewish Youth*:

"We have had to pay for your sins! The race hatred, the religious hatred, with all their terrors, have fallen mostly upon us. You kindled the fire that devours us. We have you to thank for it that the name Israel has become a curse. The entire Jewish people, suffering and astray, must suffer more than all other peoples because of your greed. It is your fault that we have been exposed to calumny. International speculators, who have dragged our name through the mud, you do not belong to us!"

Besides the Jewish bourgeoisie Lieberman attacked the Rabbinate, whom he blamed for the spiritual stagnation of the Jewish masses in Russia. He accused the representatives of Jewish theology of having forgotten the living word of the ancient prophets, and said that instead of working with the people, they were working against it, to make its spirit amenable to its social enslavement. The prophets of the Bible had stood with the people against their oppressors. But the present-day representatives of the Jewish religion defended the rich and tried to make the poor accept their exploitation. We shall understand Lieberman's indignation better if we remember that the Rabbis in Vilna at that time publicly preached in the synagogues against the socialists, to try to gain the friendship of the Russian government.

Lieberman appears to have been contemplating his call to the Jewish youth while he was still in Vilna. But in June 1875 the secret group to which he belonged was discovered by the Russian police, and dissolved. Sundelewitch, Jochelson, Wainer and Lieberman managed to get away abroad in time. Sundelewitch went to Koenigsberg; Lieberman and Wainer fled to London. The publishers of *Vperiod* transferred the paper from Zurich to London, and Lieberman learned typesetting on this Russian paper; he was probably thinking of returning to Russia, where this accomplishment would have been valuable for his work in the underground movement.

Vperiod belonged at that time to a secret group, from which the Zemlia i Wolia organisation developed soon after. The agreement with the group seems to have provided for Lieberman to be typesetter, artist and literary contributor to the paper. In addition, he was appointed editor of a Hebrew socialist paper which was to have appeared in London, under the name *Hapatish* (The Hammer). Lieberman had already drawn up the programme of this paper, but its publication was postponed for lack of funds.

During his first stay in London, Lieberman maintained close relations with the German comrades of the Communist Anarchist Group and with the International Revolutionary League formed by the Polish socialist Valerian Wroblewski.

But his work was mainly among the Jewish workers in the East End. On May 13th, 1876, he founded in Whitechapel, with his friends Wainer and Lazar Goldenberg, the Association of Jewish Socialists, whose statutes were printed in No. 37 of *Vperiod*. It was the first association of Jewish socialists. Lavrov and Smirnov were present at the inaugural meeting, and Smirnov seems to have taken an active interest in the group; he helped Lieberman considerably with both advice and assistance.

The Association of Jewish Socialists was an elite of thinking people, who were acquainted with socialist thought, and wanted to improve the lot of the Jewish workers in London. At its second meeting the question already under discussion was how to get the Jewish workers interested in the formation of trades unions. It was decided to hold public meetings to show the victims of the sweatshop system how they could improve their lot by fighting for it through the organisation of their own forces. But the result of this propaganda was not very successful. Taking into consideration the background and composition of the great majority of those early Jewish immigrants from Russia one could hardly have expected more. But it was the first attempt to create a trades union organisation among the Jewish workers in Britain.

Soon after the establishment of the Association, Lieberman went to Berlin, where there was an active group of Russian-Jewish students, in close contact with another such group in Koenigsberg, and also with the German socialist movement. He thought of interesting them in his projected Hebrew socialist paper. He returned to London in a few weeks. He had just published in London his *Call to the Jewish Youth*, which caused a stir, for it was the first socialist manifesto directed to the East European Jews.

Lieberman's manifesto was on the lines of the similar manifestoes circulated by the Russian revolutionaries to the student youth of the time. It was in Hebrew, and was signed by "The Volunteers of the People of the House of Israel".

"Private property leads to class war," it said, "and places personal interest above the interests of society. The governments established on the principle of nationality incite one nation against another, causing war. Religion has elevated folly and deceit above sound human reason. Those who think they can achieve anything in this way range themselves between the friends of the people and their enemies. Your future does not lie in the old commandments of the past, which have long lost their moral value. Emancipate yourselves from the power-lust that lies at the bottom of your privileges. Stop praying to gold and might! Away with the cult of the past! Ally yourselves with the people and its true friends! All nations are preparing for battle. The proletariat is uniting to shake off the yoke of capital and tyranny. Oppressed humanity is organising positions to regain its rights and liberties. The social revolution has raised its banner, and calls you to community of labour, community of labour production and of social wealth, the free fraternity of the workers of all lands, the removal of all rule by force and of everything that is opposed to the demands of justice. It is time for the working masses of the Jewish people to join this great work. Human brotherhood knows no division according to nations and races; it knows only useful workers and harmful exploiters. Against these the working people must fight. You have to thank for your education this despised people, that has had to pay with its suffering and its blood for your privileges. Go to the people, and suffer with it, inspire the one, and strengthen the other in the great fight against the lords of the world, against the oppressors and the exploiters of creative labour!"

This call found its way to the Jewish ghetto towns of Russia and Poland, and became the starting point for the life-work of many young idealists there.

In England, the Anglo-Jewish community, headed by the Chief Rabbi, Dr Adler, opened a campaign against the Association of Jewish Socialists, like that which the Rabbis in Vilna had conducted previously. The *Jewish Chronicle* started an agitation against the foreign nihilists who, it said, had come to London to incite the Jewish immigrants to disorder. Sermons were preached against them in the East End synagogues. Many members of the Association of Jewish Socialists were dismissed from their employment. Some yielded to this economic pressure and withdrew from the Association. But most of the members stood firm, and were only fortified in their convictions by this persecution, as often happens in such cases.

In December 1896 Lieberman left London, and went first to Berlin and then to Koenigsberg. During this time he succeeded in raising some money for his projected Hebrew paper, which he called *Haemeth* (The Truth). The first number appeared in May 1877, in Vienna. There were altogether only three issues. The contents were rich and varied, a social novel, poems, book reviews, political essays, and articles on "The Jewish Question", "The Social Status of the Jews in Hungary", "The Jews in London", "The Life of Johann Jacobi", etc.

The paper circulated mostly in Russia. There was such a demand for it that it had to print a second edition of the first issue. Its existence seemed assured. Then Lieberman was suddenly arrested in Vienna, in February 1878. He had been living there on a false American passport made out in the name of Arthur Freeman. On November 11th, 1878, after he had been in prison for ten months, he was sentenced to one month's imprisonment on a charge of inciting the Slav peoples in Austria. Meanwhile the Prussian government had demanded his extradition to Berlin. The Anti-Socialist Law had come into force there. The Austrian government did not send Lieberman to Prussia direct. It sent him to Bavaria. He was arrested in Munich and was transported to Berlin.

Most of the members of the Russian-Jewish student group to which Lieberman had belonged were under arrest there. They were all, including Lieberman, put on trial. It was the famous Nihilist Trial of 1879. Lieberman was sent to prison for eight months. So he spent nearly two years in prison in Austria and Germany, including the time he was in custody awaiting trial.

On his release in 1879 he was deported from Germany. He went back to England. He found things had changed considerably there since he had left London. The Association of Jewish Socialists no longer existed. But most of its former members belonged to a new organisation, the Third Section of the Communist Workers' Educational Union. *Vperiod* had stopped publication, and its publishers had left London. Lieberman's two closest friends, Zuckerman, who had stood at his side when he was publishing *Haemeth* in Vienna, and Sundelewitch, had gone back to Russia, where they were soon arrested and sent to Siberia. But he also found new friends in London, among them Morris Wintchevsky, whom he had got to know in Koenigsberg. Wintchevsky had left Germany because of the Anti-Socialist Law.

His imprisonment had very much affected Lieberman. It had cut him off from developments in the movement in Russia, where the Narodniki Party had split. Lieberman belonged to the old school of socialists who put all their trust in propaganda. The new movement in the Party had decided to engage in political terror. A series of bold actions won over to it many daring spirits who thought this method would bring the Czarist regime crashing down. Lieberman did not know where he belonged. His letters to Smirnov show how perplexed he was. He wanted to go back to Russia to offer the new movement his services. But he was full of ideological doubts. It made him melancholy.

During his second stay in London Lieberman renewed his contacts with the German movement. He lectured frequently to the First Section of the Communist Workers' Educational Union. He got to know Johann Most, who had since 1879 been publishing his *Freiheit* in London. Most invited Lieberman to write for *Freiheit*. He contributed several articles and also wrote several reports for it about the revolutionary movement in Russia, which he translated from the Russian. He was torn with longing to go back to Russia. In the end he made up his mind; he offered his services to the new party in Russia. But the party turned him down. Leo Hartmann, a prominent terrorist, had been asked for his opinion of Lieberman. His report was that Lieberman would not do for the new terrorist activity. Life meant nothing more to Lieberman. He could not bear to stay in London. His inner unrest drove him away. He was full of dissatisfaction with himself and with everything round him. Towards the end of 1880 he emigrated to America. Soon after, in November 1880, he took his life. He was 31.

Chapter 9

After Lieberman

The attempt made by Liebermann and his friends to start a new movement among the Jewish workers in London did not succeed. They were pioneers, working on a hard soil. Yet from that time the East End of London was never without a small group of convinced socialists, who continued Lieberman's work. Morris Wintchevsky had come to London in 1879, shortly before Lieberman left London for America. His name was Benedikt. But in Jewish life and literature he is known as Wintchevsky, the pen name he adopted for his writings. He was born in 1856 in Yanova, a small place in the Kovno district, in Lithuania. At the age of 13 he was sent to Vilna to study at the Rabbinical Seminary. He was 17 when he got hold of a copy of Lieberman's *Call to the Jewish Youth*, and became a socialist. He left Russia at 18. He went to Koenigsberg, where he was active in a group of Russian Jewish students engaged in socialist activity. When Lieberman was arrested in Vienna and his *Haemeth* stopped, Wintchevsky started a Hebrew monthly, *Asefath Chachomim*. When Bismarck enforced the Anti-Socialist Law in Germany in 1878 Wintchevsky was arrested, like many others. The German police seem to have intended to include him in the famous Nihilist Trial of 1879, with Lieberman and the others. But they could not make out a case on which to prosecute, and released him. But they ordered him to leave Prussia. He went to London.

Wintchevsky was a man with a philosopher's mind, and the ability to develop his ideas for his readers logically and lucidly. That was his strength, He had another appeal to the Yiddish reader. He did not, like others at the time, overload his writing with high falutin German words and phrases. His written Yiddish was like the simple spoken tongue. He used the popular folk language. The subjects he chose for his writing made it necessary. For instance, his *Fragmentary Thoughts of a Mad Philosopher*, which appeared regularly in the *Arbeter Fraint*, were written in the form of talks between a grandfather and his grandson; they had therefore to be conversational and easy. "The Mad Philosopher", the name by which Wintchevsky was known, rendered a great service in this way not only to socialism but to the development of the Yiddish language and literature.

In 1884 Wintchevsky started in London *Der Poilisher Yidl*, the first socialist paper in Yiddish. It was to have been a weekly, but couldn't get enough circulation, so it appeared irregularly. Only 17 issues were published in a period of about nine months.

A year later another, more successful attempt was made with the publication of the *Arbeter Fraint*, which started as a small eight-page monthly. Most of the young people who were connected with the new paper were immigrants who had arrived in England in the 80s, like Philip Krantz,

B. Ruderman, William Wess, S. Freeman, L. Rutenberg, and a little later J. Friedental, H. Kaplansky, A. Kisluk and others. Most of them were anarchists, or very close to the anarchist movement. Philip Krantz was the only social democrat in that group, but he was also the only one in the group, except Wintchevsky, who could take charge of the editorial side of the paper. None of the others had that ability.

So on Wintchevsky's proposal they appointed Krantz editor, though his knowledge of Yiddish at the time was poor. Krantz's real name was Jacob Rombro. He was born in 1858 in a small town in Podolia, in Russia. He left Russia in 1881, and went to Paris to study. He started his literary career by contributing to Russian papers. He began writing Yiddish only after he had come to London, under Wintchevsky's influence. The first thing he wrote in Yiddish was an article on the pogroms in Russia, which appeared in Wintchevsky's *Poilisher Yidl*.

The *Arbeter Fraint* began as a non-party paper, giving space to all trends of thought in the socialist movement. The differences between the socialist parties were not so acute yet among the Russian-Jewish immigrants; so long as they could express their own ideas in the new paper they were willing to work together. It was not really difficult, because the Jewish anarchists at that time and for some time after accepted the idea of economic materialism; differences arose only in drawing practical conclusions from the Marxist conception of history. The questions of parliamentary activity and centralism, over which the socialist camp in most countries was split ever since the days of the First International concerned the immigrant Jewish socialists from Eastern Europe only in theory. The great majority of this immigrant Jewish working class population in the East End of London did not acquire British citizenship. Naturalisation was comparatively easy in America. In England it was difficult and expensive. So most of the East European Jewish immigrants remained foreigners in England, living their own separate life, speaking their own language, and thrown upon themselves in every regard.

This was the situation in which the *Arbeter Fraint* came into existence. The motto chosen for the paper and printed at the top of the front page was the wise saying of the great Jewish sage Hillel: "If I am not for myself, who will be? And if not now, when?"

The idea of the founders of the *Arbeter Fraint* was to spread socialism among the Jewish workers. But the paper was hardly fitted for that purpose in its early days. Its language for the ordinary reader was stilted and doctrinaire. What the Jewish workers needed at that time was the development of a trade union movement. Yet this was ignored; was treated as something unimportant, even actually harmful to socialism. The reason is that Philip Krantz and some of his close collaborators were completely influenced by Lassalle's ideas, and believed that the so-called iron law of wages was an economic and social fact, which made it impossible that the workers' standard of living in a capitalist society could ever improve, as any rise in wages would inevitably lead to an increase in prices, so that everything after a brief fluctuation would go back to the same level.

But this of course is not true. Marx himself disproved it, and he supported the work of the trades unions. The standard of living of the working class does not remain always at the same level. We need only think of the way the workers lived fifty years ago, and how they live today. But the belated Lassallians in Whitechapel at that time were convinced that the iron law theory was true. There was an article by Isaac Stone in the first issue of the *Arbeter Fraint*, called "Trades Union Movement and Socialism", which said: "The trades unions can be of little use now to the workers. Their effect is even actually harmful, because they divert the workers from the right path, which is socialism." In the second issue Krantz said much the same thing in his editorial. He argued that in a capitalist society the worker can't earn more "than he must needs have to buy absolute necessities, no more and no less than is required to keep him from starving."

Obviously such articles could not inspire the Jewish workers to organise trades unions. The socialists of that period were all convinced that the social revolution was near, and were unwilling to get involved with things not directly related to the ultimate aim, socialism. Yet the practical needs of everyday life forced them slowly but surely to change their attitude. The *Arbeter Fraint* staff was not big. There was the editor, Philip Krantz, and there were Morris Wintchevsky and Isaac Stone, who wrote regularly for it. And there were the reports that came in from the provinces and from America. The fifth issue contained an article by J. Jaffe, "What is Anarchism?" Jaffe, who was living in Paris at that time continued to contribute to the *Arbeter Fraint*, and in 1887, when he settled in London, he was asked to join the Editorial Board. For the first two years of its existence he was the only one who put forward anarchist ideas in the *Arbeter Fraint*. Later other writers came in who represented anarchist views. In London they were notably Simon Freeman and Harry Kaplansky, both young working men, who played an active part in the early period of the Jewish labour movement in England; and S. Yanovsky and Michael Cohn contributed frequently from America. The judicial murder in Chicago in 1887 contributed considerably to the expression of anarchist sentiments in the paper. The speeches of the accused in court, and their farewell letters, which were published in the paper, helped to awaken interest in anarchism among Jewish workers.

In February 1885 the radical movement among the East End Jewish workers started a club in Berner Street which, beginning with Number 12 of the paper became the proprietors of the *Arbeter Fraint*. This club was for years the centre of propaganda and social life among the Jewish comrades. It was also used by non-Jewish comrades, Russians, Poles, Germans and others, and it maintained connections with the different revolutionary clubs in the West End. The members of the Mile End branch of the English Socialist League used the club for their meetings. Its closest contact was with the German comrades. The young Jewish movement had few good speakers. Neither Krantz nor Wintchevsky could speak; Freeman, Kaplansky and Wess took an active part in discussions, but they were not yet able to make public speeches or to deliver lectures.

So in the first years there were more German comrades among the speakers than Jews.

Most members of the publishing group were not particularly pleased with the *Arbeter Fraint* in its first years. They wanted a fighting organ, that would speak up about the daily needs of the workers. No paper so small as the *Arbeter Fraint*, appearing once a month, could possibly do that. So the comrades began in the summer of 1886 to discuss the possibility of publishing the *Arbeter Fraint* as a weekly. That was not easy. But there was so much enthusiasm and readiness to contribute materially that with the first issue of its second year the *Arbeter Fraint* became a weekly. The whole tone of the paper changed. The contents and the language were more popular, nearer to what the workers understood and wanted; the circulation went up. The paper had found itself.

The tireless propaganda by word of mouth and in writing gradually had an effect on the Jewish working class masses, and there were the first signs of a real independent Jewish labour movement. Small trades unions sprang into existence among the cigarette makers, cabinet makers and stick makers, as well as in the tailoring and shoe-making industries. Not only in London, but also in the provinces, especially in Leeds, where the Jewish socialists formed a Workers' Educational Union, and laid the foundations of one of the first and strongest trades unions in the clothing industry. Socialist societies were organised in Glasgow and Liverpool, and later in Manchester and Hull. The same thing happened in Paris, where an active group was formed among the East European Jewish workers soon after the *Arbeter Fraint* had started publication. In December 1887 the *Arbeter Fraint* won a new regular contributor, S. Feigenbaum, who was then living in Antwerp. Born in Warsaw in 1860, in a Chassidic family, he had very early thrown off his religious beliefs, and proclaimed himself a free-thinker. He emigrated to Belgium in 1884. His first contributions to the *Arbeter Fraint* were histories of the socialist movement in different countries. His chief field of work was in popularly written criticisms of the Jewish religion, an examination of the origin of the religious customs and rites, on which he based socialist arguments. His articles may nowadays be found not very profound; they should not be judged by our later knowledge and understanding, but according to the conditions of the time when he wrote them. For the *Arbeter Fraint* of that period he was just the man. We must not fall into the error of minimising today what Feigenbaum did. It is a fact that his pamphlet *Where Does Man Come From?* was the most widely-spread piece of propaganda writing of that period.

On Krantz's invitation Feigenbaum came in 1888 to live in London. He was not only a valuable writer for the *Arbeter Fraint*, but also a great gain to the movement as a clever and popular speaker. He carried the new ideas to wider circles of Jewish workers. At first Feigenbaum stood fairly close to the libertarian movement; later he went over completely to the social democrats.

It so happened that Feigenbaum joined the movement in London just when certain events had in a way prepared the ground for his anti-religious campaign. The representatives of the Anglo-Jewish community considered the *Arbeter Fraint* and the young Jewish socialist movement a danger to the Jewish name. They tried hard to get the paper stopped. They thought money could do it. The *Arbeter Fraint* was printed at that time by a Jewish printer who seemed to be very much inclined to its ideas. The back page of each issue carried a call in heavy type: "Workers, do your duty. Spread the *Arbeter Fraint*." The compositor was bribed, with the result that when No. 26 appeared it carried the legend in this way: "Destroy the *Arbeter Fraint*". The bribe was enough for the man to take himself off to America. The next move was to bribe the printer himself. He refused to continue printing the paper. The *Arbeter Fraint* had to stop suddenly on May 6th, 1887, giving it no time to advise its readers. Not till July 29th was the group able to get out a leaflet explaining what had happened.

The *Arbeter Fraint* resumed publication on August 5th. No Jewish printer could be found in London with enough courage to resist the leaders of the community. But the news of what had happened, how the free expression of opinion had been suppressed, started a spontaneous movement, especially in America, to raise money to buy a printing press. The result was that the *Arbeter Fraint* became independent of outside printers.

In January 1889 the *Arbeter Fraint* doubled its size to eight pages. Philip Krantz resigned that year as editor, and went to America. The new editor was Konstantin Gallop, a Russian social revolutionary, who had worked on the paper with Krantz. His first articles had to be translated into Yiddish from Russian. In time he learned to express himself in Yiddish. He obtained several new contributors, M. Baranov, a social democrat, and Michael Cohn, P.A. Frank (Dr Merison) and from America S. Yanovsky, anarchists. The two anarchist Yiddish poets David Edelshtat and Joseph Bovshover also sent contributions from America. The social democrats had lost Krantz. But the anarchists too lost Jaffe, who went to America in 1889. The anarchists were still however the largest and most active element in the movement of that period. In 1888 they formed the Knights of Labour group, whose chief task was publishing anarchist pamphlets. It also made an attempt to change the tide which had been taking comrades away from England to America. The next comrade who went to America, Rutenberg, took with him an offer to Yanovsky to come to London to take over the *Arbeter Fraint*.

Yanovsky's arrival in London in March 1890 opened a new epoch in the Jewish labour movement in Britain. It expressed itself of course also in the *Arbeter Fraint* . Yanovsky was then at the height of his powers; he was a man of great ability, a first-rate journalist and a very fine speaker, who could hold his own with any opponent.

He was born in 1864. He received the usual Jewish education; he also attended a Russian school. He was 20 when he went to America; he became active there in the anarchist movement, and belonged to the New York group which in 1889 started the *Wahrheit*, which was the first anarchist paper in Yiddish. After twenty issues had appeared, it was replaced by the *Freie Arbeter Shtimme*, which is still published regularly in New York.

Yanovsky brought a definite party line into the London movement. The non-party element lost their hold. The movement had begun to grow up, and wanted a clear programme. Yanovsky arrived just when the time was ripe for him. He hastened the natural development. It made the differences between the groups more acute. By the early part of 1891 there was a definite split in the Berner Street Club.

The anarchists, who were by far the strongest section, remained in possession of both the club and the *Arbeter Fraint*. The social democrats and the non-party people withdrew, including some of the regular contributors to the *Arbeter Fraint*, like Wintchevsky, Feigenbaum, Baranov and Gallop, who tried to start a paper of their own. They issued the *Freie Velt* as a monthly; it only survived ten issues. In 1892 Wintchevsky made another attempt with the *Veker*, a weekly. It survived only for eleven issues. Eighteen months later Wintchevsky emigrated to America, where Baranov and Feigenbaum had preceded him. Only Gallop remained in London; he died in London a year later.

The *Arbeter Fraint* had lost most of its contributors. For months on end Yanovsky filled the paper himself, using several pen names. The movement stood by him. In some ways the movement and the *Arbeter Fraint* gained by no longer having to keep a united front on questions about which there were disagreements. For instance, the so-called iron law of wages, and the attitude to trades unionism. Philip Krantz and his followers had believed in the iron law of wages, and did little to encourage trade unionism. Yanovsky on the other hand flung himself into the battle for the trades unions and the fight against the sweating system. As an anarchist he held that the trades unions were an essential form of organisation for the defence of the working class. At that time Lewis Lyons was active in the Jewish trades union movement. He called himself a social democrat. He was really an opportunist. He maintained relations with the socialist movement, and he often wrote for the *Arbeter Fraint*. But at the same time he tried to organise a combination of the small master tailors, who were employers, and of the workers' trade union. He said it was the only way to bring an economic improvement for the workers in the trade.

Yanovsky fought Lyons in the paper and at public meetings. He denounced his plan, which he said was trying to establish an unnatural alliance, from which only the employers could gain. He set out the principles of trade union organisation and struggle. In his controversies with opponents Yanovsky was hard and harsh. The result was that Lyons became an irreconcilable foe of the *Arbeter Fraint* and of Yanovsky. The conflict was more embittered because some of the people who had left the Berner Street Club ranged themselves in their opposition to Yanovsky on the side of Lyons.

Yanovsky went on grimly. He came to every public meeting that was held in connection with this question, no matter which side called the meeting, and he insisted on putting his points. Most of the trades unions backed him. Lyons had support for some time in the tailoring trades unions. But Yanovsky fought him there too, and finally forced him to withdraw from the

Jewish labour movement.

Yanovsky nearly paid for it with his life. One night, on his way home from a meeting he was attacked in a small street, and banged on the head with a heavy iron. He was found bleeding and unconscious in the street, and taken to London Hospital. The doctors said the thick cloth cap he wore had saved his life.

Yanovsky had a hard time in London. But his will was iron, and he held on. He was almost alone in the *Arbeter Fraint*. He did not claim to be a theoretical thinker himself. In general he represented the ideas which Kropotkin had formulated. But he had a keen sense of logic, he could grasp the connections between things, and present them clearly to his readers. His language was natural and alive, and he made his readers think. He was a born journalist. He was the ablest propagandist in speech and print among all the socialists in the Jewish East End at that time.

But he could not make the *Arbeter Fraint* self-supporting. Early in 1892 it stopped publication for three whole months. When it reappeared it had these words printed under the name: Anarchist-Communist Organ. The paper had an anarchist character from the time Yanovsky had become editor, but now it had proclaimed itself the organ of the movement. It remained that till the end. Though Yanovsky had a bitter struggle all the time he was in England, for the *Arbeter Fraint* had no material gifts to offer, it was not for that reason he left London with his family in January 1894, and returned to New York. His attitude to the so-called Propaganda of Action had caused a conflict in the movement, which made him withdraw from the editorship.

Yanovsky regarded the acts of terror which were being committed in France and other countries as a danger to the movement, and he did not hesitate to say so very forcibly in the paper and at public meetings. Some young hotheads attacked him for it. That was why he left London, In America he remained in the movement till he died on February 1st, 1939, at the age of 75. He restarted the *Freie Arbeter Shtimme* in 1900, and was its editor for the rest of his life. No one among all the comrades in America achieved so much as a writer and a speaker for the movement as Yanovsky did.

In England there was no one to take his place. Kaplan, who became editor of the *Arbeter Fraint*, was an excellent popular speaker, but without the literary qualifications the paper required. It stopped publication after six issues. It reappeared eighteen months later with William Wess as editor. Wess was one of the pioneers of the Jewish labour movement in Britain; he had belonged to the original group which first started the *Arbeter Fraint*. He died in London in 1946, over 80 years of age.

Wess, who was a native of the Baltic city Libau, came to London as a very young man. He soon found his way into the small group which was beginning to create the Jewish labour movement in the East End. He learned English, and got a good knowledge of English conditions. He was active in the English anarchist Freedom movement. It was certainly not personal ambition that moved Wess to become editor of the *Arbeter Fraint*.

For he was the most modest of men. But as there was no one else, and the movement needed the paper, he yielded to the comrades who persuaded him to take it on. He was not of course Yanovsky; but he put a lot of hard work into his job, and he was conscientious. The result was a readable paper, which was able to fulfil its purpose. Wess's job was harder than Yanovsky's for another reason. The paper couldn't afford to pay a compositor, so Wess not only had to write the paper himself; he had to set it as well, The Berner Street Club had been closed. The *Arbeter Fraint* premises were now in the attic of a tumbledown house in Romford Street, that could he reached only by climbing a ladder. But the rent wasn't much. And that was a consideration.

Wess became editor in 1895. He held the post for about a year. In April 1896 a quiet young man, Abraham Frumkin, arrived in London from Constantinople, and went to see Wess.

Frumkin was born in 1872 in Jerusalem, where his father was a leading member of the community, a Hebrew writer of note, and the publisher of a Hebrew weekly *Havetzeleth*. He himself engaged early in Hebrew journalism, contributing to his father's paper, and to *Hamelitz* and *Hatzefirah* . He spent a year in Jaffa in 1891 as a teacher of Arabic at the Belkind School. Then he went to Constantinople to study law, having been promised a stipend. When nothing came of this he emigrated in 1893 to America. In New York he became acquainted with anarchist ideas. Eager to win converts for his new cause he returned the following year to Constantinople, and soon made two valuable converts, his friend Moses Shapiro and Shapiro's wife Nastia. The hospitable Shapiro home in Constantinople was a meeting place for all the actively thinking young people there, in all the different movements.

Shapiro, who belonged to a wealthy family in Poltava, had been caught up as a student in the revolutionary movement, and had to escape from Russia. When he came to Constantinople he was active at first in the Chibat-Zion movement. It did not hold him long. Frumkin infected him with his own libertarian enthusiasm, and in 1895 Shapiro joined the anarchist movement. He set out on a study mission to Europe, ending up in London. He read all he could get of anarchist literature, Kropotkin, Reclus, Grave and others. He sent batches of it back to the group in Constantinople to study. In London he met Wess and other Jewish and Russian comrades, and he sent the *Arbeter Fraint* regularly to the group in Constantinople. One result was that Frumkin began to send contributions to the *Arbeter Fraint* from Constantinople, articles, stories and reports. Then Frumkin decided to go to London himself. Shapiro and Frumkin afterwards opened a small Yiddish printing press in London, to publish books and pamphlets. They translated and published in Yiddish Stepniak's *Underground Russia*, and other works. So Frumkin did not arrive in London unknown. He had been a contributor to the *Arbeter Fraint* for some time. Wess and the rest received him with open arms. And soon Wess, who considered his editorship purely temporary, till someone more capable was found, offered the job to Frumkin.

Frumkin was a very good editor. He wrote well. He was an educated man, widely read, with a knowledge of several European languages and literatures. He made excellent translations, including a number of works of anarchist literature.

But except for Shapiro he had hardly any contributors, till he managed to get some of the comrades in America to write for the paper. He also had money difficulties. He had come to London during an economic crisis. There was much unemployment in the East End, and the group found it hard to keep the paper going. It lived from hand to mouth; every time an issue appeared the publishers were not sure if there would be another. Frumkin described these experiences later in his book *The Spring Period in Jewish Socialism*. He had intended writing a second volume, but he was not able to get down to it by the time he died in 1940.

Twice during Frumkin's editorship the *Arbeter Fraint* suspended publication, once for a few weeks, but the second time, early in 1897, for a very long period. Frumkin who was no speaker, and could serve the movement only with his pen, felt his enforced inactivity badly; so when Shapiro decided about that time to return to Constantinople with his family, and offered him his small printing press, he tried issuing a small paper on his own account. It was just a propaganda sheet, which he called the *Propagandist*. Frumkin wrote and printed the paper himself, and with the assistance of a few comrades also distributed it. The paper lasted only eleven issues. In 1898 Frumkin left London. He was in Paris for about a year; then he went to America.

That was the end of the *Arbeter Fraint* for the time being. Wess could not see his way to resume the editorship. So after twelve years of active existence the *Arbeter Fraint* disappeared. Then I came along. On October 19th, 1898, the first issue of the new *Arbeter Fraint* appeared under my editorship.

Chapter 10

A Difficult Start

The *Arbeter Fraint* group had its printing press and administrative office at that time in Chance Street, a narrow small bleak street in Bethnal Green, which was a typical London working-class district, poverty-stricken and depressing. It had something over a dozen active members. I owe it to them to record their names: I. Kaplan, D. Isakovitz, T. Eyges, I. Sabelinsky, B. Schatz, S. Ploshansky, J. Blatt, S. Freeeman, H. Greenberg, J. Tapler, M. Kerkelevitch, B. Rubinstein and A. Banoff. Milly had been a member of the group for a few years. I had known most of these comrades before. I was no stranger among them.

Of course the circle of Jewish anarchists in the East End was larger than this group. But most of the comrades didn't belong to any particular group. They were nearly all active in the trades unions; they came regularly to all our meetings, they spread our paper and our pamphlets, and supported our movement in every way they could. The *Arbeter Fraint* group was only a sort of inner circle of the movement, responsible for the publication of the paper and the various obligations connected with it.

The first group meeting I attended dealt mainly with the financial possibilities of getting the paper out regularly. They didn't look bright. Collection-sheets had been going round, and had brought in about £12. The group had raised in addition about £20 at its annual Yom Kippur gathering, and there were a few pounds sent by the comrades in Leeds. This was the entire sum with which the *Arbeter Fraint* had to be brought back to life. But the comrades felt confident that it could be done. They counted on some assistance from America, especially as the group there had no Yiddish publication at the time, except the monthly *Freie Gesellshaft*.

Their confidence was not misplaced. Most of the Jewish immigrants from Eastern Europe who came to Great Britain continued their journey sooner or later to America or to other countries overseas. They took with them to the United States, Canada, Argentina or South Africa the socialist ideas they had first picked up in London, They formed groups in their new homes, and maintained contact with their original group in Britain, which remained the motherland of the movement. They imported the *Arbeter Fraint* and other literature, and when they could, sent us financial contributions. London was a clearing house for the Jewish revolutionary labour movement. The threads went out from London to all countries where there were large numbers of Jewish immigrants, and later even to their original homes in Russia and Poland, when the first anarchist underground groups began to form in Bialystock, Grodno, Vilna, Warsaw, Lodz and other places.

The reappearance of the *Arbeter Fraint* was hailed with joy by the comrades both in Britain and abroad, especially in America. Messages poured in from all sides, which encouraged us in our task. But it did not make things easier for me. I had all the material and other difficulties which had defeated my predecessors and, in addition, I had to devote myself to learning the Yiddish language, in which the paper I edited was written. I had plunged into a new life, with new people, and a new tongue, all quite foreign at first to me. I knew the inner circle of comrades, but not the mass of my readers. I think I could have adapted myself more quickly to living and working among any other European people and language. There is a certain common cultural heritage among the peoples of Western and Central Europe. Their history is closely linked. This new world in which I found myself was differently moulded. There were of course the same human qualities, but these people had grown up in entirely different conditions. Their spiritual development was not the same. What we call the Christian civilisation, no matter how we judge it, had created the European man, who started out with a common belief, held together for centuries by the bonds of the Church. The Jew was outside this development. In order to find himself in this hostile world he had to create a world of his own, which was different from the Christian world. In the western countries where the Jews achieved emancipation they gradually bridged the gulf that had separated them for centuries from their Christian fellow-citizens, and were able to take their part in the general cultural life. But in the ghetto-towns of Eastern Europe, under the Russian despotism, the gulf remained for another century, so that the East European Jew was in many ways a different creature from the Jew in the West.

It is not a matter of national peculiarities. Zionism was at that time a negligible factor among the Jewish workers in London.

My job was not only to edit and write for the *Arbeter Fraint*. I had also to do a lot of public speaking. I spoke at our own weekly meetings and at a great many propaganda meetings of the trades unions. I was particularly engaged in the work of instructing the comrades in our own inner circle in the deeper meaning of our libertarian ideas. The active comrades in the Jewish movement were all at that time still strongly under the influence of the Marxist doctrine of economic determinism. I tried to show them how economic materialism could not be reconciled with the conception of anarchism. I didn't find it easy. Yet those talks over our various differences of opinion have remained among my most delightful memories of that early period of my work in the Jewish labour movement. What amazed me most was the thirst for knowledge among those ordinary working people who had received so little general education, yet had so much natural intelligence that they could easily grasp things about which they had been completely uninformed before. It made me happy to see with what zeal they pursued knowledge. I learned a great deal myself by accompanying them in their pursuit. I was inspired by them to discover new ideas, to think about things which in a different environment less foreign to me I would have taken for granted; I had to probe more deeply, to think for myself.

Of course, I put forward my critical observations on the subject of historical materialism in public. The opportunity arose at our weekly meetings at the Sugar Loaf, which were regularly attended at that time by a number of Jewish social democrats, who joined in the discussions. Those discussions, the arguments which were opposed to mine, and my replies to them, prompted me to formulate my ideas concerning historical materialism in writing. This was my first literary work.

It appeared during the first year of my editorship in a series of 25 essays in the *Arbeter Fraint* . For most of my readers it was completely unknown territory. So I had to be careful not to write above their heads, to try to explain the problems to them in a way they could understand. For the important point about the *Arbeter Fraint* was that it had to be a propaganda sheet; it was no use filling it with stuff that its readers could not follow. I intended going through those articles afterwards, to put them into shape, to add to them, tighten them up, make them more complete, and publish them as a book. I never managed it. When I look back now on that work I am well aware of its shortcomings. But it should be judged not by the standards of today, but by the conditions and the needs of that time. I had no predecessor in that field in Yiddish. As far as I know it was the first attempt in that language to subject the Marxist conception of history to a critical examination. I don't think anything more was done in that field till Dr. Chaim Jitlovsky took up the same question some years later in America.

It is a puzzle to me how the *Arbeter Fraint* managed to appear regularly every week for a whole year during that early period of my editorship. The small sum with which we had started was soon used up, and we found ourselves in a financial crisis. We never knew how we would get out the next issue. We always worried how to find the money to pay the printer. The editor didn't matter so much. I had been promised £1 a week for my work as editor. The promise was rarely kept. I was paid when there was enough money. If there wasn't I had to go without. The amounts owing to me were entered in a book. When the total owing to me became too large to consider even paying so much, they put a pen through it, and the debt was wiped out. We started afresh. It was a splendid way of keeping books, but it didn't do me any good. We lived from hand to mouth, and it was only by Milly working and by my odd jobs of bookbinding that we kept going.

The comrades did what they could. They didn't live any better than we did. They gave more than they could afford to the paper and the movement. I was always full of admiration for their devotion to the cause. The German comrades in the West End gave more, both for their movement here and for sending home to Germany to help the movement there. But they were well-paid craftsmen who could afford much more than the poor Jewish proletariat in the East End. Every penny these sweatshop workers gave us was something taken away from their own mouths. They denied themselves essentials; and they gave it willingly, gladly, ungrudgingly. If they didn't give more it was only because they hadn't any more to give. They would have pawned their last few small possessions for us. People who have not themselves lived through that dreadful period of poverty can have no idea today what it meant, under what incredibly difficult conditions the *Arbeter Fraint* appeared week after week. There was a change, later, but only with the improvement of labour conditions, as a result of the unceasing struggle which was waged by the trades unions. After that the movement made swift progress. The existence of the *Arbeter Fraint* became assured, and we even established a fair sized publishing concern, which issued books and pamphlets, that went to help to cover the cost of producing the *Arbeter Fraint*.

We had a number of comrades both in London and the provinces who were good propaganda speakers, Wess, Sachs, Freeman, Friedental, Baron, Schatz, Eyges, Feinsohn, Elstein, Salomons, and others; most of them were also active in the trades unions, where they rendered considerable service to our cause. But the best speaker among the Jewish anarchists at that time was Kaplan. After Yanovsky went back to America Kaplan was the finest speaker the Jewish movement had in England.

Kaplan came from Sager in Lithuania, where he was for a time *Maggid* (Preacher in the Synagogue). He told me he had begun to read free-thinking books in Sager; they had awakened doubts in his mind about his religion, He came to England in the 1850s. He was employed for a time as a preacher by the Jewish community in Leeds. There was a small group of Jewish socialists and anarchists in Leeds at that time, and Kaplan got in touch with them. He read the *Arheter Fraint* and the *Freie Arbeter Shtimme* and the pamphlets that were published in London and in New York. He learned English, and read secularist English literature. It made him decide to give up his post with the Jewish community. He went to work as a machinist in the tailoring industry, and he threw himself into the Jewish labour movement.

When I got to know Kaplan he was living in London. He loved speaking in public. He was a good speaker. He knew how to hold his audience. He didn't always follow the beaten path in his speeches. He liked to think for himself, and he very often worked out a new and independent line of thought in his speech. He was a redoubtable debater. He was practically the only speaker in the Jewish movement of that time who could work out his speeches logically, point by point. The people who had influenced Kaplan most in his development were Herbert Spencer, Bradlough, Ingersoll and Foote. Their ideas led him to a kind of political atheism, and later to anarchism.

When I first met Kaplan he was still very much under the influence of the Marxist idea of historical materialism. It took me a long time to shift him from that idea. His favourite subject was religion with a social content. He was, as I said, a logical thinker, and he might have done something if he had been given a systematic education.

His only interest was thought. For literature and art and aesthetics generally he had no understanding at all. He was quite impossible as a writer. The point is that he wanted to write, he tried to put his ideas on paper. But he had no literary sense of words. The same man who could develop his ideas logically as a speaker failed utterly when he tried to write them down on paper. It was strange, for in his speeches he showed that he had powers of observation, he had flashes of wit, he had a sense of humour, and he had moral courage. When it came to writing it down all his gifts deserted him.

Kaplan was good company. People liked him. Children loved him. We lived with him in the same house for a time, so that I could see it for myself. There were three young boys in the house.

Two were his wife's children by her first marriage. The third, Fred, was his own boy. Fred was about six or seven then, a clever and promising lad. When the First World War broke out in 1914 Fred was 18. He volunteered at once for the army. His parents tried to dissuade him, but he insisted that he must go. As soon as he was trained he went to Belgium; six weeks later he was killed in action. It was a terrible blow to Kaplan. The mother went mad. She died in the lunatic asylum two years later.

Kaplan's last years were spent in poverty and illness. He was a desperately lonely man. When Milly and I came to London in 1933 he was in hospital. He had just had his leg amputated. We were to visit him on Thursday. He died the night before. It fell to me to speak at his cremation in Golders Green.

Chapter 11

Germinal

The *Arbeter Fraint* had been appearing for a whole year under these difficult and trying conditions when a new unexpected blow struck us. To help to cover our costs we had been printing advertisements, which brought us about fifty pounds over the year. I didn't like the idea of advertisements, but the *Arbeter Fraint* had been doing it before I became editor, and fifty pounds a year was a considerable sum of money for us. The advertisements came from booksellers, photographers, shipping agents and such like. They settled with us at the end of the year; we were looking forward to getting the money, because we had a lot of bills to pay. Then we found that the comrade who collected the money had already spent it for his own purposes. He made up for it afterwards by giving us many years of devoted work. He had been tempted, because of some very serious trouble he had got into. I wouldn't have mentioned it, but for the fact that it compelled us to stop publication once again.

I went to Liverpool, Manchester and Leeds, to lecture and to collect some money from the comrades, to enable us to restart the paper. I couldn't get enough. The comrades in America couldn't help us either, because they were issuing the *Freie Arbeter Shtimme* again and the monthly *Freie Gesellshaft* as well.

It was November 1899. Emma Goldman had arrived in London for a series of talks in the West End. It was during the Boer War, which sent a wave of jingo feeling through the country. Even Lloyd George had to escape in Birmingham from a hostile mob disguised in the uniform of a policeman. The English comrades were naturally reluctant to expose Emma to the fury of a mob. She refused to be frightened off. She was announced to speak at the South Place Institute, near Liverpool Street Station. Her subject was patriotism. The hall was packed, and hundreds hadn't been able to get in. Tom Mann was in the chair. It was an openly hostile crowd. More than half the audience had come to make trouble. As soon as Emma rose to speak they heckled her. There was a scuffle. An attempt was made to rush the platform. Emma stood her ground. Her calm voice and Tom Mann's unflustered behaviour in the chair saved the situation. Emma got her hearing. She spoke to the end. I am sure the fact that it was a woman speaking was a great help with an English audience. But she also spoke well. She held their attention. The applause when she finished showed that clearly.

It was then I made my first personal acquaintance with Emma Goldman. She had heard of me and of my work among the Jewish workers in England. She wondered how a non-Jew had managed to fit in to life in a Jewish environment. When I told her about our difficulties she offered us a number of lectures, whose proceeds would go to help the *Arbeter Fraint*. We arranged three meetings for her in the East End. They brought in a few pounds, not much. The East End was not a place then for financially successful meetings. The people who came were poorly paid sweatshop workers, whose every penny counted. We were glad we could pay the hire of the hall and the cost of the printing, and have a couple of pounds left.

We did restart the *Arbeter Fraint*. It was a daring thing to do under the conditions; this time the experiment did not succeed. We got out another ten issues, and then we had to stop.

We had had to shift our premises to an old shed in Stepney Green, adjoining some stables, from which we got a lot of bad smells and swarms of flies and bluebottles. Yet a miracle happened to me there, the birth of the periodical *Germinal*.

Our old typesetter had left us. He had rightly come to the conclusion that there wasn't much chance for him with us. We had found instead a young man recently arrived from Russia, named Narodiczky. He was an intelligent young man, who had received a good education, and had been studying to be a Rabbi. He learned typesetting in London. He had a good knowledge of Hebrew literature, and had been an active Zionist in Russia. That did not make him an orthodox Jew. On the contrary, the opposition of the Rabbis to Herzl had led him away from the traditional religion. He got to know our group, and had come to accept our libertarian ideas, without however abandoning his Zionism. He believed that a Jewish Palestine would offer a better field for new social experiments than the old countries of Europe. He had a special admiration for me, a Goy who had devoted himself to working among the Jews.

When it was clear that we must stop publication Narodiczky came to me with a proposal that I should start a periodical of my own. I said I had no money, and that if the *Arbeter Fraint*, which had a group of supporters and a tradition of years behind it could not exist, what chance was there for a new periodical? His answer was that the *Arbeter Fraint* group was always in trouble because it had a lot of old debts, and could never get clear of them. Of course, he was right.

Narodiczky said he would set the type for a new periodical that I would edit, which would be free from the debts of the *Arbeter Fraint* group; he would be satisfied with any payment we could make. He said he had already discussed the idea with some of the younger comrades, and they had undertaken to get the money to print the first issue, and to back me in every way.

It was an attractive proposal. I asked the *Arbeter Fraint* group what they thought of it. Most of the comrades had no great hopes of it, but they all agreed the attempt was worth making. They placed their printing press at my disposal, and promised all their support. So the last issue of the *Arbeter Fraint* appeared on January 2th, 1900, with a farewell message from the group, and an announcement of the new periodical, which I had decided to call *Germinal*.

As I was not responsible to any group I thought I would give the new publication an entirely new character, to acquaint its readers with all libertarian tendencies in modern literature and contemporary thought. To have more space in one issue I decided to make it a 16 page fortnightly, not an eight-page weekly, and to have no advertisements. The first issue appeared on March 16th, 1900.

My views were closest to Kropotkin's, but I realised even then that all the ideas of mutualism, collectivism or communism were subordinate to the great idea of educating people to be free and to think and work freely. All the economic propositions for the future, which had still to be tested by practical experience, were designed to secure to man the result of his labour and to aim at a social transformation of life that would make it possible for the individual to develop his natural capacities unrestrained by hard and fast rules and dogmas. My innermost conviction was that anarchism was not to be conceived as a definite closed system, nor as a future millennium, but only as a particular trend in the historic development towards freedom in all fields of human thought and action, and that no strict and unalterable lines could therefore be laid down for it.

Freedom is never attained; it must always be striven for. Consequently its claims have no limit, and can neither be enclosed in a programme nor prescribed as a definite rule for the future. Each generation must face its own problems, which cannot be forestalled or provided for in advance. The worst tyranny is that of ideas which have been handed down to us, allowing no development in ourselves, and trying to steamroller everything to one flat universal level.

That was the spirit in which I conducted my new periodical. When I look back, though there is much I would disapprove of now in detail, I find it was on the whole not at all a bad piece of work. The publication of the new periodical was bound up with difficulties and hardships which cannot be easily described. We started with empty hands. From the material point of view it was perhaps the hardest time in the whole of my life. We were often without the barest necessities. Yet I think of those days with nostalgia. My old heart warms at the memory of those fine young people who worked at my side, and gave so much devotion and love and self-sacrifice to the cause. They were wonderful young people.

Germinal attracted a good circle of readers, not only in England and the British Isles, but in most of the big cities of America, and in Paris, Berlin, Bucharest, Sofia, Cairo, Alexandria, Johannesburg, Cape Town, Buenos Aires. When I came to Berlin after the end of the First World War the famous actor Granach told me that *Germinal* had set him on the first steps towards his career on the German stage. Granach was a young East European Jewish immigrant working at that time in a bakery. *Germinal* roused his interest in literature. He was a born actor. He recited at meetings of the small group of Jewish anarchists in Berlin to which he belonged. Someone heard him there and made him go to a school for dramatic art; he became one of the great actors in Germany. He never denied his origin or his early associations.

We published twelve issues of *Germinal*; then Narodiczky told me he couldn't go on with it. He had opened a small printing shop, and had his hands full trying to build up his business. I had feared something like that would happen, and it never occurred to me to blame Narodiczky for what he did. But it was a blow to me.

Meanwhile the *Arbeter Fraint* group had managed to pay off most of its old debts, and was thinking of restarting the *Arbeter Fraint*. That meant I would no longer be able to use its printing press for *Germinal*, for there wasn't enough type for two publications. That seemed to seal the fate of *Germinal*; even the re-issue of the *Arbeter Fraint* could not console me for its loss.

Then a young comrade, Ernst, came to me with a proposal to get some type of our own, to continue *Germinal*. Ernst was one of the best-paid workmen in our group. He worked in an English organ-making factory, was never out of work, and earned good wages. He offered to contribute towards the cost of the type; he found a place where we could get the type, and he arranged that I should pay for it in monthly installments. I had learned a little typesetting from Narodiczky, and though I was not very quick at it I felt capable of undertaking the work. Milly had also learned typesetting, and she managed by herself to set two whole articles in each issue.

When I look back at those issues today I find they were quite well set. Of course Milly and I were not professional compositors; we took much longer over our work. But the result was not bad. So now I not only wrote the paper myself, but with Milly's help also set it. We were living at that time in one large room on the fourth floor of a tenement block in Stepney Green called Dunstan Houses; it was our combined living room and bedroom. Now it also had to serve as our workshop for setting the type. It was not easy to carry the cases of type up and down four flights of stairs, but I was young and strong, and there were always comrades ready to help us. As the *Arbeter Fraint* was now reappearing we decided to publish *Germinal* as a monthly. How I managed to write both papers and to set one of them as well is still a puzzle to me. But a young man devoted to his cause can do a lot.

Chapter 12

Peter Kropotkin

My work in the Jewish labour movement brought me in frequent contact with Peter Kropotkin, who was always in close touch with the comrades in the East End. I had seen him several times at meetings, and had heard him speak, but I did not know him personally till I met him one day in 1896 at the Italian Club. After our talk he invited me to visit him at his home in Bromley. His wife opened the door when I came. Kropotkin was waiting in their simple living room, where their daughter Sasha was getting tea ready. After tea Kropotkin took me to his study. The walls were lined with books up to the ceiling. The desk was heaped with papers and periodicals. He showed me a book which had just arrived, a gift from a friend in Edinburgh. It was Paul Marat's *The Chains of Slavery*, published in England in 1774. "A fine mind, this much-abused Marat," said Kropotkin. "Of all the men of the Great Revolution he was the most significant thinker. He saw things better than Robespierre and all his followers put together."

Then our talk turned to Germany. He was intensely interested in the conditions there, for he was already at that time afraid of the coming war. He was convinced that the Kaiser's government was working in a direction which made war inevitable. He believed that the other powers would have no choice but to meet Germany's challenge. If war came it would bring, he said, a terrible reaction after it, and the loss of much freedom, even if Germany were defeated. Only an inner change in the political and social life in Germany itself could save Europe and the world from this disaster.

But Germany was at that time a consolidated state, with no serious opposition to the Kaiser's government inside the country. The middle class was solidly imperialist. The social democratic movement which had almost the entire German working class in it was a huge idol with clay feet, that would crash immediately anything happened. Kropotkin knew the conditions in Germany. He had no illusions about the influence of the small anarchist movement there.

I remained closely connected with Kropotkin from the day I first entered his house in 1896 till he returned to Russia after the Revolution in 1917. The longer I knew him the more I admired and loved him. He was a man of great personal charm and kindliness, with all his great learning modest and unassuming, and with a burning passion for justice and freedom. He was in his personal life and his personal relations the same man who wrote *Mutual Aid*. There was no cleavage between the man and his work. He spoke and acted in all things as he felt and believed and wrote. Kropotkin was a whole man. He was one of the greatest happenings in my life. I was never a man to worship an idol. I could never be blind to a man's faults, however great I thought him. What bound me to Kropotkin was his warm humanity, his unshakeable sense of justice. Justice was no abstraction to him. It was the expression of his real fellow-feeling with other people. I am sure he never made anyone feel small in his presence. He was a great soul.

When the war he had foreseen and feared came in 1914 and our paths divided our personal relationship remained unaffected. I knew that he acted as he did out of absolute conviction. Which of us was right no one can decide today. A man's inner conviction is not something that can be measured with a tape measure, or weighed in a balance, to say how far it was right or wrong.

I remember distinctly a talk a few of us had with Kropotkin at his home not a year before war broke out. He said he was convinced that Germany was preparing for war. It could begin any day. I can't tell you the exact date, he said, but it won't be long. Germany has gone too far to retreat. When you have rattled your sword so long that the whole world regards you as a menace you can't suddenly drop the trumpet and exchange it for a shepherd's reed. That would be humiliating. Germany is only waiting for the opportunity to strike.

One of us asked Kropotkin if he thought that Germany alone was responsible for this situation. Of course not, he said. But those who are in power in Germany today are more responsible for it than the others. They plunged Europe into militarism. Britain and France have nothing to gain by war, and they have much to lose. Even if they win they will suffer terribly, and it will take them a great many years to recover. It will shake the whole world. It is impossible to foresee what a cycle of political and economic crises the war will start off.

Germany is much more favourably placed. If she wins the war she will be for a long time the undisputed dictator of Europe. Her rulers will squeeze all they can out of the other countries, to make good her own losses quickly. If Germany loses the war she will be a problem to the victors, and the problem may not be solved without a European revolution. If Germany is broken up by the victors, it will create an irredenta that will give Europe no peace.

The only hope is that a new movement may come from a defeated Germany. But such movements come only if the conditions exist in the minds of the people, and I am afraid they do not exist among the German people. If the Germans are defeated they will brood over their wounded national pride rather than want to listen to the voice of reason. We asked Kropotkin if a general strike in all countries could not prevent the war. It could, he answered. But it would have to be simultaneous in all the countries concerned, and it would have to be complete before the fighting starts. If it waits till war is declared it will be too late.

I remember Tarrida asking me if I didn't think the German socialists would do something to stop Germany going to war. I answered that I was afraid the German socialists would do nothing at all. The German working class had lost all understanding for direct action. They had put all their hope in parliamentary activity. The most we could expect was that the socialists in the Reichstag might vote against the war credits, but even that was not certain.

76

Then there is no hope of preventing the war, Tarrida said. If the German workers won't do anything how can we expect it from the French and Belgian workers?

Tcherkesov thought the fact that Russia would be in the war on the side of France would add to the confusion. How could Russia be presented as fighting a war of democracy against German militarism? I said I agreed. But I also said I was convinced that Germany was now a much greater danger to Europe and the world than Russia.

Kropotkin was ill when the war came, and he was a sick man all through the war years. As I was of German birth I was soon interned as what was called an enemy alien. Kropotkin wrote to me in the internment camp as often as he could; and he sent me books from his library to read. That was not easy, because his books were all full of marginal notes, which he had to erase very carefully, or the censor might think he was trying to pass secret information to me. He wrote to me in one of his letters that he could understand my attitude about the war: "It is essentially a matter of conviction. One should never make a stand for a cause if one's heart is not in it. This terrible catastrophe will come to an end, and then we shall stand together again, as we did before, in the great cause of human liberty, which is the cause of us all."

Kropotkin was a scholar and a thinker, a man of extraordinarily wide reading and learning, a historian, geographer, economist and social philosopher. He had made his name by his geographical and geological exploration of Siberia before he came to associate himself with the anarchist movement. In his book *Mutual Aid* he gave us a picture of nature utterly different from the conception of a continuous struggle for existence presented by what is called Social Darwinism. He revealed the fallacy of the Malthusian theory of over-population and put the relationship between man and society in a new light. His book *Fields, Factories and Workshops* opened a wide new vista of the future relations between industry and agriculture. His history of the *Great French Revolution* looked at that vast uprising which did so much to shape the historic development of all Europe from a new point of view, as a movement of the people.

Kropotkin was no utopist. He had a practical view of life. He showed it in the way he sensed what was happening to the Russian Revolution. He saw long before any of us did in what direction Bolshevism was leading. When Kropotkin said goodbye to me before he left for Russia I had a feeling that I should never see him again. But I did not realise what a terrible fate awaited him in the land of his birth. For years men like Kropotkin had worked and hoped and suffered imprisonment to liberate Russia from despotism. Then the Revolution came, and instead of liberty it brought a new despotism, dictatorship and the totalitarian state.

Kropotkin realised it very soon; and as he was never a man to be silent in the face of oppression he said what he felt, openly, firmly, though he was an old man, and ill. His open letter to Lenin, protesting against the methods of the new regime, and his *Appeal to the Working Class of Western Europe*, which he wrote shortly before he died, and which Margaret Bondfield brought back from Russia, were his last proclamations against the tyranny which he had fought all his life. While the so-called political realists were jubilant about the coming of collectivism, Kropotkin saw the death of liberty.

Chapter 13

Leeds

The crisis in the Jewish labour movement in London continued. There seemed no way of getting over our difficulties. The suspension of the *Arbeter Fraint* affected our whole propaganda; the entire Jewish labour movement suffered because of it. Even *Germinal* appeared only intermittently. It was the hardest time I had since I entered the Jewish labour movement.

David Isakovitz suggested that Milly and I should move to Leeds, and publish *Germinal* there. Leeds had a fairly large Jewish trade union organisation among the workers in the clothing industry. Our friend Louis Elstein was very active in it. Also a number of comrades had gone to the provinces because things were hard in London, many of them to Leeds. We left London at the end of October 1901; the first Leeds issue of *Germinal* appeared in December.

We found Leeds a small place, and after London not very attractive. But there was a close friendship among the comrades; we were like one big family. We didn't have the big distances there were in London. We could see each other almost every day, and it was altogether easier to do things than in the big city.

Most of the Jewish socialists in Leeds belonged to the anarchist wing. But there were also a number of social democrats. Relations between the two sections were friendly. The reason lay in the character of the Jewish population of Leeds as a whole. They were mostly rigidly conservative, and uninformed. They could not understand the difference between anarchists and social democrats. Both were to them departures from their accepted rut. These people lived differently. They thought about things; they challenged the old beliefs and traditions. Therefore they shut them all out from their common Jewish life. The small minority of Jewish socialists and freethinkers of all kinds found themselves surrounded by a Chinese wall of intolerance and dislike. The result was that they got together more among themselves, were dependent on each other much more than in London.

In the summer months the comrades held open air meetings every Saturday in North Street Park. In winter it was practically impossible to get a suitable hall in the Leeds ghetto. No proprietors would hire a hall to Jewish socialists. They were afraid of the official Jewish community. The Jewish Tailors' Trade Union had its own premises, but it needed them for its own purposes on most occasions when we had to hold our meetings. Shortly after we arrived in Leeds the difficulty was overcome by opening a socialist club in Meanwood Road. We held our meetings there every Saturday and Sunday; we also used it as a club every other evening. While we lived in Leeds I went on many propaganda lecture tours to other towns, Manchester, Liverpool, Birmingham, Hull, Glasgow, Edinburgh. Just when the movement was at its lowest in London we had a big upward swing in the provinces.

There were active groups of comrades in all these places. Our best centre after Leeds was Glasgow. I first met there Zalman Vendroff, who afterwards made a name in Yiddish literature. He went back to Russia at the time of the revolution and became one of the leading Yiddish Soviet writers. When I first knew him he was inclined to Zionism; we had long arguments about it. When he came to live in London afterwards he found himself much nearer to our views, and was a valued contributor to the *Arbeter Fraint*.

The Jews in Leeds hated us and all our activities. They attacked our comrades in the streets. They tore our posters off the walls.

One Yom Kippur the comrades had arranged a meeting in the club, and brought Kaplan from London as the speaker. A mob attacked one of our comrades who was distributing leaflets announcing the meeting. We were warned that our meeting would be broken up. We feared a lot of our people would stay away, not to be involved in a fight. But the hall was packed. There wasn't an empty seat. I had been asked to take the chair. I introduced the speaker briefly; he was already speaking when we heard a lot of shouting in the street. Our audience jumped up. Before I could do anything Louis Elstein asked me to come to the front door. I found two of our comrades there, Agursky and Perlman, who told me there were hundreds of people outside, ready to storm our club.

To understand how we were placed I should explain that our club was on the second floor of a rear building, divided from the street by a courtyard, through which people had to pass to reach a steep narrow staircase, which led to the hall. I saw that we must keep the mob from getting to the stairs. For once they found their way up nothing could hold them back. It was lucky for us that the narrow staircase could be easily defended, if only nobody came out from the hall at our back thinking to help us, and diverted our attention. Agursky was a big fellow. So was I. I took my stand at the bottom of the stairs, two or three steps up. Agursky stood a little higher; Perlman's job was to see that no one came out of the hall.

We had no sooner taken our positions than the mob rushed in, led by a tall lanky fellow. He was calling the others to follow him. But when he saw me and Agursky waiting for him he stopped. Then he shouted at us to stand aside, or they would rush us.

"Back!" I cried. "Not one of you will get up these stair's alive!"

The man was no hero. He wavered. I took out my watch, and I said: "I give you one minute to clear off. If you're not gone by then, on your head be it."

It was of course an empty threat. But it shook him. I looked at my watch. "Ten more seconds," I said.

"Back!" the leader shouted. "He's got a knife!"

We were unarmed. But the crowd thought the man had seen me wave a knife at him. They all turned tail. I heard them shouting in the street. The danger was over. Somebody had called the police, and presently a police inspector and two constables came and wanted to know what we were up to.

The lanky mob leader appeared again, and told the police that we were a gathering of anarchists and God-blasphemers, and that I had a knife, and had threatened him with it. I told the inspector what had happened. He came up with me to the hall, looked round, and saw a lot of people sitting quietly, listening to the speaker. It seemed to satisfy him. He ordered the constables to disperse the crowd in the street. That was the end of it.

There were well-meaning folk who said we should not have provoked people by holding our meeting on such a day. I don't agree. Progress would be impossible if people didn't hold different opinions. The conflict between fathers and sons exists in every generation, and it does no good to try to ignore it. People must learn tolerance. It would never occur to me to upset anyone engaged in his religious devotions. People who can think of breaking into a Synagogue or a Church to prevent others practising their religion are no better than those fanatical zealots in Leeds who tried to break up our meeting. The right to act according to your own belief belongs to everyone. The place for a believing Jew on Yom Kippur is in a Synagogue, not in the street trying to deny somebody else's right to do what he wishes on that day. No civilised society could exist otherwise.

But Leeds was a place where people generally had queer ideas at that time. I used to hear them grumbling about foreigners; they usually meant Jews. They were under the impression that all foreigners were Jews. One day I stood setting type when there was a knock at the door. A shabbily dressed man came in, and told me that he had something for me. He brought out a *Tallith* (prayer-shawl) and a pair of *Tephilin* (phylacteries) which Jews use when they pray. He asked me for a shilling for them. I explained that I wasn't a Jew, and had never used such things in my life. He plainly didn't believe me. "But you're a foreigner, aren't you?" "Yes," I said. "Then you're a Jew." "Why?" "Because all foreigners are Jews."

Of course it never worried me that people took me for a Jew. It was sometimes amusing. We lived in Leeds almost on the edge of the town, in Buslingthorpe Lane, a good distance from the Leeds ghetto. As most of my visitors were Jewish comrades the neighbours took it for granted that I was a Jew. I had two close friends, William McQueen and Toni Petersen, both like myself of Christian origin; Petersen was a Dane. When the three of us went to the ghetto on a Saturday afternoon to see our Jewish comrades, the Jewish women in the street told us off for smoking on the Sabbath. When we got back to where I lived, where there were few Jews, the children ran after us, shouting, "Jews! Christkillers!"

Besides the Jewish comrades we also had an active English movement in Leeds. William McQueen was the best of a group of English speakers there. He also edited a small monthly, *The Free Commune*. He was an able and an extremely likable young man. He earned his living as a commercial traveller. Going about the country on his job he always used the opportunity to do propaganda for our cause. Johann Most was responsible for McQueen emigrating afterwards to America, where he became editor of *Liberty*. He was active in the American movement till he was arrested for a speech at a strike meeting, and was given the savage sentence of five years imprisonment. He came out a broken man. I saw him when he returned to England. He died soon after.

Also prominent in the English movement was a young man named Moskovitz; he was a fine speaker. He was born in Manchester, of Jewish parents, and was diverted at an early age to the secularist movement. He was a follower of Benjamin Tucker. For his living he sold a harmless patent medicine called Yesurum Killer. The first word is Hebrew, meaning pain. It is also Yiddish, with the same meaning. The outlandish name therefore meant simply pain-killer. He didn't do particularly well out of it, and he often went hungry. But that never disturbed him. He never lost his happy-go-lucky good humour.

Then there was Mat Solid, a delightful old man. He was 67 when I knew him, but he was full of vigour and vitality, more than many younger people. He attended every meeting, and he was always a ready and a lively speaker. He was tall and lean, completely bald, but he had an impressive grey beard. He had fine features, and wise eyes. I saw a good deal of him, and found that he had read an amazing amount of philosophy and natural science. He had a gift of expressing himself clearly and briefly. His great fault was his quick temper. He always got furious when his opponent in an argument wandered away from the subject or didn't follow his point logically. He was a first-class lecturer. If his audience showed any grasp of the subject he would develop it in a really masterly way, like a trained university professor. But if his temper was roused he was a fighter. He was a stormy petrel. At the time of the Boer War, when no socialist in Leeds dared to speak against it in the open air, he stood up and got a hearing. I think he would have preferred to be stoned to death by an infuriated mob rather than be silent. Once McQueen had been badly knocked about, almost lynched at an open-air meeting; the following Sunday Mat Solid appeared at the same spot, and seemed by what he was saying in his speech to be inviting the crowd to treat him as they had treated McQueen. Yet nothing happened. They listened to him. Sometimes an angry murmur ran through the crowd. But they heard him to the end, and they let him go without making a move against him.

Mat had been a sailor for many years. He had got a knock on the head one day from a falling spar. It nearly brained him. He was operated on three times. He was a different man after that. He had never shown any particular interest before in reading; his intellectual capacity had seemed small. Now he became a voracious reader. He gave up the sea, and settled in Leeds, where he worked as a french polisher. He used to tell this story at all his public meetings; he said that everybody ought to get a knock on the head to make him think.

I spent a year in Leeds. Things were beginning to improve in London, and the comrades there urged me to return to restart the *Arbeter Fraint*. London was of course a more important position for our work than Leeds; I agreed to go back. The last issue of *Germinal* in Leeds appeared in September 1902. The next issue came out in London the following month.

Chapter 14

The Movement Goes Forward

I found a new spirit in our London movement. Everything seemed to be going forward. Our public meetings had never been so well attended. The trades unions which had suffered during the depression of the South African war recovered, and a lively agitation was started for better labour conditions. The *Arbeter Fraint* group was very active. My year in Leeds had served one important purpose. The contact between our groups in London and the provinces was much closer. Isakovitz also came to London, to help to restart the *Arbeter Fraint*. Some of the comrades had wanted to begin publishing as soon as I arrived. But my past experience made me insist that we must first assure ourselves of sufficient means, so that we would not have to stop publication again after a few months or a year.

We held a conference of Jewish anarchists during Christmas week 1902, in London. There were four questions on the agenda: restarting the *Arbeter Fraint*, opening a club, issuing pamphlets and books, and linking the different groups in London and the provinces into a Jewish Anarchist Federation. The decision was to get the *Arbeter Fraint* out again on March 20th, 1903. We reappeared therefore in March 1903. The *Arbeter Fraint* group was again in charge of the administration, but there was now a note under the heading which said that it was the organ of the Federation of Yiddish-Speaking Anarchist Groups in Great Britain and Paris.

March 1903 also saw the publication of the last issue of *Germinal*, till it was started again in January 1905, no longer my own paper, but that of a group, which however made me the editor, so that it remained the same paper it had been before. But for two years there was no *Germinal*. I felt its loss keenly. It was my own child. I had not only started it and edited it. I had also set it myself and printed it myself. But it was physically impossible for me to continue to do that. The work of getting out the weekly *Arbeter Fraint* regularly was enough to engage all my energy. I was also in constant demand as a speaker, not only in our own movement, but for hundreds of trade union meetings and for lecture tours in the provinces. I had no time left to do *Germinal* as well.

We were all overloaded with work. But we were young and we were enthusiastic, and the times were pregnant with hope. The labour movement was making great progress everywhere. There was a big movement in Great Britain. Syndicalism had spread among the working class in France. The old ideas of the First International were in the air again. The crippling influence of German social democracy on the international labour movement seemed to be diminishing; the centre of gravity was returning to the Latin countries. This new movement, which was aimed not only against the economic monopoly of a privileged minority, but also against the danger of a state-bureaucracy arising in the future, was growing astonishingly in the Latin countries.

I tried to acquaint the Jewish workers with the significance of this new movement, in the *Arbeter Fraint* and at our meetings. But most of all I tried to rouse them against the terrible sweating system under which they were working. I knew it was not enough to agitate against it. People who are active in a social movement must always ask themselves by what methods they can best move and serve the people. There is no final and complete answer to this question. Our work is always determined by the conditions in the world outside, in which we must live. We can be guided only by practical experience. The word "propaganda" has left a bad taste in people's mouths because it is too often only a batch of empty slogans. True propaganda must be directed not to make people repeat slogans, but to make them think for themselves.

It is not enough to be always talking about the material and social ills with which we are afflicted. It is also necessary to open new intellectual and spiritual horizons for the people, to make them want a better kind of life. Preaching class-consciousness won't help us. People's lives are not determined so much by their membership of a particular class as by their daily experiences of the society as a whole in which they live. The fact that most of the pioneers of socialist ideas in all countries came not from the proletariat but from other classes of society should warn us against such illusions.

What brings people into the movement is not so much the material effects of modern economic life as a sense of outraged justice. The smallest wage struggle would be impossible without an ethical motive behind it. The stronger the sense of justice is in people the more it influences their thoughts and actions. The idea of justice is not merely material. It derives from our general cultural life, which is the creation of countless generations of people of all social classes. Our culture cannot be judged from the point of view of class or of economic conditions. Economic life is itself a consequence of our general cultural level. Modern industry and modern production forms did not create our culture. They are the result of our culture. Without the immense progress of scientific culture in the 19th and 20th centuries and its application to machinery and chemistry, modern industry and modern production forms and the whole revolution in economic life could never have happened.

That brings me to the point that we cannot condemn everything in our present society as equally bad, and ripe for decay. The inadequacy of our existing social order for large sections of the people and the glaring injustice of many aspects of our political and social life must not lead us to the mistake of measuring our entire culture as such by this one standard. What human civilisation has created over many centuries in spiritual and social values can be estimated only by considering it as a whole. What the human spirit has created in science, art and literature, in every branch of philosophic thought and aesthetic feeling is and must remain the common cultural possession of our own and of all the coming generations. This is the starting-point, this is the bridge to all further social development. There is not only a hunger of the body. There is also a hunger of the spirit, of the soul, which demands its rights.

Chapter 15

The Kishineff Pogrom

In April 1903 the world was shaken by reports of a terrible pogrom against the Jews in Kishineff. Later pogroms made it clear that this was not a spontaneous outburst by an ignorant populace, but a carefully organised massacre prepared in cold blood by the Tzarist police and authorities.

Antisemitism had been for a long time used as an instrument of policy by the Tzarist government to divert the attention of the people from the true cause of their misery and poverty. Protest meetings were immediately held in both the East and West End of London, and early in May there was a huge demonstration in Hyde Park, called by the Friends of a Free Russia, in conjunction with other bodies. Of course, we were there. Outstanding among the many speakers was Peter Kropotkin. I still carry a picture in my mind of Kropotkin as I saw him that day, his face pale with emotion, his grey beard caught by the wind. His first words were hesitant, as though choked by his deep feeling. Then they came rushing out fiercely, each word like the blow of a hammer. There was a quiver in his voice when he spoke of the suffering of the victims. He looked like some ancient prophet. All the thousands who listened to him were moved to their depths. Who could have imagined then that the pogrom in Kishineff would seem like child's play afterwards against the mass slaughter of millions in the Hitler period?

We also had a separate Jewish labour demonstration, which was held in Hyde Park on June 21st 1903 The initiative came from the Jewish Cabinet Makers' Union, which called a conference for the purpose of all the Jewish political and labour organisations in London. All the Jewish trades unions sent representatives, as well as the Federation of Jewish Anarchists and the Jewish branches of the Social Democrats, the Social Revolutionaries and the Polish Socialist Party.

Unfortunately, the two delegates of the Social Democratic Federation brought an unpleasant note into the proceedings. Immediately we met they declared that they would take part only on two conditions — first, the Zionists must be barred from the conference and, secondly, the conference must adopt a resolution expressing sympathy and support for the Jewish Labour Bund in Russia and Poland. It was a presumptuous demand for an organisation which represented only a small minority of the Jewish working class in England. The Zionists had no following of any consequence at that time in the Jewish working class movement. The Zionist press had besides accused the revolutionary movement in Russia of being in a way to blame for the pogromist activity of the Russian government. For this reason no invitation had been sent to the Zionists, and they for their part had made no attempt to be represented at the conference and to take part in its work. It would have been absurd to adopt a resolution excluding an organisation which was not seeking to be represented. The second condition too was unacceptable, because the policy of the Tzarist government against the revolutionary movement in Russia was aimed at the entire movement, not at one particular party. A special resolution of sympathy with the Bund would have been a slap in the face for all the other organisations.

The two delegates refused to withdraw their demand. The whole first day of the conference was wasted in fruitless discussion about it. On the second day they threatened that if the conference did not accept their resolution they would publicly brand the London Jewish trades unions in the Russian press as enemies of the Bund.

I got up and protested that it was an outrage that socialists, no matter to what party they belonged, should exploit the terrible tragedy of Kishineff for their own party ends. If, I said, the Social Democratic Federation would hold a protest demonstration of its own, it could adopt any resolution it wished; but it could not force its ultimatums on other organisations. Most of the other delegates supported me. When the vote was taken only two small trades unions, whose combined membership was under a hundred, voted with the social democrats; the two representatives of the Social Democratic Federation thereupon withdrew. We had no further trouble at the conference.

The two Yiddish dailies in London at that time, the *Jewish Express* and the *Jewish Telephone*, denounced the conference and all it was trying to do as an anarchist manoeuvre. The *Jewish Express* went so far as to question Kropotkin's friendship for the Jews. It told the Jews of the East End that if they went to our demonstration they would find that it was not directed so much against the pogrom in Kishineff as for socialism. It said that the Russian government had accused the Jews of Russia of being engaged in the socialist movement. Such a demonstration would give the Russian government an excuse to say that the charge was true, that the Russian Jews were linked with socialism.

The demonstration was held on a Sunday afternoon. It was the biggest manifestation of Jewish workers that London had seen till then. Thousands of Jewish proletarians marched in closed ranks from Mile End to Hyde Park. It was a dull, unfriendly day, fitting for the angry, sullen mood of the marchers. Thousands more had gone straight to the park, especially women who did not feel that they could go all that way on foot. The speeches were in English, Yiddish, Russian and Polish. The London dailies estimated that there were at least 25,000 people assembled round the three platforms. Besides our East End Jewish speakers there were Herbert Burrows, John Turner, Ted Leggatt, Harry Kelly, N. Tchaikovsky and W. Tcherkesov. Kropotkin was not well, and said he could not speak; but he came to the demonstration. He arrived late, and the crowd round our platform was so dense that he couldn't get through to us. But some of the crowd recognised him; they lifted him shoulder-high and so passed him along over their heads till he reached our platform.

Having got there he made a short speech, first in Russian and then in English. His speech appeared in full in the *Arbeter Fraint* and in *Freedom*. But some of the English daily papers published fairly long extracts from it.

The demonstration had succeeded beyond our expectations, in spite of the incessant campaign against us in the two Yiddish London dailies, and the way in which the Rabbis in the East End Synagogues had, with a zeal worthy of a better cause, preached for weeks past to their congregations to get them to boycott the demonstration.

We had the same campaign against us in the provinces. When I came to Manchester and Liverpool to speak against the Czarist pogroms, our comrades couldn't get a hall in which to hold our meeting. But we had packed meetings in Leeds and Glasgow and Edinburgh.

I understand that the main motive for the opposition we met from the representatives of religious Jewry was their fear that such mass demonstrations abroad might endanger Russian Jewry still more. I am sure their fear was exaggerated; such huge demonstrations must have impressed the Tzarist government, and made it realise the extent of the feeling its progrom policy aroused throughout the world. But it was an understandable fear, considering the state of continual uncertainty in which Russian Jewry had to live.

Chapter 16

The Campaign Against
the Sweating System

The Jewish working class movement in London had demonstrated its strength. There was a new active spirit among the Jewish workers. We played our part, of course, in the awakening. There were enough grounds for arousing their discontent.

We decided to start a big campaign against the evil sweating system, from which the Jewish workers suffered most. The British government had for years been concerned with this problem. It had set up a Select Commission to enquire into it, and to recommend ways of dealing with it. But nothing was done. It was all on paper. Even the Factory Inspectors who were appointed to see that women and young people should not work all the hours of the day and night did not stop it. They could not be altogether blamed for it; as long as the workers were not properly organised, to prevent it themselves, there were countless ways in which they could be circumvented. Even if the inspectors did their best they could easily be outwitted. For the most important of the sweated industries was tailoring which was mainly in the hands of foreigners, whose ways were beyond the understanding of English officials. The whole system of factory laws and regulations at that time was so complicated that they could always be got round. Also, the skilled workers who, with the sub-divisional system had unskilled or less skilled workers under them, were as much interested to cheat the regulations as the master-tailors for whom they worked.

The clothing industry in the East End was run by hundreds of small master-tailors who were sub-contractors for the big firms in the City and the West End. In order to get the contract they under-bid each other mercilessly, thus creating their own hell. They passed that hell on of course to their workers. The new immigrants, the greeners, as they were called, who had just arrived from Poland or Russia or Romania and had to earn their bread, went to these small sweatshops to learn to be pressers or machinists. They started as under-pressers or plain-machinists, working for about six months for a skilled presser or machinist, doing the first preparatory work for him, till they learned to work for themselves. This lower grade of workers was employed and paid not by the master-tailor, but by the presser or the machinist. Sometimes a presser or machinist employed three or four under-pressers or plain-machinists. It suited the master-tailor, because it placed the responsibility for driving the workers on the upper grade of the workers themselves.

The evil of the sweating system was that it was so contrived that each drove everybody else. The big firms in the City and West End drove the sub-contracting master-tailors to compete ruthlessly one against the other. The master-tailor drove his workers, and they in their turn drove their subordinate workers. It was a vicious circle, each trying to squeeze as much as possible out of those under them.

It is understandable that trade union organisation was difficult under such conditions. The subordinate workers had other interests than the skilled workers who employed them. They formed their own unions, but these could not be lasting, because their members in time learned their trade and became skilled workers; then they employed others themselves. As long as this system existed the effort to organise the workers in proper trade unions was a labour of Sisyphus. To add to the trouble, there were a great many young women in the industry who had no interest in trade union organisation, because they went to work only until they got married.

The first step had to be to persuade the higher-grade skilled workers to stop employing subordinate labour, to leave that for the master-tailors to do. But most of them didn't want it. They refused to think of the improved labour conditions that organisation could secure for them for the future. They thought only of the money they would lose now.

It is hardly possible to conceive today the conditions in which the mass of the Jewish workers in London lived at that time. They were mostly engaged in the clothing industry, under what was then the new system of sub-divisional labour. Each part of the work was done by a different worker who did nothing else, only that one part of the work all the time. The workshops were ordinary living rooms, completely unfitted for the purpose, heavy with the sweat of many working people, to which was added the damp of the pressing irons on the cloth. There were no regular hours of work. Employment was completely seasonal. In the busy season the people worked all the hours of the day and night, to save something for the slack season, when they earned next to nothing. It was slave-driving. In the busy season the pace was killing. In the slack season it was hunger and hopeless despair.

When we took up the fight against this terrible system we were told that we were out of touch with the realities of life, that we thought people could feed their families with promises of a distant better future. There is no truth in the charge. We were aware of the present needs of the workers, and we were concerned to help them now. The files of the *Arbeter Fraint* over the years show that we were telling the Jewish workers all the time that they must stand out for an immediate betterment of their lot. There was no trade union meeting, no strike, no smallest effort that the workers made to fight for their daily bread in which we did not take part. The fact is that all the Jewish trades unions in the East End, without exception, were started by the initiative of the Jewish anarchists. The Jewish labour movement grew largely out of the ceaseless educational work that we carried on year in year out. Even those who disagree with our views cannot deny what we did in the field of Jewish trade union organisation and activity.

It is completely wrong to suppose that anarchists reject the idea of an improvement of conditions in present-day society. What we said was that the people must work and fight for that improvement. It would not come by itself. All social and political progress, from Magna Charta to the eight hour day, was the result of popular demands to which the authorities had to agree. We told the people that they must always stand on guard to defend their rights and liberties.

So when the Jewish labour movement in England had demonstrated its strength, we considered that the time had come for a big practical effort to improve the conditions of the Jewish workers. We called them to join in a united effort against the sweating system.

We were of course thinking primarily of lifting the evil yoke of the sweatshop system from the Jewish workers. But we also had a second object, which seemed no less important to us, to establish better relations between the Jewish workers and the English workers and the English trades unions. They were far from good then. They couldn't be. The English workers could not feel happy about the development of new industries in the East End of London which were not subject to trade union discipline and control, especially when those industries kept growing through the immigration of more foreign workers. The English workers didn't know the circumstances which brought those Jewish immigrants to England and made them work under those evil conditions. The result was that they were prejudiced against the Jews; and this might have led to a very ugly situation. Some of the English trades unions had tried to get the Jewish workers to join them, but there was a lack of understanding of their peculiar conditions, and nothing came of these efforts.

There is no doubt about the anti-Jewish prejudice which existed not only among the English workers, but also among the English trade union leaders. We had an example of it in connection with our protest demonstration against the Kishineff pogrom. We had asked James MacDonald, the Chairman of the London Trades Council, to be one of our speakers, and he refused. He said that Jewish workers in London had acted as strike-breakers, doing work that strikers in Edinburgh had refused to do. He even published his accusation in *Reynold's Newspaper*. We could not find out if it was true; there were so many hundreds of small workshops in the East End of London that no real control was possible.

Of course MacDonald was wrong to confuse the two issues. We had asked him to protest against the inhuman pogrom policy of the Russian Tzarist government, and the innocent victims in Kishineff were not to blame for what a few Jewish workers had done in London. Besides, we who had organised the demonstration were as much against strike breaking as MacDonald. MacDonald apologised, after the Jewish trades unions had protested sharply. But his charge may not have been unfounded; it shows the kind of feeling that existed.

I kept calling in the *Arbeter Fraint*, in article after article, for the Jewish workers to take the initiative to improve their relations with the English workers. We denounced the sweating system, and we carried on an agitation among the Jewish workers for a general strike for its abolition. We roused tremendous interest, and we won a great deal of support. Early in 1904, we had enough support to increase the size of the *Arbeter Fraint* to twelve pages, with four pages of literary supplement. On April 6th, 1904, we held a public meeting in the Wonderland, in Whitechapel, to deal with the question of the general strike. There were five thousand seats, and every one of them was occupied, and there were crowds outside who couldn't get in. The police had the doors closed. Besides our East End Jewish speakers we had all the leading speakers in our movement in London, Malatesta, Tarrida del Marmol, Tcherkesov, Tchaikovsky, Mainwaring, Ted Leggatt, Kelly, John Turner, Kitz. Mowbray took the chair. Kropotkin was not well enough to come, but he sent a long message, which was read out to tremendous applause.

There was a small strike at the time, called by the Jewish Bakers' Union. It should be mentioned here, both because it was the prelude to a series of such strikes, and because it showed how even a small thing can become an event if it has public opinion behind it. The strike was started to get better working conditions for the bakers. Feeling in the East End was so strongly on the side of the workers that the employers' organisation would hardly have stood out long against them if the workers had not introduced a new demand — they wanted a trade union label on the bread, so that the public could see if it came from a bakery that observed trade union conditions.

The whole East End seemed to be solidly behind the workers. A few days after the strike started some of the smaller bakers agreed to use the trade union label on their bread. The Jewish women of the East End refused to buy any other. In the East End bread was sold not only in the bakers' shops, but in all the groceries. The women would buy their provisions first, and then ask for a loaf. If it had no trade union label they would hand it back. The result was that the grocer was left with so much bread on his hands that he took no bread the next day from the non-union baker. The strike was won in a few weeks. The label helped the Jewish Bakers' Union to get better conditions in their part of the trade; they were for a long time in advance of the conditions of the workers organised in the English bakers' unions. It added to the sense of their strength among the Jewish workers generally, and helped to prepare the way for the big general strike later against the sweating system.

Chapter 17

The Impact of the Russian Revolution

Of course much of the increased activity in the Jewish labour movement in London was the result of the interest and enthusiasm roused by the news of the great Russian Revolution of 1904–1905. Everybody said that the days of the Czarist regime were numbered. No one believed at that time that it would take almost another fifteen years before the Czarist regime collapsed, and that it would happen under conditions we could not possibly have foreseen. I saw with what eagerness the Jewish workers watched the course of events in their former homeland. It was incredible to me that people who had suffered so much in Russia, where Jews were treated as pariahs from the cradle to the grave, should retain such affectionate feeling for the country. These Jewish proletarians seemed to belong in spirit still to Russia. It could hardly be called patriotism. It was love of their native places, of the towns and villages where they had grown up and spent their early years.

The Russian war with Japan hastened the progress of the Russian Revolution. There were big demonstrations everywhere against the war and the autocracy — in Moscow, Petersburg, in Poland, South Russia and the Caucasus. On July 28th the Minister of the Interior, von Plehve, was assassinated by the Social Revolutionaries. He was one of the main pillars of the Russian reaction. The same month Tolstoy issued his powerful protest against the war. We can imagine the feelings with which the Czar and his supporters read those damning words of the sage of Yasnaia Polanya. Yet no one dared to lay hands on him. All that happened was that the Orthodox Church excommunicated him, and the Holy Synod placed his books under its ban. What would have happened to Tolstoy if he had lived in Stalin's Russia or in Hitler's Germany?

The Czarist government lost its head. Promised reforms were withdrawn. The people rose in revolt. There were demonstrations everywhere. In Smolensk, Vitebsk, Mohilev, Kiev the reservists who had been called up refused to serve. In January 1905 there was the terrible Bloody Sunday in Petersburg, when the soldiers shot down men, women and children who were marching in a peaceful demonstration to the Winter Palace, with the idea of presenting a petition to the Czar.

It roused a storm of indignation all over the world. There were protest strikes in Finland, in Riga, Tiflis, Batum, Baku, in every part of the Russian Empire. The crew of the Potemkin mutinied.

The moving spirit of the Potemkin mutiny was a sailor named Matutchenko, who soon after came to London, where I got to know him. I lived at that time in Dunstan Houses, in Stepney, where Kropotkin's paper, *Listki Chlieb i Wolia* had its printing office. I knew the printer; whenever

Matutchenko visited the office of the paper they both came up to have a cup of tea with me.

Matutchenko was a good-natured, smiling Russian peasant type; about medium height, and powerfully built. It was hard to believe that this simple, kindly man had been the ringleader of the Potemkin mutiny.

Matutchenko had been a member of a secret group of the Social Revolutionaries when he was called up as a naval reservist at the beginning of the Russo-Japanese war. He managed on the ship to maintain contacts with his group on land. He was an active propagandist among the crew of the Potemkin and other ships of the Black Sea Fleet, and succeeded in forming several secret revolutionary cells among them. He always spoke very modestly about his own share in the Potemkin mutiny. If anything he blamed himself for having failed to make it a general rising throughout the fleet.

Matutchenko wasn't happy in London. He felt out of touch. He fretted at the inactivity to which he was condemned. He was homesick for Russia. His spirits drooped. His friends helped him to go to Canada. But a few months later he was back in England, and insisted that he must return to Russia.

His friends warned him of the danger he would be running into in Russia. They tried to dissuade him. He refused to listen. He crossed into Russia. Not long after there was a report in the English press that Matutchenko had been arrested. He had gone straight back to his old home in Sevastopol. He was too well known there to escape detection. They court-martialled him, and sentenced him to death. He died like the brave man he was.

In October 1905 there was a general strike of workers in all the Russian industries. For four weeks everything was at a standstill. It forced the Czar to issue the famous October Manifesto, promising a Constituent Assembly, dismissing Pobedoneszev from his post as Grand Procurator, abolishing the censorship, and giving an amnesty to all political prisoners. The manifesto was received with satisfaction by the liberal elements in Russia. But the workers and the peasants no longer trusted the Czarist government. The strikes, the peasant risings and the mutinies in the army continued. The sailors in Sevastopol and Kronstadt revolted. There was a military rising in Kiev. There were mutinies among the troops in Siberia. What was lacking was a united leadership and a planned, concerted movement. These were all sporadic, isolated local incidents. Otherwise Russian absolutism might have been overthrown in 1905.

The final act in the revolution was the battle at the barricades in Moscow from December 22nd to December 30th, 1905. It ended with a complete defeat of the revolutionary forces. They were spent. The counter-revolution had won.

The Jewish workers in London followed these events with passionate interest. Each time something happened there was a big mass meeting in the East End, which thousands of people attended.

A number of our younger comrades made their way back to Russia, to take their part in the events. We were all elated. We were sure that we stood on the threshold of Russian liberation, of a world-shaking event that would like the French Revolution start a new era.

People may shake their heads wisely today over us and call us dreamers, and say that we had no sense of the reality of history. They fail to see that dreams are also a part of the reality of life, that life without dreams would be unbearable. No change in our way of life would be possible without dreams and dreamers. The only people who are never disappointed are those who never hope and never try to realise their hopes.

Chapter 18

The Jubilee Street Club

Our movement was growing fast. When we restarted the *Arbeter Fraint* in 1903 our circulation was 2,500. Within the year we doubled the size, and our circulation increased to 4,000. The number of our readers was of course much larger than that, because those who bought the paper always passed it on afterwards to others who were interested. When I think of the miserable conditions in which the Jewish workers in the East End of London lived I marvel at their devotion and their self-sacrifice. I myself knew people who didn't earn enough to keep body and soul together and yet, year in year out denied themselves the bare necessities of life in order to contribute to our funds. Young girls who slaved in the sweatshops for a weekly pittance of ten or twelve shillings, literally took the bread from their mouths to give the movement a few pennies. They did it gladly, with a sense of dedication, a sacrifice which they made willingly for a cause to which they looked for the coming of a better world.

In many workshops the workers nailed a cigar box to the wall, and dropped their pennies in it: "For the *Arbeter Fraint*".

We owed much to those ordinary working men and women, who were devoted heart and soul to our cause, people whose individual names are never mentioned, but who were the backbone of our movement. I have two of them in mind; they may be regarded as symbols of them all, representatives of the larger mass of whom they were part — Tapler and Kerkelevitch.

Their lives were hard, from childhood till death. They belonged to the very poorest section of the Jewish working class. Tapler was a shoemaker. Out of his small earnings he contributed his few pence regularly to the movement. He was at all our meetings. He came at any hour of the day or night, like a faithful watchdog. Nothing was too hard for Tapler or Kerkelevitch to do that could in any way constitute a service to the cause or to any of us who worked in it. When we celebrated in 1906 the 20th anniversary of the *Arbeter Fraint* it was one of the oldest organs of our movement. There were papers in Spain, Italy and France that had been started earlier, in the days of the First International, but they had sooner or later fallen under the ban of the authorities, and had to be replaced by new publications. The *Arbeter Fraint* and *Freedom*, the English anarchist paper, appeared continuously under the same name. There were only two papers in our movement that were older, Johann Most's *Freiheit* in New York, and *La Révolte* in Paris.

We published a sixteen page issue for the anniversary, with articles and messages from all our earlier editors and contributors, including Wintchevsky, Yanovsky, Philip Krantz and Frumkin, and from Kropotkin,

Tcherkesov and Johann Most. On the night of the celebration, March 17th 1906, we were having a ball. The dancing was just starting when a telegram arrived from New York that Most had died. Of course the ball was abandoned.

Meanwhile *Germinal* had made its reappearance. The first issue came out in January 1905. A group of young comrades had approached me towards the end of 1904 to ask me to renew the magazine. They said they needed something more than the *Arbeter Fraint*. They wanted a periodical devoted to literature and contemporary thought. I told them I would gladly do the editorial work, but I could not again shoulder the burden of being also the printer and manager. They offered to form a separate *Germinal* Group, which would be responsible for everything except the editorial side, which would be my province.

There were about a dozen young people in this group, fine young people, who gave their services freely, enthusiastically. None of us ever took a penny in payment for all the work we did on *Germinal* during the whole of its existence.

I had a long essay in the first issue, which over the course of years appeared as a separate publication in a dozen different languages. The first time was in 1906, in a hectographed sheet produced in Vilna in Yiddish and Russian, which was circulated secretly in Russia. The latest was in 1947, in Chinese. It appeared at Cheng Tu, translated by our old comrade Lu Chien Bo. In 1922 the Argonauta Press in Buenos Aires published a 300 page book of my collected essays from *Germinal* in a Spanish translation, under the title *Artistas y Rebeldes*.

Germinal appeared as a 16 page paper till April 1906, when we increased the size to 48 pages; it continued in that increased size till the middle of 1908. The circulation was between 2,000 and 2,500.

We also published many books and pamphlets, translations into Yiddish from some of the leading contemporary writers, like Tolstoy, Ibsen, Tchechov, Gorki, Andreiev, Hauptmann, Anatole France, Maeterlinck, Knut Hamsun, Oscar Wilde, Israel Zangwill, as well as works by Kropotkin, Louise Michel, Reclus, David Edelshtat, myself and others, which belonged to the literature of our movement. They were an important contribution to the enrichment of Yiddish literature at that time, and they were widely read in every country where the growing Yiddish literature had a following. Frumkin, who did much of this translation work, holds his place as one of the first who brought modern European literature to the Yiddish reading public.

The *Arbeter Fraint* was also able to help the movement in Russia and in Poland. We received and printed a great many reports from our secret groups in Warsaw, Vilna, Grodno, Bialystock and other places about events in the lands of the Czar. Sometimes emissaries from the Russian groups arrived in London, and consulted us about smuggling our literature into Russia. The result was that the *Arbeter Fraint* and *Germinal* and our books and pamphlets were widely distributed throughout the Czarist Empire.

Much of our literature went into Russia through the connections which one of our comrades, Ruderman, who kept a bookshop and newsagent's in Hanbury Street, had with the famous Yiddish publishing house Kletzkin in Vilna. Ruderman imported from Kletzkin Yiddish papers and periodicals and books which appeared in Russia. He sent him in return the Yiddish papers and periodicals and books that appeared in England and America. There was an arrangement by which the big cases were filled with illegal literature, covered over with layers of innocent publications. The censor in Vilna must have been bribed not to look deeper into these consignments. This arrangement, of which of course only a few of us in London knew, went on for years, without interruption or discovery.

The growth of our movement in London led to the opening of the *Arbeter Fraint* Club and Institute in Jubilee Street, which played a great part for years in the Jewish social and intellectual life of the East End. It was a big building, with a large hall, which with the gallery held about 800 people. There were a number of smaller halls and rooms. One hall on the second floor was used as a library and reading room. A smaller building adjoining the club served as the editorial and printing offices of the *Arbeter Fraint*.

The club was opened on February 3rd, 1906. The big hall and the gallery were packed. Long before we were due to start we had to lock the doors, because there was no more room. Almost every Jewish trade union in the country had sent us messages of congratulation. There were also messages from Malatesta, Louise Michel and Tarrida del Marmol. I was reading out the messages when a storm of cheering and clapping cut me short. Peter Kropotkin had arrived. His doctors had warned him not to appear at any more public gatherings, because of his heart. But this was an occasion from which he felt he must not stay away.

I begged him not to speak. He waved me aside. He spoke for over half an hour. He was utterly exhausted when he finished. And when he got home he had a heart attack. We felt very guilty when we heard of it; but we had tried to stop him, and he had refused to listen to us.

The other speakers included John Turner and Ted Leggatt. It was a great occasion. Most of us did not go home till the early hours.

The Jubilee Street Club played such a great part in East End Jewish life because it was open to everyone. Anyone could use our library and reading room, or join our educational classes, without being asked for a club membership card. This made it impossible for us to sell drinks in the club, from which most of the other clubs got the greater part of their revenue. For the law restricted the sale of intoxicants in clubs to club members. We sold only tea and coffee and food. So we had to find other ways of meeting our running costs.

Other organisations could rent the club for their meetings. Indeed, most East End meetings were held there. It was only when some very big demonstration was planned that the Wonderland or the Pavilion Theatre, which could seat about 5,000, were used. Otherwise the meetings were held in our club. The smaller trades unions, the branches of the Workers' Circle, our own branches, the branch of the Russian Social Revolutionaries, and our English comrades used the club for their regular meetings.

The classes included one in English, for the younger immigrants. I taught history and sociology. On Sunday mornings I took my classes to the British Museum, whose treasures richly illustrated what I had been trying to teach them. The British Museum authorities gave us every possible facility and help.

We also had speakers' classes, and a Sunday School, conducted by Nelly Ploshansky, her husband, Jim Dick, and my elder son, Rudolf Rocker. Dick afterwards went to Spain, where he studied the methods of Ferrer's Escuela Moderna; he and his wife were then active for years in the Ferrer School in Stelton, and later they started a free school in Lakewood, New Jersey.

There was no other movement at that time in the East End of London which could compare with ours in numbers or activity. Zionism was a small movement then, and had few adherents among the Jewish workers. The only other movement which had any following were the Jewish Social Democrats; but they were never a strong body. They tried several times to start a party paper of their own; it never lasted long. There were a number of Bundists among the Jewish immigrants. They started a weekly in 1904, *Di Naie Zeit*. It continued, with several breaks, till 1908. Then it disappeared. Many former Bundists, who had been active social democrats in Russia and Poland, joined our movement in London.

The leading figures among the Jewish Social Democrats were Beck, Finn and Saul Elstein, of Leeds, and later Morris Myer. Beck who was the editor of the *Naie Zeit*, was like myself not a Jew. He was a Russian Marxist who had, as I did, learned Yiddish. It was a strange coincidence that the editors of both Yiddish labour papers in the East End were not themselves of Jewish origin.

Though Beck and I were always at loggerheads over our opposing ideologies, it did not disturb our personal relationship. He was a dogmatic Marxist, rigid and unbending, with an unshakeable belief in the infallibility of scientific Marxism. But he was honest and decent, and devoted to his conviction, for which he was prepared to make any sacrifice. One had to respect the man. He was not a particularly good speaker, nor a very lively journalist. He was unimaginative, stolid and plodding, and he had no sense of humour. I sometimes tried pulling his leg, but he could never see it.

Beck stood at the wheel of the *Naie Zeit* for about eighteen months. He realised it was hopeless, and gave it up. He went back to Russia with a false passport, was caught and sent to Siberia, That was the last we heard of him. There was a rumour that he had died in Siberia. As I said, he was an honest man, devoted to his cause, and I can speak of him only with respect.

Morris Myer succeeded him as editor of the *Naie Zeit*. He hadn't Beck's theoretic knowledge of his subject, but he was a much livelier journalist and a better public speaker. He came to London in 1902 from Romania, where he had translated some of my articles in the *Arbeter Fraint* into Romanian for the anarchist monthly *Revista Idii*. I was living in Leeds when he arrived in London, and I got to know him only the following year, when we restarted the *Arbeter Fraint*. He contributed several articles to the *Arbeter Fraint*. When Beck left, he took over the *Naie Zeit*. But the paper couldn't get enough support; in 1908 it stopped publication. Morris Myer joined the Yiddish daily *Jewish Journal*. After that he founded in 1913 his own paper, the *Zeit*, a popular daily in Yiddish, which existed till 1952, a few years after his death. In Jewish politics Morris Myer became a prominent figure in the Zionist Labour Party, Poale Zion, and later in the English Zionist Federation.

Chapter 19

Our English Movement

I first came to London I found there was a very active anarchist movement among our English comrades. We had groups in all parts of London and in all the big provincial towns, conducting open-air propaganda at street corners and in the public parks. This was something quite new to me. I don't think there was any other country with so many open-air meetings, political and religious. I was struck by the mutual toleration of the rival groups and the fair play of the crowds that gathered round the different stands. We had nothing like it in Germany.

One of the best-known of the anarchist open-air speakers at that time was Ted Leggatt, a big, burly Cockney carman, who played a big part in the Transport Workers' Union. He was a man of the people, racy of speech, with a rich Cockney humour, and a stentorian voice, which he used to good advantage to proclaim his ideas. He would start his speeches with: "I am Ted Leggatt, the anarchist". He was a good fellow, and a good comrade, a frequent visitor among the Jewish comrades, who were always glad to see him.

Most of our English comrades were veterans of the movement, who had come to anarchism through William Morris and his Socialist League. Sam Mainwaring was born in 1841 in Wales. He came to London and found his way into the socialist movement. He was one of William Morris's close associates in the Socialist League. He died in 1907.

His friend, Frank Kitz, was another Cockney, who had been with Morris in the Socialist League. He died in 1922. There were many others, including younger men like M. Kavanagh, S. Carter, W. Ponder, M. Bentham, Guy Aldred, A. Ray, S. Presburg, and George Barrett, the editor of the *Voice of Labour*

John Turner was an outstanding figure in the English anarchist movement, and in the English trade union movement. He too had been in the old Socialist League; he was one of the founders of the *Freedom* group. He was of course an anti-Marxist. Once at my home he met a German comrade who had never been quite able to shake off his Marxist dogma. This comrade was worried over Eduard Bernstein's revisionism in the socialist movement. Turner told him revisionism was a good thing, because the revisionists were undermining Marxism from within. They were freeing socialism from the fatalistic conceptions with which Marx shackled it. The revisionists were true revolutionaries, he said, because they challenged the old dogmas.

When it became the fashion for trade union leaders to go into parliament his trade union wanted to send John Turner to parliament. He declined. He said he preferred to work for the labour movement in the trades unions, rather than waste his time in parliamentary debates.

Lothrop Whittington and Harry Kelly were both Americans. Whittington did not live in England. He came over every year on business, and during the time he was in London he took an active part in our movement. He was a very popular speaker at our meetings. He lost his life in the Titanic disaster.

Harry Kelly was born in 1870 in St. Louis. He had got to know the English anarchist Charles Mowbray in Boston, and when he came to England he joined the *Freedom* group. He was tremendously active, especially as a public speaker, both at the meetings of the English comrades and at the meetings of our Jewish group.

It was at the London home of Harry Kelly and his wife Mary that I met Voltairine de Cleyre, whose writings and speeches were so valuable in our libertarian movement, especially in America. She lived with the Kellys in London in 1903, and as she had heard of me from the Jewish comrades in America she asked them to let her meet Milly and me. We spent a day together. It was the only time I met her. When I was in Chicago in 1913 I visited her fresh grave, beside that of the Chicago martyrs.

Kelly afterwards went back to America, where he continued working for the movement. He was a close friend of Emma Goldman and Alexander Berkman, and had a good deal to do with their organ *Mother Earth*. He died at New Rochelle, near New York, in 1953, at the age of 82.

The new anarchist movement in England grew out of the Democratic Federation, which was founded in 1881 by Henry Hyndman, Joseph Cowen MP, Helen Taylor, John Stuart Mill's step-daughter, Herbert Burrows, Joseph Lane, and a few old Chartists. William Morris, Belfort Bax and Edward Carpenter joined it, and several people from the working class, like Sam Mainwaring, Harry Quelch, Jack Williams, Charles Mowbray and Frank Kitz. It was Edward Carpenter who gave the money to start *Justice*, the organ of the Federation.

At first, the Democratic Federation, which afterwards became the Social Democratic Federation, was a socialist propaganda organisation, embracing socialists of many different ideologies. But Hyndman was determined to turn it into a political party. Hyndman had started out as a Tory, and he remained a Tory at heart. He was a Jingo, and showed it by his attitude during the First World War. He was dictatorial by nature.

The result was that there was a great deal of resistance to him and his methods in the Federation, and in the end there was a split. In 1884 William Morris and a number of others left the Federation, and formed the Socialist League. Some left for different reasons than others. Marx's daughter, Eleanor Marx-Aveling and her husband, and Friedrich Lessner, for instance, were no doubt animated by the old enmity which existed between Engels and Hyndman.

But most of the members of the Socialist League were libertarian socialists, and a number, like Mainwaring, Lane, Kitz, John Turner, Mowbray and others were anarchists.

The soul and spirit of the Socialist League, of course, was William Morris, a great artist and a great poet, one of the finest figures that English socialism has produced. To him socialism was something much more than a scientific economic theory. He had no patience with Marxism. Economic justice and security was no ideal for him; it was only the necessary basis for a new community life, where people would be free and would be able to express themselves freely in life, in art, in culture and civilisation. Man's free spirit was what mattered to him most. He made that clear in his books, *News From Nowhere*, and *The Dream of John Ball*, and in his many other writings and poems. It rings out in his poem "No Master", "We've heard and known that we no master need," the true anthem of the libertarian movement. When I came to London in 1895, Morris was already a sick man. But he still took part in the movement, and he sometimes came to public meetings. But I saw him for the first time in the studio of an artist friend of mine, in Hammersmith, where Morris lived. One day, out for a walk, Morris came in to see how my friend was getting on with a work he had been commissioned to do for a theatre. I happened to be there at the time. The one-time Viking was now bent, leaning heavily on his stick, and he looked ill. But his magnificent head was still imposing, and his voice still boomed. We could not converse much. For Morris knew only English, and my English, in those first few months of my stay in England, was poor. Before the twelve-month was out, Morris was dead.

It is a pity Morris and Kropotkin never got more together, though Kropotkin had been living in London since 1886. Kropotkin always spoke to me of Morris with the greatest admiration. They were both active at the same time in very similar fields. In 1886 Morris was editing the Socialist League's paper *Commonweal*. And in 1896 Kropotkin started the Freedom group, and its organ *Freedom*, with a number of comrades some of whom belonged to Morris's Socialist League. This group included Charlotte M. Wilson, John Turner, Sam Mainwaring, T. Pearson, A. Marsh, T. Canwell, T.H. Keel, W. Tcherkesov, and William Wess, of the Jewish group, and his sister, Doris Zhook.

Another great libertarian socialist of those days was Edward Carpenter, who wrote *Towards Democracy*. He too, like Morris, was not a scientific socialist. He was no Marxian. He detested the thought of socialism as "nothing but an envious shriek and a threat, a gospel of bread and butter". He thought of socialism as "the signal for the advent of the true life of the People". To him the socialist movement was "carried on by bodies of men very various both in name and in methods". This was the essence of free socialism, which the rigid Marxists and authoritarians could not understand nor tolerate.

Edward Carpenter came of a wealthy English family. It was his social conscience that brought him into the socialist movement. He made it clear in his autobiographical book *My Days and Dreams*, that socialism was to him not another economic system, but a new society, a new civilisation, a new and higher ethic. It was an appeal more to the social conscience of the rich and the men of education, to lift up those who were less fortunate. "In this sense," he wrote, "I am working for the ideal of anarchism." His great socialist hymn "England Arise", is a passionate call to freedom.

103

When the 1914 war broke out, there was a split in the ranks of the Freedom group. Kropotkin, Tcherkesov and a number of other members were pro-war. Keel, who was then editor of *Freedom*, and others were, like Malatesta, anti-war. Keel gave space in the paper for both points of view, He printed articles by Kropotkin and Tcherkesov explaining their attitude in support of the war, and he printed articles against the war by Malatesta and others. The anti-war articles drew the attention of the censor, and Keel spent several months in prison because of them. When victorious Bolshevism dazzled some anarchists with its promise, deluding them with the idea that the dictatorship of the proletariat would lead to the new free society, Keel stood firm by his old beliefs, and followed his straight line. He died in 1938 at Whiteway Colony, in Gloucester, at the age of 72.

Another remarkable figure in the movement was Thomas H. Bell. Born in Edinburgh in 1867, he became a ship's engineer, and as such knew all the Mediterranean countries, as well as South Africa, the United States and South America. He knew French, Italian, Spanish and German. As a young man he belonged to the Scottish Land and Labour League. About the end of the 80s he joined the anarchist movement, and became active in London in the *Freedom* group. He returned to Edinburgh in 1892, and with his friends Blair Smith and McCabe carried on a regular propaganda there. He was connected in Edinburgh with Patrick Geddes, the biologist, sociologist and town planner in his work for educational reform, He got Geddes to bring Elisée Reclus, the anarchist and geographer, to lecture at Edinburgh University.

Tom Bell went back to London in 1898 as Secretary to Frank Harris, a position he held for seven years. It brought him in touch with Edward Carpenter, Bernard Shaw, Havelock Ellis and others. He quarrelled with Frank Harris over his biography of Oscar Wilde, which he considered unjust to Wilde. He went to New York in 1905, and in 1911 finally settled in America with his family; he became a farmer at Phoenix, in Arizona. He spent the last twenty years of his life in Los Angeles, where he died in 1942, at the age of 73.

I saw him again in Los Angeles, when he was an old man. He was ill. His mop of red hair and his bushy beard were now white. His giant frame (he was well over six foot) was bent. But his mind was active; he was still working and speaking for the movement. Others who stood close to us in that period were J. Morrison Davidson, who wrote *The New Book of Kings*, *Scotia Rediviva* and *The Book of Lords*, and John C. Kenworthy, author of *The Anatomy of Misery* and *From Bondhood to Brotherhood*. Davidson and Kenworthy were both greatly influenced by Tolstoy, and were Christian Anarchists. Henry W. Nevinson, whose works include *Essays in Freedom and Rebellion*, and *England's Voice of Freedom*, also stood close to the Freedom group in the 1890s. He was a contributor to *Freedom*. I remember his speech at the dinner held in 1911 for the 25th anniversary of *Freedom*, when he emphasised the great influence of *Freedom* on him.

I must also mention Sir Herbert Read, who came later, after the First World War, in which he fought at the front as an officer. He was much influenced by Kropotkin and Edward Carpenter. Besides his important books on art, and his poetry, Sir Herbert has written *Poetry and Anarchism*.

Others who contributed to the literature of libertarian thought were Havelock Ellis, Francis Adams, who wrote *Songs of the Army of the Night*, Auheron Herbert, author of *A Politician in Sight of Heaven. Being a Protest against Government of Man by Man*, Wordsworth Donisthorpe, Henry Seymour, Robert Harding and William Gilmour.

England is a country with a liberal tradition, a land of tolerance and fair play. Those liberal traditions had their influence on the development of the socialist movement in Great Britain, in all its different trends, in a way I never saw it in Germany, with its Prussian barrack-room spirit. I learned a great deal during the years I lived in England, for which I am grateful, which helped to shape my development, and opened my eyes to many new ideas and outlooks.

Chapter 20

Trouble With New Immigrants

We had a lot of trouble with a number of our young comrades who had been in the underground movement in Russia and couldn't adjust themselves to life in England. Many went back to Russia in the end, though they knew it might mean imprisonment or death. Perhaps the danger attracted them.

We did what we could to help them to find their feet. But it was hard. They had come to regard themselves as engaged in a war against established society, and they could see no difference between England and Russia. Some of them were dangerous people. There were also Russian police agents and spies among them. The Azeff Affair had shown how widespread the Russian police spy network was in the revolutionary movement; we didn't know whom to trust.

There were also rogues among them. There was one man who came to us with a letter from the International Group in Warsaw, which had sent him abroad to buy propaganda literature and arms. He was boastful and aggressive. He wanted us to give him a quantity of our pamphlets. We agreed. He wanted more copies than we had. We offered him stereos, so that the group in Warsaw could print as many as it wanted. Then he demanded money from us, to pay the cost of the paper and printing. We had no money. We had sent our literature free for years to Russia. But the *Arbeter Fraint* group was never a rich organisation, with money to give away. He flew into a rage. He was abusive. He told us that our work was useless, that we were wasting our time. What we were doing in England was of no importance. The only thing to do was to give money for those who did the work in Russia. It was very unpleasant.

The next thing we heard was from comrades in Paris that he was there, and living rather extravagantly. Then I got a letter from Warsaw, through roundabout channels, asking if we knew where he was; they hadn't heard from him for a long time. The letter said the group had given him four thousand roubles for buying literature and other things.

I wrote back to tell them of our experience with him. I said we were surprised that they had found no better man to send on such a mission.

About a week later he came to see me in London. He said he had completed his mission, and wanted to go back to Warsaw. He had spent all his money on his purchases for the group, and hadn't enough left for the return fare. Would I lend him the money?

I asked him how much the comrades in Warsaw had given him. Two hundred roubles, he said. I brought out my letter from Warsaw. He went white. He tried to argue that the figure in the letter was a mistake. I saw no point in arguing with the man. I showed him the door.

He went back to Paris. We had warned our comrades there, and he was cold-shouldered. We heard afterwards that he did go back to Russia, and was unmasked there as a police spy. That was the story we got. I don't know whether it is true that he was a police spy. I shouldn't be surprised. He was a very unpleasant fellow, and no good to any movement.

There was a much worse case, a man who called himself Tchishikoff. He had been engaged in Russia in a number of "expropriations", armed raids on banks, and suchlike, to get the funds for the revolutionary work. The police had caught him on one of his raids, and had put him in prison in Vilna. He escaped, while awaiting trial. He climbed the prison wall, and fell and broke his leg. Comrades waiting for him outside carried him off, hid him, and helped him to escape abroad. He went to Paris, and then came to London, where the Russian comrades welcomed him with open arms. His leg had healed by the time he came to London. But he limped.

I met the man several times. He seemed to me to talk much too much about his daring deeds. He was something of a dare-devil. His ideas about revolution and about anarchism were very crude. That was not surprising. Lots of people had joined the Russian revolutionary movement to fight, and not to study. I thought that with all his faults he was devoted to the cause.

He collected a group of young people round him, who had worked in the underground in Russia, and admired the kind of work he had done. This group spoke only about Russian affairs, and planned activities in Russia. They had no patience for our work in England. We were not revolutionary enough for them.

Revolutionary work without "expropriations", without armed bank raids meant nothing to Tchishikoff. The fact that we held public meetings and conducted our activity openly was sufficient proof to him that we were not really against the authorities. Otherwise they would not have allowed us to hold meetings and distribute our publications. Revolutionary activity, as he saw it, had to be secret, conspirative.

Then something happened which made me decide not to have anything more to do with this man. There was a nice young girl in our movement, whom we all knew by her first name, Zlatke. She was naive, impulsive, all heart. She had little theoretic knowledge of our movement; she had come into it believing that we were working to improve conditions for all people, and she was devoted to us. There was nothing too hard for her to do for us. We were all very fond of her.

Tchishikoff got hold of that poor girl. He told her all about his deeds of daring for the movement, made her think of him as a great hero. They took a room, and went to live together. It lasted a couple of months. Then we heard that Tchishikoff had turned Zlatke out of the house one night. She was pregnant. A few days later his wife arrived from Vilna, and those two lived together in the same room where he had lived with Zlatke.

I was furious at this blackguardly behaviour. So were most of our comrades. We refused to have anything to do with Tchishikoff. But his own group remained loyal to him. They said that his private life did not concern them.

Shortly after there was a wave of arrests in our movement in Russia. Clearly there was a spy at work in the movement. Thirty of our most active comrades were caught by the police. As a result the contacts were broken with our groups in Poland and Lithuania. Tchishikoff proposed to his group that he should go to Russia, to restore the contacts. The group agreed, and started to raise the money for his journey and for the work he would have to do in Russia.

One of our comrades, Nagel, an engineer, who had been a political refugee in London for some years, and whom we all held in high regard, came to ask me to help to raise some of the money. I told him I didn't like Tchishikoff, and I wouldn't do anything to help him.

"I know," said Nagel. "He did behave like a skunk. But that is his private life. I am concerned with his usefulness for the movement. We need him to restore the broken contacts between our groups."

I repeated what I had said. I didn't like the man, and I didn't trust him. After all, I said, a man's character matters. His private life showed the sort of man he was. I didn't believe that he could be one man in his private life, and another in his public life.

Nagel tried to make me see his point about the good of the movement. I was firm in my attitude. He went away disappointed with me.

They managed to raise the money. Tchishikoff went to Russia. He succeeded in restoring the contacts between the groups; he organised a secret conference which comrades from Poland and Lithuania attended. The conference was raided by the police; everybody there was arrested.

Tchishikoff was the traitor. It was all proved against him. Even his escape from the prison in Vilna had been arranged by the police, to win for him the confidence of the comrades.

Fearing the vengeance of the comrades he fled to Switzerland. A young Russian student entered his home there, and shot him dead.

Of course, not everybody who came from Russia at that time was like that. But there were many who couldn't possibly fit in with our activity in England. It wasn't their fault. They had been brought up with the idea that revolutionary activity meant secrecy, conspiracy, and terrorism. They couldn't understand the difference in the political and social conditions in England. Our work in the trades unions was meaningless to them. They treated us as though we were playing at being anarchists. There were often unpleasant scenes between them and our older comrades, who had lived for years in England.

We were haunted by the fear that some of them might do something desperate that would put our whole movement in danger. I discussed that danger with Kropotkin, Tcherkesov and other Russian comrades, who were as much worried by it as we were. Our fears were not unfounded. One day, at the beginning of November 1909, a young Russian comrade came to see me. He told me that a small group to which he belonged had completed a plan to throw a bomb at the Lord Mayor's Show.

I couldn't believe my ears. But the young man gave me names and details; he convinced me. I asked him why he had revealed the plan to me. He said that he had thought it over, and he had realised that many innocent people watching the show would be hurt or killed. I explained that it would also have raised an outcry against all political refugees in England; it might have meant the withdrawal of the political asylum we enjoyed.

We discussed how to prevent the plan being carried out. He told me that the group was to meet the following evening at the home of one of its members in Whitehorse Lane, in Stepney. I arranged with my friend Lazar Sabelinsky to go there with me, to talk to these young people. We found five of them there, including my informant, and one young girl. I told them we knew of their plan. I explained what a terrible blow it would be to all the people who had been able to find refuge in England. I asked them why they wanted to kill the Lord Mayor, and innocent spectators. At first they denied the whole story. In the end they admitted it was true. I said that I was sure some Russian police agent had incited them to such a stupid and senseless outrage, to discredit the whole revolutionary movement, and to close England to all political refugees.

I don't know whether I convinced them by my arguments, or whether it was only the fact that their plot had been discovered that decided them to drop it. There may have been a Russian police agent who had incited them for the reasons I feared. Or they may have been simply blind fanatics who had come from the unhealthy atmosphere of the conditions in Russia, where every policeman and every public dignitary, Governor or Mayor was an instrument of despotism and oppression. Those conditions in Russia had given rise to such terrible things as the theory of unmotivated terror, directed against the entire bourgeoisie as a class, no matter whom it hit.

That small group in London broke up soon after. All the members went back to Russia, except the young man who had revealed the plot to me. He was active afterwards for years in our movement; he was one of my most devoted followers. He told me once that the group had seriously discussed killing Kropotkin, to get him out of the way, because his moderate views were holding back the revolutionary forces. That is the sort of thing fanatics can do.

But the great majority of the immigrants from Russia who joined our movement in London in those years did gradually manage to adjust themselves to the new conditions. Many rendered great service to the movement. One of them, S. Freedman, was afterwards for many years manager of the *Freie Arbeter Shtimme* in New York.

There was an interesting young woman named Judith Goodman among the comrades who found refuge in London in those years. She had been a leading figure in the movement in Bialystock. She wore a wig, because the Cossacks had torn all the hair out of her head.

Judith arrived in London with the same terrorist ideas as many others who had worked in the Russian underground She had her own group round her in London. But she came to our meetings, and she talked to us. She was willing to listen, and to learn. She became a frequent visitor to our house; she was very friendly with Milly. At first she was a little distrustful of us, as though she feared that we would try to damp down her revolutionary zeal. But I think she came to understand us in the end. We tried to make her see that there were methods that might be unavoidable in Russia that were impossible in other countries.

She emigrated afterwards to America with her husband. She died there in 1943. All the comrades in New York knew her, this quiet, modest woman, with her wise, kindly eyes; few knew what a turbulent past she had behind her. For she was one of those who do not talk about themselves.

Her London group included a young man, Moishe Tokar, whose daring in the terrorist activity had won him a great name in Russia. He had laughing blue eyes, and fair hair; no "race scientist" would have believed that he was a Jew. He was a member of the International Group in Warsaw. By incredible good luck he escaped arrest with a group of sixteen of his comrades, who were shot out of hand, without trial. He was for a time a hunted fugitive; the police caught him in the end. His luck held again. He had no papers on him to identify him, and they put him in the notorious Citadel in Warsaw, where they tortured him, to make him say who he was. The torture did not make him speak. In 1907 he escaped. He got away to Paris; then he came to London.

He didn't like the life in Paris or in London. It was too tame for him. He left London. He went back to Paris, intending to return to Russia. In Paris he met a group of young Russians, who also wanted to return to Russia. They wanted to take back funds for their revolutionary activity, so they planned to rob a Paris bank. One of the group informed the Paris police. They were all arrested, and were told at the Paris Prefecture that they must leave Paris by the first train. If one of them were found in France ten hours later he would be punished with the full severity of the law.

This was in February 1908. It seems strange that the French police treated them so leniently. It appears that Clemenceau, who was then Prime Minister, had been informed of the affair, and he said he didn't want to punish young idealists, who didn't realise that what they were trying to do was criminal. It shows how easy it was to misdirect the revolutionary ardour of these young people into the wrong channels.

Moishe Tokar came back to London. He stayed nearly a year in London. He couldn't stand it any longer. He told us that he was going back to Russia. He didn't care what happened there. We could not dissuade him. In January 1909 he returned to Russia. There were reports in the press in England and elsewhere at the time about terrible tortures inflicted on political prisoners in the Vilna Fortress. The man responsible for this was the military commander of Vilna, whose name was Hershelman.

Tokar, who was living in Lodz, read these reports, and decider that he would assassinate Hershelman. He went to Vilna. On December 6th he fired at Hershelman as he drove in his carriage through the street. Hershelman escaped uninjured. General Fenga, who was in the carriage with him, was wounded.

On January 13th 1910, Tokar was sentenced to death. A couple of days before the execution he poured the paraffin in the lamp in his cell over his clothes, and set fire to himself. When the warders unlocked the cell he was still alive. But his burns were too terrible for them to save him. He died soon after.

The most important member of Judith Goodman's group in London was Baruch Rifkin, who became an outstanding Yiddish writer, and exercised an important influence on Yiddish literature, as a critic and a thinker. His early writings appeared in the *Arbeter Fraint* and in *Germinal*. He had joined the anarchist movement in Russia when he was very young. But I am sure he must have felt from the beginning that there was much more to the anarchist idea than a barbaric warfare against the barbaric system which ruled in Russia. He was a man who thought and searched, and could not be kept in the narrow limits of his party group. His later development as a writer proved it. What bound him to his group in London was much more the memory of common youthful experiences in Russia than any intellectual understanding they could have for his groping, questing and questioning character.

He was, like Judith, a frequent visitor at our home, and at the Frumkins. We discussed all sorts of things, not only party matters and the ideas of the movement. One evening we came to discuss materialism and idealism. I said they were both only different views on life, by means of which we tried to explain life, without really discovering its true secret. Life had its material and its spiritual aspects, but however much we tried we could never find absolute truth.

He was taken aback. He had clearly not expected that from me. "If that is so," he said, "then anarchism is no final goal for the future."

"Of course, not," I answered. "There is never an end to the future. So it can have no final goal. I am an anarchist not because I believe anarchism is the final goal, but because I believe there is no such thing as a final goal. Freedom will lead us to continually wider and expanding understanding and to new social forms of life. To think that we have reached the end of our progress is to enchain ourselves in dogmas, and that always leads to tyranny."

Chapter 21

Francisco Ferrer

October 9th, 1909, Francisco Ferrer, the founder of the Modern School (*Escuela Moderna*) was sentenced to death by a military court in Barcelona, on a charge of organising the July rising in Catalonia. Everybody called it a judicial murder. There was no evidence against Ferrer. It was a deliberate attempt by the Church and the monarchy to get rid of one of its most powerful opponents. There were protest demonstrations in London, Paris, Rome, Berlin, Amsterdam, Brussels, Vienna, Geneva, all over the world. Anatole France, Maurice Maeterlinck, Maxim Gorki, George Brandes, Cunninghame Graham, Kropotkin, Jean Jaures, Keir Hardie and hundreds of others protested against the sentence. University professors, trades unions, political parties petitioned the Spanish government to release Ferrer. The press of Europe and America demanded his release. Even in Spain itself, except in Catalonia, where there was a state of siege and all assemblies were prohibited, there were protest meetings, and most of the Spanish papers joined the demand for Ferrer's release.

I was in Paris on a lecture tour when the news of Ferrer's sentence reached me. There were big street demonstrations the same day. Crowds assembled at the Place de la Bastille, the Jardin Luxembourg, and the Place de la Concorde. I was asked to address one of the protest meetings held at the Hall L'Egalitaire. I was only one of several speakers. It was a packed meeting. There were no incidents. Yet the next morning two police officers came to my hotel and told me that I must leave France within 24 hours.

On October 12th I was back in London. The following day the press reported that Ferrer had been executed. It started an outburst of protests everywhere. The press of all countries were full of it, There were numberless articles published about Ferrer and about his educational work. His portrait sold in millions of copies.

59 City Councils in France named streets and squares after him. The City of Brussels erected a Ferrer statue. A week after Ferrer's execution the Spanish government which had sent him to his death fell. The new government had to listen to the voice of the civilised world. There was a world-wide demand that those who had been arrested in connection with the July rising in Catalonia should be released. In January 1910 the new government opened the gates of the prisons, and thousands were set free, many of them people who had been active participants in the July rising. Ferrer had by his death brought them liberty.

I had met Ferrer for the first time only six months before, in London, during the May Day demonstration in Hyde Park. I had read his works. I had published some of his essays in *Germinal*, essays about his theories and methods of teaching. We had tea together after the demonstration, in a cafe

112

near Marble Arch, Ferrer, his wife, Malatesta, Tarrida, Tcherkesov, Shapiro and I.

A few days later I met Ferrer again at Tarrida's house, with Malatesta, Tcherkesov and Lorenzo Portet, whom Ferrer had named in his will to continue his educational work. Ferrer had made a tremendous impression on me. Every word he spoke breathed sincerity. He had no pose. There was a warmth about him. His face lighted up when he spoke of his plan to establish a Free University in Barcelona. He said that he knew he would encounter a great many difficulties, but he was sure he would succeed. About his existing schools, he told me that there were about 8,000 children attending them. The problem was not to get children to attend, but to keep them from losing the school influence in their homes. They were trying to do something about it by arranging regular meetings between parents and teachers. The great thing, Ferrer said to me, "is to educate them to be complete human beings. A man who is a complete Catholic is better than a man who is only half a free man."

I treasured the memory of this meeting with Ferrer. How could I have known then that a few months later his life would be ended at the hands of a firing squad in the old Barcelona Fortress of Montjuich.

It was pure chance that Ferrer happened to be in Barcelona during those fateful days in July. He had left Spain with his wife in March, to see his publishers in Paris and London. He also wanted to discuss his project for a free university in Barcelona with a number of well-known educationists in England, France and Belgium. His plans were to return to Barcelona in September.

But in the second week of June he received letters that his brother's wife and her small daughter, Ferrer's niece, were seriously ill. He rushed back to Spain, without even saying goodbye to his friends in London. He left a note to explain his sudden departure. His niece died a few days after he returned. Ferrer was on the point of leaving Spain again, to continue his discussions in London and Paris, when the July rising began, quite unexpectedly. No-one had foreseen it. It was a completely unorganised and spontaneous movement, which grew out of the opposition of the Spanish people to the Moroccan war. There were anti-war demonstrations in Valencia, Saragossa, Bilbao and other towns. There were serious disturbances in Madrid. Regiments mutinied and refused to leave their barracks. In Catalonia, so the Civil Governor of Barcelona reported, half the reservists called up deserted. It was asking for trouble, therefore, for the government to order the troops to embark at Barcelona for Morocco. On July 16th, a Sunday, while the troops marched through the streets of Barcelona to the docks, thousands of people, including many women and children, tried to hold them back, shouting "Down with the war! Throw down your arms!" The officers ordered the soldiers to fire at the crowd. Not a shot was fired.

Till then the movement had been spontaneous. But at this moment the Solidaridad Obrera, the Catalonian organisation of trades unions, intervened. It called a delegates conference for July 23rd to consider the situation. The civil administration prohibited the conference. Nevertheless,

113

the conference met, with delegates from the trades unions, the anarchists and the socialists. It decided to call a general strike. A strike committee of three was elected, Miguel Moreno, the Secretary-General of the Solidaridad Obrera, Francisco Miranda, for the anarchists, and Fabra Ribas for the socialists. On July 26th the general strike took place. The stoppage was complete throughout Catalonia. Every factory was closed. The railways, the telegraphs, all transport and communication stopped. The following day the military Governor of Barcelona proclaimed martial law throughout Catalonia. This started the so-called "Red Week", in which the general strike developed into open insurrection. There were barricades in the streets. Government buildings and churches were burned down. Things looked critical for the government. Many of the troops sided with the insurrectionists. If the strike had spread to other parts of Spain the clericalist-monarchist regime would have been overthrown. But the strike did not spread. The government sent strong forces of loyal troops to Catalonia, and the insurrection was suppressed with great bloodshed. But not before many of the barricades had to be subdued by heavy artillery. On August 1st it was all over; and the white terror began.

It was under such conditions that Ferrer was arrested and tried before a military court. Had he appeared before a civil court there is little doubt that he would have been acquitted, for there was not the slightest evidence that he had taken any part in the rising.

It is significant that the clericalist paper *El Universo* wrote in connection with Ferrer's arrest: "Civil courts have a tendency to demand absolute proofs of the accused's guilt. Military courts of honour need no concrete proof. It is enough for the Judges to form a moral conviction that accords with their conscience."

Miguel Moreno, the Secretary-General of the Solidaridad Obrero, and one of the three members of the strike committee which had called the general strike in Catalonia from which the rising had developed, fled to Paris. There he met a young Russian Jewish comrade, Morris Schutz; he sent Schutz to Barcelona with a letter, to open contact with the comrades there. Schutz was arrested at the Spanish frontier, and the letter was found on him. It gave no indication however of the people to whom it was addressed. The Spanish police couldn't make Schutz talk. In the end they decided, as he was born in Russia to deport him there. With Schutz's revolutionary past it meant sending him to his death.

As it happened, most of the crew on the ship on which Schutz was being deported belonged to the Solidaridad Obrera, and they hit on a plan to save him. When the ship stopped at Marseille they spirited him ashore. The French police refused to hand him back to the Spanish authorities.

Schutz afterwards came to London, where I got to know him. He was quite a young man, very wide-awake, and completely devoted to the cause. He emigrated from London to the United States, and then to the Argentine. He was active for a number of years in the American and South American movement. In the end he was caught up by other affairs, and we lost touch with him.

As I am dealing here with events connected with Spain I may be forgiven for mentioning that my name was quite well-known over the course of the years both in Spain and in the Spanish-speaking countries of America. Most of my books and some of my shorter writings appeared in Spanish translation. In fact, my book *Nationalism and Culture* first appeared in Spanish; so did my autobiography.

I knew many of the Spanish comrades who were living in London, notably Tarrida del Marmol, Lorenzo Portet, Vicente Garcia and José Prat.

Prat was in London only a few months. He returned to Spain, where he remained till he died, shortly before the Spanish civil war. But while he was in London I saw him almost every day. And I continued all the time to be in touch with him. He was an engineer, like Tarrida. He first directed my attention to the Spanish libertarian movement, and supplied me with Spanish periodicals and books. He first introduced me to Pi y Margall, who was President of the first Spanish Republic, which lasted from 1873 to 1874. The new monarchist regime undertook the repression of the revolutionary and republican movements. Revolutionary strikes and risings followed all over the country, including the peasant revolt of 1892. In 1896 there was the terrible Montjuich affair. Prat and his friend Ricardo Mella, the outstanding intellect of the Spanish anarchist movement, wrote a book about it, *La Barbarie Gubernmental en Espana*.

A religious procession was going through the streets of Barcelona when someone threw a bomb. It killed several people. No-one knew who had committed this senseless crime. The entire anarchist movement and press condemned it as stupid and inexcusable. Nevertheless, the Spanish government seized on it as a pretext to start a campaign of repression against the anarchists. 380 people were arrested; most of them were anarchists; some were republicans. Many were put in chains and kept in the hold of an old warship in Barcelona harbour. But the greater number were imprisoned in the old Barcelona fortress Montjuich. For months nothing was heard of the prisoners. Gradually rumours began to go round that they were being terribly tortured. Letters were somehow smuggled out by some of the prisoners, which told what was going on. The letters were sent to Paris and London, where they started an outcry. They recalled the tortures of the Spanish Inquisition.

George Clemenceau, Keir Hardie, Robert Blatchford, Walter Crane, August Bebel, Wilhelm Liebknecht and hundreds of others protested. Meetings were held in London, Paris, Rome, Brussels, Amsterdam, New York, all over the world. Even in Spain the Liberal papers like *El Pais, La Justicia, El Pueblo*, and others spoke of the shade of Torquemada looming again over Spain.

So when Ferrer was arrested, public opinion all over the world remembered what had happened not many years before at the same Montjuich, where Ferrer was imprisoned, and where in defiance of justice and of world opinion he was shot without trial, on conviction by a military "court of honour".

Chapter 22

Houndsditch

On 17th December 1910, the London papers reported a terrible crime in Houndsditch, a street mostly of business houses in the City, running from Aldgate to Bishopsgate, hard on the borders of Whitechapel. Three policemen were shot at and killed by desperados, who turned out to be aliens.

About three weeks before someone had rented a house next to a jeweller's shop in Houndsditch, with the intention of entering it at night, to rob it. On the night of the 16th a Jewish shopkeeper, who had stayed late in his shop, heard sounds suspiciously like digging; he informed the police. Five uniformed police and a plain clothes man arrived, and knocked at the street door. The door opened; as the police entered someone fired a revolver from the stairs. Three of the policemen were shot dead, and two were wounded. The plain clothes man, who escaped injury, ran off to get help. While he was gone the men disappeared.

It all happened in a matter of minutes. By some incredible chance one member of the gang had been hit by the fire of his own friends and was badly wounded. But for that the gang might have got away undiscovered. As it was, they had to carry their wounded comrade with them; and this put the police on their track.

They took him, mortally wounded, to the home of a girl they knew, in Grove Street, and made off, after having warned her under no circumstances to call a doctor. The poor girl didn't know what had happened. She disregarded the warning, and called a doctor, who found the man was dying. He immediately informed the police. By the time they arrived the man was dead. The body was removed to London Hospital, and the girl was arrested. The evening papers reported all this, and also that Nihilist literature had been found in the girl's room. That made it clear, they said, that the Houndsditch murderers were East End foreign revolutionaries.

The morning papers carried a police description of four men. They had got their information from the arrested girl. It was very vague. It seemed that she did not know much about them. She didn't know their names. There was no information about the dead man, not even his name. But they printed his picture in every newspaper, hoping that someone might recognise it. The second man was described as Peter the Painter; he was said to be the ringleader. The third was called Fritz; his surname was not known. The fourth man hadn't even that much to identify him.

We soon discovered that the arrested girl, whom we knew only by her first name, Rosa, had been regularly attending the weekly meetings and social evenings at our club. The Nihilist literature in her room consisted of a few copies of the *Arbeter Fraint* and *Germinal*, some pamphlets and some Russian periodicals.

People who knew more about her than we did said she worked in a tailoring workshop, and lived poorly and honestly by her meagre earnings. We never found out how she had got to know the Houndsditch murderers. Quite possibly she had met them in our club, which was visited by hundreds of people who came to our meetings or used our reading room without our knowing anything about them. Rosa couldn't explain. The poor girl's mind gave way under the shock. She was sent to a lunatic asylum, where she committed suicide soon after.

The way the newspapers linked Rosa and the Houndsditch murderers with the foreign revolutionaries made us fear the affair would be used to work up an agitation for withdrawing the right of asylum in Great Britain. It was the only country where political refugees really enjoyed the right of asylum, where they did not live with the constant dread of expulsion hanging over their heads, as in France, Belgium or Switzerland. If the press campaign resulted in public opinion demanding the withdrawal of the right of asylum many refugees would be left without protection. We were aware of that danger, and we were apprehensive for the future.

But we had not expected what happened the next day. Malatesta was arrested in connection with the Houndsditch murders. It never entered my mind, of course, that he had really had anything to do with the crime, but it showed how far we could be dragged into it by the suspicion that was being spread about us in the public mind. Then I heard Malatesta had been released, only an hour or two after his arrest. I rushed off immediately to see him. He told me what had happened.

About four months before the Houndsditch murders he had been approached in our club by a man who said he was a Lettish refugee, and came to our club to read the Russian papers. He gave his name as Muronzeff. I don't know if that was his real name. Most refugees had taken new names. It had become a general practice in the conspirative movement. Malatesta said he had found it difficult to understand what the man was saying because he spoke only Lettish, Russian and German, while Malatesta only knew Italian, French, Spanish and English. So they carried on their conversation through an interpreter. Our comrade Siegfried Nacht, who had met Muronzeff before, at the Polish Club, acted as interpreter. A few weeks later Nacht told Malatesta that Muronzeff had spoken to him about an invention on which he was working, which was held up because he had no workshop and no proper tools. Nacht said that a Russian comrade had introduced Muronzeff to him as a man who had been active in the movement in Lettland, and had to flee when the big repressions started in the Baltic provinces. Nacht had found Muronzeff a taciturn, uncommunicative person, who seemed unwilling to lift the veil over his past. Such uncommunicativeness was not uncommon among the political refugees. That too was part of the tradition of the conspirative movement. People were afraid of talking too much.

When Muronzeff had complained to Nacht about his lack of tools, Nacht thought of Malatesta, who earned his living by running a small machine-repairing workshop in Islington. Malatesta was always ready to help anyone, so he said that Muronzeff could of course use his workshop and his tools. The result was that Muronzeff came several times to Malatesta's workshop, and did some work there. One day he brought another man with him, to explain to Malatesta in French that he had decided to return to Russia, where he could be of more use to the movement. He wanted to take back with him an oxygen blow-pipe; it was hard to get in Russia, he said, and it was essential for his work.

Malatesta, who suspected nothing, told him that he could buy one at the place where he bought his machine-parts and tools, and he gave Muronzeff his card to show there. He hadn't seen the man since.

That was a few weeks before the Houndsditch murders. When the police entered the house in Houndsditch they found an oxygen blow-pipe there. Every oxygen blow-pipe has a number on it, so it was soon traced back to the firm where it was bought, and there Malatesta's card was produced.

Malatesta was having breakfast the morning after the murders when two Scotland Yard men arrived, and took him to Scotland Yard. He hadn't seen the papers yet, and had no idea of what had happened in Houndsditch. He asked why he was being taken to Scotland Yard; the detectives wouldn't say.

At Scotland Yard an Inspector told Malatesta that they wanted him to go to Whitechapel to identify someone in hospital. Malatesta asked what it was all about. The Inspector wouldn't tell him. The same two detectives who had brought him to Scotland Yard took him to London Hospital, where he was shown the dead body. He recognised Muronzeff. The detectives asked if he knew the man. He told them the whole story.

Then he was brought back to Scotland Yard, where he repeated his story to the Inspector. There was nothing he could add; he hadn't known where Muronzeff lived, nor anything about him. When his statement had been taken down the Inspector passed a morning paper to Malatesta. That was the first he knew of what had happened at Houndsditch. Malatesta's story bore the stamp of truth. He was immediately released. He said the police at Scotland Yard had behaved admirably. I am sure that in any other country the police would have played up Malatesta's political beliefs in such a way as to implicate him in the affair.

But some of the London newspapers did not behave as well as the London police did. They started an agitation against the anarchists, against the political refugees, and against the aliens generally. They tried to stir up prejudice against the aliens, and to force the government to take action against them. There was talk of sending all aliens back to where they came from.

Papers like the *Daily Mail* were writing: "Even the most sentimental will feel that the time has come to stop the abuse of this country's hospitality by the foreign malefactors." Strangely enough, a leading English socialist, Robert Blatchford, the editor of *Clarion*, joined the cry against the aliens. Even the Social Democratic organ *Justice*, which largely shared his views,

118

rebuked him for it. "It is greatly to be regretted," it said, "that Robert Blatchford should lend himself to the wicked and mischievous cry against the alien." It contended that "the Houndsditch affair appears to be a brutal crime without any political significance whatever", and that "the law here is sufficiently strong for dealing with criminals, native or foreign". If the cry achieved its purpose "it would bring to the Czar's shambles those whom fate had mercifully spared. It would strengthen Russian reaction and be a crime against civilisation." But I shall come back to something less pleasant in *Justice* later.

A number of liberal and non-sensational conservative papers, and also the *Jewish Chronicle*, drew attention to the causes in Russia of this kind of criminal activity. The weekly *Graphic* published an article by Albert Kinross, "The Letts, their Land and their Lawlessness", which said, "these men are the products of the Russian system; no immigration laws will keep them out; so long as the Russian system of government is what it is, men desperate as these will be produced. Lucien Wolf, also in the *Graphic*, wrote: "This type of desperado will only cease when the conditions in Russia have been swept away." The *Jewish Chronicle* wrote in an editorial: "Who can say that with rational, merely decently-civilised government in Russia these men and men like them, instead of becoming mad desperados, would not have been rational, decent, civilised members of society?"

But the agitation against the aliens went on. Our club was presented as a meeting place of criminals, where only conspirators and initiates found admission, by secret signs and passwords. It was a den of thieves and murderers. Peter the Painter had delivered lectures there to teach the use of explosives.

We were helpless against these calumnies. Shapiro and Linder, the secretaries of the club, sent a short letter in January 1911 to the editor of the *Daily Chronicle*, stating categorically that Peter the Painter, Muronzeff and Fritz had never been members of the Club. The letter was not printed. *Freedom* did print it, with an editorial headed "Gentlemen of the Press". But of course *Freedom* did not reach the wide public.

Sir Philip Gibbs, the novelist and journalist, visited our club, and had an article about us in the weekly *Graphic*. He wrote ironically: "I spent some hours with the anarchists of Whitechapel. I felt rather heroic and also rather nervous when I set forth upon the perilous journey." He found us in a large bare room furnished with a few wooden benches, a deal table and a number of wall-posters in Yiddish. Here was the anarchists' club. "I was a little reassured and a good deal astonished," he went on, "when a number of women entered the room. They were all young women, most of them neatly dressed. One woman who sat behind the table where the pamphlets lay, and who seemed in some authority, had the face of a tragedy queen." He meant Milly, who always sat at the table where we sold our literature.

He continued: "So I sat, a solitary Englishman, among all these foreign anarchists, for more than an hour, during which nothing happened except friendly greetings, handclasps, voluble conversation in subdued voices and a foreign tongue, and a quiet scrutiny of myself. Then there was silence, and from the back of the room two men came forward. One was a tired-looking man with dreamy eyes which looked out with a kind of soft benevolence. This anarchist had a winning smile."

Then he described me: "A tall, stout man with immense shoulders, and a big powerful head and a strong face, which might have been brutal but for the thoughtful look behind his spectacles." Gibbs gave a fairly correct idea of what I said. He explained that he knew German, and so had been able to follow me and understand.

He concluded: "Nothing happened to me. I could laugh now at my fears. These alien anarchists were as tame as rabbits. I am convinced that they had not a revolver among them. Yet remembering the words I heard, I am sure that this intellectual anarchy, this philosophy of revolution, is more dangerous than pistols and nitro-glycerine. For out of that anarchist club in the East End come ideas."

I printed an article in the *Arbeter Fraint* of 24th December 1910, explaining our position about the Houndsditch murders. *Freedom* also had an article, headed "The Houndsditch Tragedy. Who is Responsible?" But of course our reading public was limited.

Some papers interviewed people like Malatesta; but the interviews appeared in a distorted form, and did not properly convey what had been said. The papers were out for sensation, not to make clear our beliefs. We finally agreed not to give any more interviews to the press.

Then a reporter from the *Morning Post* came to see me, with a note from an English trade union leader who was a friend of mine. He wrote that he knew the man, and he could be trusted to report what I said without distortion. *The Morning Post* was a conservative paper, but it was not sensational. I told the reporter that our experiences with the London press so far had been very unfortunate, and we had decided not to give any more interviews. He assured me that he would not misreport what I said. I asked if it would all appear in the way I said it. He answered frankly that he could not guarantee that. It depended on how much the editorial staff could find room for. What he could guarantee was that the report he sent in would be a true report, and what appeared in the paper would not misrepresent me.

He sounded honest. So I gave him the interview. He asked questions, and I answered. I told him exactly how we felt about the Houndsditch criminals. He asked me what explanation I had for what these people had done. I said it was not easy in England to understand what had driven such men to becoming desperados. It was necessary to consider the situation in Russia, where the government had instituted a reign of terror. Thousands of people were arrested and shot without trial. Every sort of barbarism was used to suppress every expression of liberalism or freedom. In Lettland three thousand people had been shot without trial, on the orders of so-called field-courts. The entire populations of many villages had been publicly flogged, including old men, women and children. Their homes were burned down, and the people were living in the forests like wild beasts. It was important that the Houndsditch murderers all appeared to be Letts.

I gave him a copy of Kropotkin's *The Terror in Russia*, which the Parliamentary Russian Committee had published in London in 1909. I said that people living under such terror would think little of their own lives or of others. The guilt lay not so much with them as with the Czar and his regime. How would people in Britain feel if their government imprisoned and shot its political opponents? I said the British and French financiers who provided the Czarist regime with the loans without which it could not exist were largely responsible.

He seemed impressed by what I told him. He assured me that his report would be a true report of what I said. The next day the *Morning Post* carried nearly three columns of my interview, giving almost everything I had said, and in the way I had said it, including even my remark about the British and French financiers. Several other papers were as decent as the *Morning Post*, notably the *Manchester Guardian*, the *Morning Leader*, and the *Weekly Times and Echo*. The *Manchester Guardian* fought courageously against the attempt to make a political issue of the criminal murders in Houndsditch. The *Morning Leader* emphasised that the anarchist movement had no programme of robbery and murder, and that even if the Houndsditch criminals were proved to have been anarchists, which they had not, it would still not implicate the anarchist movement, any more than criminals belonging to other political movements implicated them, or Catholic or Protestant criminals implicated the churches. The *Labour Leader*, the organ of the Independent Labour Party, stood firm for the continued traditional British policy of asylum for political refugees.

Meanwhile the police were continuing their search for the murderers. Muronzeff's picture in the press had been seen by a man in whose house he had lodged, and he had come forward. He was a law-abiding, religious Jew, a member of a synagogue. He belonged to no political movement. He had had a room to let, and had no idea what sort of a lodger he had got. The police found in the room Muronzeff had occupied, firearms, chemical stuffs and burglar's tools, but no literature, nothing at all. Muronzeff's mistress, Nina Vasileva, two Lettish social democrats named Peters and Duboff, and a Jewish barber named Rosen were arrested, and were held for questioning.

Then on January 3rd came the siege of Sidney Street. The police had received information that the men who had been with Muronzeff in Houndsditch were hiding in a house in Sidney Street. Warned by what had happened in Houndsditch, the police took precautions. About three hundred police surrounded the house at night. All the approaches to it were closed with a cordon. All strategic positions round it were occupied. The other people living in the house and in the adjoining houses were wakened and evacuated. The police force waited till daybreak.

As soon as it was light two detectives approached and flung stones at the window of the room where the criminals were known to be sleeping. Immediately the window opened, and one of the detectives was shot. The murderers did not show themselves. A big body of police fired at the house from behind shelter. Then the troops were called in. A detachment of Scots Guards arrived from the Tower, near by, and opened fire. Winston Churchill, who was then Home Secretary, came with the Chief of the Criminal Investigation Department, the Assistant Commissioner of the Metropolitan Police, and other high officers. More soldiers were called out. A Maxim gun was brought up. Finally the Horse Artillery was summoned to destroy the house with shell fire. We lived near the scene of the battle, and we heard every shot.

In the end the house was set on fire. The flames spread, and the house became a furnace. The criminals inside the house had been firing all the time. Suddenly there was silence. When the police entered the ruins they found two bodies. According to the police one was Fritz. The name of the other was never officially established. But from information that reached us afterwards it may be assumed that he was a recent immigrant from Russia, whose first name was Yoshka. He used to go about with Muronzeff and his crowd.

The press was full of it. It made much of the fact that Muronzeff, Fritz and the missing Peter the Painter, who became a kind of legendary bogeyman, were all Letts. It must have seemed to the average reader that the Letts were all a people of robbers and murderers.

Some papers asserted that Muronzeff was suspected of being a Russian secret police agent, working for the Ochrana, to discredit the Russian revolutionaries abroad; if the British right of asylum had really been withdrawn it would certainly have been a great victory for the Russian Czarist regime. But it seems impossible. A police agent working among the revolutionaries would have incited them to crimes, but he would not have stayed to the end, to fall a victim to his own plot. If the story of a Russian police agent had any basis it pointed rather to Peter the Painter, who had got away. Some papers said there was no such person as Peter the Painter, that he was an invention, a myth. That is not true. Peter the Painter was a real person. How he escaped that night of the Houndsditch murders is a mystery. But it is certain that eight years later, in the early days of the Russian Revolution, he appeared in Russia, and was appointed by the Bolshevik government as an official of the terrible Cheka, becoming one of its most notorious agents. Our comrade Alexander Shapiro, who had seen Peter in London, met him in Russia, working as an agent of the Cheka.

The four people under arrest, Peters, Duboff, Rosen and the woman Nina Vasileva, came up for trial in May. Peters and Duboh were members of the Lettish Social Democratic Party in London, which arranged for their defence. Rosen had a lawyer to act for him. Nina Vasileva belonged to no organisation, and nobody bothered about her. A few of our comrades had met her when she had sometimes come to the club, to our public meetings. The press said there was no charge against her, and that she had been arrested only because of her association with Muronzeff.

It came out that Muronzeff had been associating with other women as well, had in fact been deceiving Nina Vasileva as he had deceived Malatesta. Her case was important to us, because of the effect it might have on the British attitude to the political refugees. We therefore decided to see if we

122

could do something to help in her defence. Milly volunteered to visit her in prison, to find out what we could do.

When Milly arrived the poor girl stared at her in amazement and burst into tears: "You come to see me! Then I am not forsaken by everyone!"

Milly explained why she had come. She discovered that a young lawyer had already offered to defend Nina, without a fee. So that problem was settled.

The trial showed that the police had failed to establish any political motive or connection with the Houndsditch affair. Duboff, Peters and Rosen were acquitted and released. All that could be said about them was that they had known Muronzeff and Fritz.

Nina Vasileva was sentenced to two years imprisonment. It seemed odd. For if she had known what Muronzeff was doing the sentence should have been more severe. If she hadn't, two years was a lot for having an affair with Muronzeff.

Indeed, only about three months after she was sentenced, Nina Vasileva was released. She wasn't told why. She was just told to go, that she was free.

She went to the people where she had lodged. They showed her the door. She tried her Russian friends. They all cold-shouldered her. I imagine they were not so much unfriendly as afraid of getting mixed up with somebody who had been connected with a very dangerous business, and who might direct police attention to them. She was desperate. She had no money. She had nowhere to live. She turned to us to help her.

We hadn't really known her before. It was the first time she came to our door. I doubt if Milly hadn't gone to see her in prison whether she would have thought of coming to us. We told her she could stay with us till she found work, and could get a room elsewhere. She stayed with us nearly a month. We sometimes talked about Muronzeff. She always said that she had never had any suspicion of what he was doing.

The London press left her alone. Even the sensational papers which had featured her case, behaved decently in that regard. The issue of the political refugees and the right of asylum was dropped. I must say that in any other country the consequences would have been more serious.

* * *

There was a very unpleasant sequel. And neither the police nor the sensational press were at fault; *Justice*, the organ of the Social Democratic Party, published a note in its issue of 13th May about the Houndsditch and Sidney Street affairs, which went on to suggest that anarchists incited people to such crimes, and that one explanation was that there were *agents provocateurs* among the anarchists, who tried in this way to discredit the socialist movement, and to get the right of asylum withdrawn in England. It then made this infamous statement: "It is not generally known that Emma Goldman is in the pay of the police, though the fact has leaked out recently. At one time she was employed by Mr. A.E. Olarovsky, of the Russian Secret Police in San Francisco, as an agent and spy."

123

There was no attempt made to produce any evidence of this monstrous charge. I still can't understand what prompted even so bitter an antagonist of the anarchists as Harry Quelch, the editor of *Justice*, to publish this calumny. He knew that Emma Goldman would never go to a court of law to defend her name against his slanderous attack.

Our comrades of *Freedom* protested in a letter signed by John Turner, A. Marsh and T.H. Keel, published in *Justice* the following week. "This monstrous and outrageous statement," they wrote, "is the climax to the unscrupulous misrepresentations of anarchists which have appeared in the social democratic press for years. The writer of the article gives not a tittle of evidence in proof of this infamous charge. While asking for no apology or retraction, as we have long since grown accustomed to these calumnies — venomous as stupid — we do wish to indignantly protest against a vile and cowardly statement in reference to a brave woman, who has fought during the best years of her life, and suffered imprisonment again and again, for principles which we and others hold dear."

Quelch replied: "We naturally expected some such protest. We have however nothing to retract. The statements were made on the most reliable authority, or they would not have been made. We do not say that there are no good men and women among anarchists; but we do say that every anarchist who has been betrayed has been betrayed by a fellow-anarchist, who has proved to be a police agent; that police agents have been the instigators of almost every anarchist crime and plot, successful or unsuccessful, which has been discovered; that the principles of anarchism lend themselves to azeffism; and that, with few exceptions, anarchists are either agents or dupes of the police."

John Turner brought up the matter at a meeting of the First of May Celebration Committee, most of whose members belonged to the Social Democratic Party and the Independent Labour Party. As a result, this committee wrote to *Justice*, which published the following note: "C. Cook forwards the following resolution of the First of May Celebration Committee: 'This meeting expresses its opinion that the statement appearing in *Justice* without proof or evidence is unjustifiable, and asks that the evidence should be published.'"

At the same time Quelch published this note: "Anarchist Agents. Dear Comrade, The information concerning Emma Goldman was conveyed by a definite statement to that effect made in my hearing by Mr A.E. Olarovsky himself. I am fraternally, Your Informant."

We couldn't credit it — that the editor of *Justice* accepted the word of a known representative of the Russian Secret Police.

Even branches of the Social Democratic Party protested. *Justice* published a letter from D. Carmichael on behalf of the Battersea Branch: "I am instructed to forward you a resolution carried unanimously at the Battersea Branch meeting — The members of the Battersea Branch SDP are of opinion that the editor of *Justice* has failed to produce any justification for the charge against Emma Goldman, and they desire that the name of the informant be published or a complete withdrawal of the statement, as the members of this branch desire the policy of the paper to be the same as its name implies — not Injustice."

Quelch refused to publish evidence, or to withdraw his charge. He repeated it: "We have nothing to add and nothing to withdraw. The statements would not have been made had we not been convinced of their truth."

Quelch never withdrew his absolutely groundless charge. It is impossible even now to understand what moved him to make it in the first place, and to stand by it so stubbornly in the face of the demand that was made that he should either substantiate it, or withdraw. He did neither.

It did Emma Goldman no harm. Nobody believed the story. It was an early example of the technique that was later developed into a fine art, of the lie as a propaganda weapon, used in this case against us, whom he described as "our enemies". "We shall not be deterred," he wrote in *Justice*, "even by the censure of friends and comrades moved by misguided sympathy with our enemies." He refused to publish the name of his informant. All he said was: "Social democrats surely do not need to be reminded of how necessary it frequently is for one whose bona fides are above suspicion, to remain unknown."

It is a most unpleasant chapter in the history of British social democracy.

Chapter 23

Workers' Circle.
The Great Strike

Our movement among the Jewish immigrants in the East End of London was different in a number of ways from that of the other foreign revolutionary groups in England. It was much larger. It was the only foreign movement of the kind that could fill a big public hall with five to ten thousand people. And above all, these Jewish immigrants did not contemplate as the others did returning one day to the countries from which they came. They therefore tried to adjust themselves to the conditions on the spot; and one of our activities had to be to help them to establish trades unions and other organisations to protect their interests.

Our difficulty was the continuing flow of Jewish immigrants from Britain across the Atlantic, to the United States and Canada, which offered better opportunities. The journey cost little. There was much competition between the shipping companies, at that time, and they cut the fares down to as little as five dollars, which was one pound sterling. This impermanence, the constantly shifting population, prevented the establishment of stable organisations. Yet eventually, by about 1909, we had a large body of Jewish workers in London and elsewhere who had more or less decided to make their home in Britain, and were striking roots.

Also new comrades had come into the country, and replaced those who had gone to America. David Isakowitz's place as manager of the *Arbeter Fraint* was taken by Solo Linder, who went to America much later; he is now editor and manager of the *Freie Arbeter Shtimme*. We also gained a valuable young worker, Sam Dreen, who has remained active in London all these years and is still, at over 70, working with the *Freie Arbeter Shtimme* group in London, in the Poale Zion, and in the Workers' Circle (*Arbeter Ring*). The Workers' Circle recognised Sam Dreen's lifelong services by a dinner given in his honour and a presentation to mark his 70th birthday.

The Workers' Circle was one of the organisations we helped to form. It came into existence first in the United States as a mutual aid organisation, to help its members, Jewish workers, in sickness and need. It was different from the many other mutual aid organisations in being a workers' organisation, devoted to progressive and socialist effort. It described itself as "an order of workers for workers, and for progressive thought". Its members belonged to all branches of socialist thought, and each group or branch or division could conduct its cultural activities within its own framework, and according to its own ideas. It used its financial surpluses to support progressive schools and progressive cultural work.

The first attempts to establish the Workers' Circle were made in 1892. It was not till 1900 that it began to develop as the powerful organisation it has become. It has over 70,000 members now in the United States and Canada. In England we started the Workers' Circle in the years between 1903 and 1905. It established itself firmly by 1909, and by the end of that year it had a membership of 50. By the end of 1910 there were 220 members. The first annual conference of the Workers' Circle was held in London in May 1912. It then had 814 members. In 1921 the membership was 1,103. Today the Workers' Circle has twelve branches in Great Britain, with a membership of 1,200; it is an important organisation in Anglo-Jewry.

The *Arbeter Fraint* played an active part in the establishment and growth of the Workers' Circle in the early years, and our comrades have throughout its existence been prominent in its work. I have already mentioned Sam Dreen. Arthur Hillman was one of our group, and our friend Wiener was General Secretary for many years.

* * *

The nightmare period of the Houndsditch and Sidney Street affairs in 1911 and the anti-alien agitation of the time had passed. By 1912 we felt that the Jewish labour movement in England, and especially in the East End of London, was strong enough to challenge the detested sweating system. The opportunity was provided by a strike of tailors in the West End of London in April 1912. It was called by the London Society of Tailors, and was soon actively supported by the members of the Amalgamated Society of Tailors, though the leaders of the Amalgamated were against the strike. It did not take them long however to realise that their members would do nothing against the strike.

There were about 1,500 tailors on strike, all highly-skilled craftsmen, doing the very best class of West End work. Those tailors of the West End were an international crowd, Englishmen, Germans, French, Italians, Czechs, and a few Jews. It was a completely different kind of work from the mass-produced sub-divisional sweatshop tailoring of the East End Jewish workers. It soon became clear that strike-breaking work was being done in small East End tailoring workshops. There were so many of these that it was impossible to know of them all and to control them. The Jewish trades unions had never been able to accumulate enough funds to call a general strike. Their members didn't earn enough to pay contributions large enough for strike pay. There was also a big mass of unorganised workers, some of whom were strike-breaking. We felt we must do something to remove the stigma of strike-breaking from the Jewish workers. If the West End strike collapsed, the Jewish workers would be blamed for it. The entire British trade union movement would become hostile to the Jews. As it was, the English workers distrusted the Jewish immigrants, because of the sweatshop system, which they rightly saw as a danger to working class conditions. They couldn't go into the reasons which had created the sweatshops. And it wouldn't have altered the facts if they did.

It was therefore a point of honour with us to rouse the Jewish workers to abolish the sweatshops. It was even more important morally than economically. We knew it would be a hard struggle, but there was no other way. If we failed we would at least have shown that the Jewish workers were not a willing party to the sweatshop system.

Our comrades in the Jewish trades unions brought up the question of the general strike in all of them. On 10th May I published a call in the *Arbeter Fraint* explaining to the workers what was at stake.

Our efforts got things moving. Over eight thousand Jewish workers packed the Assembly Hall for a meeting called by the united Jewish tailoring trades unions, which adopted the decision to strike. More than three thousand others stood outside, because the hall couldn't hold more, waiting to hear what was decided. There was feverish excitement, and a real determination to act.

Kaplan opened the meeting. He was followed by MacDonald, the Secretary of the London Society of Tailors and Chairman of the London Trades Council. Then I spoke. I repeated more or less what I had already said in my call to the Jewish workers in the *Arbeter Fraint*. There was so much tension in the hall that no other speakers could get a hearing. The workers wanted a decision. When the vote was taken not one hand was lifted against the strike.

The strike was on. Eight thousand workers were out the first day. Another five thousand came out the day after. The whole clothing industry in the East End was at a standstill. A small minority remained at work, but they were so few that it made little difference.

There was a strike committee of fifty members, representing all the tailoring trades unions in the East End. There were three sub-committees — finance, to raise funds for carrying on the strike; negotiations, to discuss agreements with employers prepared to accept the workers' conditions, and one which set up the local strike committees, which were controlled by a committee of seven, to which Kaplan and I belonged.

We decided to issue the *Arbeter Fraint* for the duration of the strike as a four-page daily, to keep the workers informed of the progress of the strike.

Most of the strikers were not organised trade union members. Our problem was how they could get strike pay. Even the best organised trade unions in the strike, like the Mantle Makers, had no funds to meet anything like the call that was made on them. The other trades unions outside the tailoring industry had no funds with which to help. But the spirit of the workers was wonderful.

Except for the employers, who were interested parties, the whole East End was on the side of the strikers. The better-paid workers who had some savings refused to take strike pay. They even contributed to the strike fund. It didn't swell our treasury very much. I was the Chairman of the Finance Committee, so I knew. We needed a lot of money to help the families of those strikers who were absolutely destitute. We opened canteens on the premises of all the trade unions in the East End. We were not able to provide much more than tea and bread and cheese. But sometimes we also gave hot meals. The Jewish Bakers' Union supplied bread, and the cigarette makers provided cigarettes. All the Jewish trades unions put a levy on their members for our strike fund. Many who were not workers themselves and had no contact with the labour movement sent us money. The Yiddish theatre gave several performances to benefit the strikers. As a result we were able to pay the strikers a few shillings during the first weeks.

The strike had started in sympathy with the West End tailoring workers. Now we had to draw up our own strike demands. What we wanted was to sweep away the whole sweating system. So our first demand was a normal working day. We asked for the abolition of overtime, higher wages, and above all, no more small workshops where decent hygienic conditions were impossible, and closed union workshops in the rest. Without trade union labour there could be no guarantee that the better working conditions we obtained would last.

The employers' organisation was as little prepared for the strike as the workers were. The Masters' Association had about 300 members, which was only a fraction of the many hundreds who had small tailoring workshops in the East End. But the Masters' Association had the backing of the big city firms for whom its members worked. The city firms had decided not to give any of their work to master tailors who accepted the workers' conditions.

It was no secret that we had no funds. The Masters' Association was therefore sure that we could not hold out more than a couple of weeks, and that sheer hunger would drive the workers back, ready to agree to anything. They had in answer to the strike retaliated with a three weeks' lock-out. They had no doubt at all that before the end of the three weeks the workers would come begging to let them return.

The spokesman of the Master Tailors' Association, a man named Samson, tried to create feeling against the strikers by alleging in statements to the English press that they had no real grievances, and were being used as tools in a plot by foreign anarchists to disrupt the industry. He produced false wage-sheets according to which the workers were earning anything between six pounds and ten pounds a week. Reading the reports he put out one got the impression that the infamous sweatshops of the East End were a paradise.

But the workers who slaved in those sweatshops knew what they were really like, and they were determined to stay out on strike whatever happened, in order to win better conditions. All our agitation would have been useless if the workers had not themselves stood firm. People often say the masses don't know their own mind; this time they did. Attempts were made to play on the natural fears of the womenfolk, for whom the strike meant literally no bread in the house. But the women too of the Jewish East End stood firm. There were big mass meetings of women at which they proclaimed their determination to stand by their menfolk in the strike till the end.

It so happened that the big London Dock Strike was on at the same time. The common struggle brought Jewish and non-Jewish workers together. Joint strike meetings were held, and the same speakers spoke at huge joint demonstrations on Tower Hill and on Mile End Waste.

I was busy attending all the meetings of the strike committee, acting as Chairman of the Finance Committee, and editing the daily *Arbeter Fraint*. I worked on the paper from six in the morning till eleven. I addressed three or four strike meetings every day. I never got finished before two in the morning. It left me only three or four hours for sleep. Luckily I had a robust constitution. I wasn't the only one who worked all those hours. We were all at our posts day and night.

Three weeks after the strike started the workers and employers in the West End reached a settlement. The result was that the East End workers employed in men's tailoring, including uniforms, also went back to work, their employers having agreed to their most important demands — shorter hours, no piecework, better sanitary conditions, and the employment of union labour only.

The strike in the women's garment industry continued. This was the branch of the industry in which the East End Jews, masters and workers, were overwhelmingly engaged. Both sides were suffering badly. The master tailors had lost their season's trade and were getting worried. The workers had no funds left, and were going hungry. The Masters' Association decided to meet the men's representatives, and said they would agree to shorter hours and higher wages, but not to closed union shops.

The strike committee called a meeting of the strikers in the Pavilion Theatre. It started at midnight, after the performance was over. The place was packed. Crowds who couldn't get in stood outside waiting to hear the decision. Kaplan, as Chairman of the strike committee, opened the meeting. The strikers listened to him silently. There was no interruption, no opposition, no applause. A murmur ran round the building when I stood up as the first speaker. I saw those pale, pinched, hungry faces, those thousands of people who had come together at midnight to decide what to do about this strike for which they had sacrificed so much. I felt that I dare not conceal anything from them. I must tell them the whole truth. I explained the position to them. I said that if they held out a few more days I was sure they would win. If they decided to go back now the masters would make them feel that they had lost. "But the decision," I said, "rests with you. I am not going to tell you what to do. You must decide for yourselves." There was an outburst of applause, and from all sides came the cry: "The strike goes on!"

When the Chairman took the vote, not one single hand was raised against the decision to continue the strike.

The Masters' Association met the following morning. Samson insisted that they must hold out. But the great majority had had enough. They withdrew from the Association, leaving only a few members to continue the opposition to the workers' demands. Negotiations started the same afternoon. We were astonished to find that Samson was one of the first who came to ask the trade union to let him reopen his workshop. Our answer was that we could not deal with him until we had settled with all the other master tailors. He had been the leader of the opposition to our demands and would therefore have to wait to the last. Even after he had signed the agreement nobody wanted to go to work for him.

That was the death-blow to the sweatshop system. The English workers looked at the Jewish workers with quite different eyes after this victory. It was important to us materially, but it was much more important morally.

I had played a leading part of course in the organisation and the conduct of the strike, but legends began to grow up around me as though I had been the sole organiser and architect of the victory. People ascribed to me things I had never done and had never even heard of. There were many others who had done as much as I did. But the popular mind and tongue insisted that I had done more, that I had done most of it. It was terribly exaggerated, it was fantastic. It was most embarrassing. I couldn't put my foot out in the street without becoming the object of a demonstration. One day as I was walking along a narrow Whitechapel street with Milly, an old Jew with a long white beard stopped me outside his house, and said: "May God bless you! You helped my children in their need. You are not a Jew, but you are a man!" This old man lived in a world completely different from mine. But the memory of the gratitude that shone in his eyes has remained with me all these years.

The London dock strike was still dragging on. A great many dockers' families were suffering real want. The Jewish workers who had just won their own strike felt they must do something to help their fellow-workers. The *Arbeter Fraint* took it up; we started a campaign. We called a conference of the Jewish trades unions. A committee was set up, and our comrades Ploshansky and Sabelinsky were elected secretary and treasurer. It was decided to ask Jewish families in the East End to take some of the dockers' children into their homes. Offers poured in. Unfortunately we couldn't accept them all. Members of the committee always went first to see the house and too often the family couldn't feed its own children properly. When we found a suitable home, Milly would go to the docks area with one or two other women to fetch the children. They were in a terribly undernourished state, barefoot, in rags. We placed over 300 dockers' children in East End Jewish homes. Shopkeepers gave us shoes and clothing for them. Trade union leaders and social workers in the docks area spoke publicly of the kindness shown by the East End Jews. The docker parents used to come to the Jewish homes in Whitechapel and Stepney to see their children. It did a great deal to strengthen the friendship between Jewish and non-Jewish workers.

Chapter 24

The Peak of the Movement
Canada and the United States

The period between the successful strike of 1912 and the outbreak of the war in 1914 was the peak of our movement. We were kept busy in every direction. The Jewish trades unions grew and increased their memberships and their activities. We had big meetings almost every day. Our organisations expanded. The *Arbeter Fraint* appeared regularly as a twelve page paper till the war came. On the publicity side we issued a large number of Yiddish books and pamphlets, which found a wide circulation in Britain and abroad. We had weekly lectures, concerts and dramatic performances, all very well attended. There was something going on all the time. Dr Jitlovsky came to England, and lectured under our auspices. The great Yiddish poet Abraham Reisen visited London; we gave him a reception and printed several new poems of his in the *Arbeter Fraint*.

1913 was the time of the Beilis ritual murder trial in Kiev; the *Arbeter Fraint* was foremost in the protest movement among the Jewish working class against this terrible accusation. The pages of the *Arbeter Fraint* were full of it week after week. "The accusation is absurd," I wrote in one of my editorials. "No one believes that Jews commit ritual murder. The Beilis affair is another move by the Russian Czarist regime against the Jews; Beilis is a symbol of the long and cruel martyrdom of the Jews under the bloody regime of the Czars."

The first months of 1914 were probably the most active period in the history of the Jewish labour movement in Great Britain. Who could have foreseen the collapse which followed the beginning of the Great War?

My work in London was interrupted for a while in 1912 by an invitation I accepted from the comrades in Montreal to go to Canada on a lecture tour. They assured me it would benefit our movement in Canada, and would also bring money and readers to the *Arbeter Fraint*. I felt I needed a change. But I could not easily decide to leave London, even for a short time. I had come to be such an integral part of the London movement that the comrades did not see anyone who could replace me. We wrote to Frumkin, who was living in Paris with his family, and asked him if he would come to London for three or four months, to edit the *Arbeter Fraint* while I was away. Frumkin had commitments in Paris, but said if we would give him a couple of months to arrange his affairs he would come. I couldn't have wished for a better editor. The administrative work of the *Arbeter Fraint* was in Linder's very capable hands. So that was settled.

My elder son had long wanted to try his luck in America, and he welcomed the opportunity to travel with me. We left early in February 1913 on board the "Corsican" from Liverpool, going to Halifax, because Montreal is inaccessible during the winter months, when the St. Lawrence River is frozen. It wasn't a very pleasant voyage. It was cold and stormy all the way, and there was thick fog for days, so that we couldn't see the ocean from the deck. The Corsican was a small steamer of five or six thousand ton, that groaned and wheezed every time a wave came along and hurled her up and down. We were hardly ever able to set foot on deck during the whole voyage. The tables and chairs in the dining-room were kept screwed down all the time.

When we reached Halifax our boat was an astonishing sight. The whole deck was one glittering sheet of ice; huge icicles hung down everywhere. An icy wind bit into us. My London clothes had not been made for such Siberian cold. Halifax looked bleak and uninviting. It may be different in summer. But in winter it is a dreary place. It was very small at that time, with hardly 30,000 inhabitants. Snow lay high, reaching nearly to the roofs of the houses. The people in the streets were wrapped in heavy furs, like Eskimos. The streets were empty but for a few sledges. Wheeled traffic was impossible in winter. I felt as though we had landed at the North Pole. I was relieved when I got into the train a couple of hours later to continue my journey to Montreal. It proved even worse. The train was what they called the immigrants' train; it had no conveniences, no comforts whatever for that long 36 hour journey. It was over-heated, and the windows being thickly frozen outside we couldn't open them, to get some fresh air. I felt stifled. On top of that the train had been freshly painted, and the smell of paint in that stifling atmosphere made me feel ill. I hadn't been sea-sick on the boat. But I was on the train. I have never forgotten that terrible journey from Halifax to Montreal. I feel sick every time I think of it.

We reached Montreal about 11pm. A group of comrades were waiting for me at the station, including old Schaffler, who had belonged to our Liverpool group when they persuaded me in 1898 to make my first experiment as a Yiddish editor with the *Freie Vort*. I got a very warm welcome from them. No one seemed to notice the miserable state in which I arrived. But it hadn't escaped their attention. Someone produced a heavy overcoat to replace the light coat I had brought from London. They also gave me a thick shawl and a fur cap with ear flaps, and I felt better equipped for the Montreal winter.

I spent the next few days in conference with the comrades, among whom were several old friends from England, like Louis Elstein and his wife, Bernstein, Baron, Weissmann, Schutz. I also met again Conrad Bercovici, who writes Romanian gypsy stories; I had known him in Paris, where he was active in our Jewish and our French movements.

Montreal is beautifully situated, but when I saw it in winter, hidden by ice and snow I could hardly appreciate its beauty. It looked all the same everywhere, terribly monotonous. The comrades took me through the city in a sledge. What struck me immediately were the large number of churches, priests, monks and nuns we saw in every street. The Roman Catholic Church is immensely powerful in Montreal and in the whole of Quebec. There are few places in Europe where the Roman Catholic Church holds such undisputed sway as in the French part of Canada. Things have changed in Montreal since my first visit, but even today it recalls the middle ages. Even the French language they speak stopped still in the 17th century, and my knowledge of modern French wasn't much use to me. Modern French literature is practically unobtainable in Quebec. Most modern French writers are under the ban of the church; their books are on the Index. But they can all be got not many miles away, in Ontario, where they are sold openly.

Shortly before my arrival in Montreal, the French Theatre had arranged to bring over Sarah Bernhardt. The Archbishop of Quebec put her under his ban, as a freethinker. The theatre was helpless. It paid Sarah Bernhardt for breach of contract.

I spent three weeks in Montreal, addressing over a dozen big public meetings. The people who came had all sorts of political beliefs, so that we had some very lively discussions after my talks. The comrades said that I had been a success.

Then I went to Ottawa. It isn't much distance from Montreal, but the contrast between these two cities was enormous, like two different worlds. The streets were broad and clean, and the houses were modern and well-kept. At that time Ottawa had less than 50,000 inhabitants. I stayed with the Polinskys, whom I had known in England. I had two public meetings in Ottawa which they said were the largest ever held among the Jewish population of Ottawa till that time. I have never forgotten the second of those two meetings. It was a Sunday afternoon. Ottawa is a Puritan town, where there is no public transport on Sundays. When I was there the first time few people had cars. So we walked to the hall, about a mile from where I stayed. It was bitterly cold, but there was no wind, and the sun shone. I enjoyed the walk. But during the meeting the weather changed, and we had to make our way back through a blizzard. The wind cut like ice. The snow fell heavily. My thick overcoat was little protection against that terrible weather. We were blinded by the snow. It took us two hours to cover that mile to the Polinskys' house, and we arrived nearly frozen.

My next stop was Toronto, where the weather was much milder. It was early March, and spring was in the air. In Toronto I met a number of other old London friends, Desser, who had belonged to my *Germinal* group, and had been active in the London Jewish trade union movement, L. Steinberg, M. Londbord, M. Simkin, and my hosts the Yudkins.

I had that same experience in every town I visited on the American Continent, not only on that first visit but every time, over a period of many years, in all parts of Canada, from Montreal to Vancouver, and in the United States from New York to San Francisco and Mexico. There was no place where I did not meet old friends from London, Glasgow, Leeds, Manchester, Liverpool. I found them in the most out of the way corners. They had never forgotten the old days in England. It made me realise what an important influence our London movement had been.

When I was the first time in Toronto it had a population of over 300,000, and was an imposing modern city, with a good organised labour movement, and a very effective Trades Council. The Jewish workers, mostly in the tailoring industry, were active trade unionists, and I received an invitation to address a big trades union meeting, called under the auspices of the Trades Council. It was the first time an anarchist had been invited to speak under its auspices.

Our movement held first place in the Jewish socialist movement in Toronto at that time. The Jewish social democrats were split, as everywhere in America then. There was also the Poale Zion, the socialist wing of the Zionist movement. The group wasn't large, but it had a number of very good and intelligent young people, who were active culturally; they had a school for Jewish children, which was supported by the other socialist groups.

The Poale Zionists in Toronto at that time stood much more for libertarian socialist ideas than the social democrats of the Marxist school, and their relations with our comrades were therefore very friendly. The teachers invited me to address the older children at the school. I enjoyed the experience immensely. There are still a number of socialist schools in most of the big towns of Canada and the United States, generally supported by the branches of the Jewish Workers' Circle. When I was in Toronto that time there were two branches of the Jewish Workers' Circle there.

I stayed more than three weeks in Toronto, and addressed a dozen big meetings. We had some very fruitful discussions, especially with the Poale Zionists on the national question. I found that I had to deal with intelligent people, and it was worth while. I am afraid I can't say the same about my social democrat antagonists in Toronto. After my last meeting in Toronto I decided to take a rest, to visit Milly's sister Fanny, who lived over the border, in Towanda, Pennsylvania. Comrade Rosenberg offered to go with me as far as the Niagara Falls. It was wonderful spring weather when we got there. We crossed the suspension bridge, which links Canada with the United States, and found ourselves in New York State. Niagara Falls which is now an important manufacturing city, using the immense hydroelectric power resources of the falls, was then a tiny town, living mostly on the summer tourist traffic, which hadn't started yet when I arrived, in the last week of March. The residents were nearly all owners of hotels and inns and shops, catering for tourists; everything was closed and shuttered when we walked through the empty streets. We found only one small inn open, and we were the only visitors.

We spent the whole afternoon at the falls, or walking along the bank of the Niagara River, without meeting a soul. The Falls made a tremendous impression on me, of course. They are a grand sight, majestic and awe-inspiring, one of the wonders of the world.

When we returned to our inn that night we felt crushed by the impressions of the day. I could not sleep. I sat at the window of my room for hours, staring into the night, listening to the roar of the falls.

We were dressed and ready very early next morning. It was dull and raining, but we walked for hours along the bank of the Niagara. It was my birthday. I was forty years old. I couldn't have spent the day better. I have since seen the Niagara Falls many times, but I have never forgotten my first sight of them.

Rosenberg went back to the inn with me for our midday meal. Then he returned to Toronto, and I took the train to Buffalo, where I arrived about 2pm. My train to Towanda was not due till 8pm, so I had six whole hours in which to look round the town. Buffalo was the first town I had seen in the United States. It didn't make a good impression. The poorer quarters reminded me of the French section of Montreal. The streets were dirty and neglected; the houses looked shabby and grimy, and were monotonously alike. Buffalo has changed since I was first there, but then it was a depressing sight. I was really glad when the train came, and I got away from Buffalo.

It was quite dark by that time, so that I couldn't see the country we passed through. But I remember the whole area was flooded, and the fields and meadows lay under water, not very deep, but sufficiently to cover the railway lines, so that it looked at night as though we were travelling by boat over an expanse of waters. The impression lasted till we approached the mountains.

We reached Towanda about 2am. It was pitch black, and the few lamps of the small station building did little to brighten the Egyptian darkness. I groped my way along the platform, till suddenly two figures carrying a light loomed towards me, and embraced me, Milly's sister Fanny, and her husband Morris. They had been waiting there for me for hours.

Morris had a small car, in which the three of us were soon making our way through the dark streets to their home, where we sat up till daybreak talking. We had not seen each other for a long time, and we had so much to tell each other. It was late when I woke, and met three pair of inquisitive children's eyes watching me from the doorway. When they saw I was awake they whooped and rushed at me joyfully.

I had a wonderful time in Towanda. The weather was good, and I was able to spend a lot of time exploring the beautiful countryside, which was familiar to me from my youthful reading of the Knickerbocker stories. It was a quiet, tree-lined, friendly place with less than 5,000 inhabitants. It is hardly any bigger today. There is no industry; its craftsmen and shopkeepers depend for their living entirely on the neighbouring farmers. The young people find little scope there, and usually leave it to seek their fortunes in New York or Philadelphia. I have been many times in Towanda since that first visit; it was in Towanda many years later that I wrote the first pages of this autobiography. On that first visit I was able to stay only a week. I had to return to Canada, where I had a long lecture tour in front of me.

My first move from Towanda was to London, Ontario, which lies on a small stream proudly named the Thames. I delivered two lectures there. We had no group in London, but one of our comrades, Hornstein, was about the most popular man in London. Everyone knew and liked him. The whole town came to my lectures, both because Hornstein had arranged them, and because the visit of a lecturer all the way from London, England, was an event.

I was back on 7th April in Toronto, where they gave me a big farewell dinner. The next day I started my journey to Winnipeg. It took me two whole days. Luckily it was spring; in winter there would have been a heavy snowstorm on the way, and I should have been held up for several days, because the trains would have stopped. The comrades in Toronto said my heavy overcoat that they had got for me there wouldn't be warm enough for Winnipeg. When I pointed out that it was spring they said, "Yes, but Winnipeg is cold even in the spring." I discovered on later visits that they were right. But this first time I did not freeze in Winnipeg in my Toronto overcoat.

I didn't find the long journey to Winnipeg difficult or tiring. The landscape was unusual, and held my whole attention. All the way from Toronto to Winnipeg there wasn't a single large town, and after the first eight or nine hours there were few small towns.

What struck me was the yawning emptiness of this vast stretch. One travelled for hours without meeting more than here and there a settlement of a few trappers or Indians or beaver hunters, who looked lost in this great waste of snow.

I wondered why the Canadian government made it so difficult by its immigration laws to settle and develop this rich land. Even today Canada is largely unpopulated, with less people scattered over its enormous territory, larger than the entire United States, than in the one small New York State. But the ways of governments are mysterious, like the ways of God. At a time when millions of people in Europe were driven like cattle from land to land and could find no home one asked oneself in vain why the great countries of the American continent kept their gates closed against these people, heedless of the simplest dictates of ordinary humanity.

I was received in Winnipeg by a crowd of comrades waiting for me at the station, including my old friend Matlen, whom I had known in Liverpool. It was a glorious sunny day when I arrived, and I was glad to get out of the train and stretch my legs. It was certainly not warm in Winnipeg, even with the bright sunshine, and there was still snow in the streets, But it was not the Siberia my friends in Toronto had warned me about. I stayed with comrade Prasov and his wife, whom I had known as a young girl in our London movement.

When I was there in 1913 Winnipeg had already over 100,000 inhabitants, made up of the most varied population groups, Russians, Poles, Ruthenians, Germans, Jews, French and a dozen others. In time this mixture merges into a nation, which imagines itself a unique brand of humanity. It was obviously the same with the nations of Europe, though people have forgotten it or try to forget it. On the American continent we see it happening before our eyes.

Winnipeg looked quite different from Montreal, Toronto and the other cities of the East. It still had the air of a frontier post. It seemed to have been roughly knocked together. Except for the churches and public buildings in the heart of the city the house's were all of wood. Most streets were unpaved. It was strange in a city of over 100,000 people.

The shop windows were full of the oddest things, broken bits of old furniture, small barrels of bent rusty nails, used parts of machinery, old tins, things nobody in the East would have dreamt of buying. My friends assured me that this old junk was in great demand in Winnipeg. The farmers round about were ready buyers. They couldn't afford better. But food was fabulously cheap. The best meat could be bought in Winnipeg at that time for five cents a pound. The great menace to the farmers were the wheat speculators from the East, who offered the farmer an absurdly low price for his whole harvest before there was a stalk of grain in the field. The farmers who needed the money simply gave their wheat away.

When I was in Winnipeg again twelve years later it had grown immensely. The population had doubled. The streets were well paved, and most of the houses were of stone. The farmers had organised themselves in sales cooperatives, and the wheat speculators didn't get a look-in.

I hadn't expected anything like the success my lectures had in Winnipeg. Our group there had used the weeks before I came to prepare the ground carefully. Winnipeg also had a good Yiddish weekly, which was printed by our comrade Simkin. The editor, Goldstein, was sympathetic to our ideas. He had written me up so well that everybody in the town wanted to hear me. There was a good intelligent Jewish public in Winnipeg, and I felt very happy among them. I stayed in Winnipeg a whole month. I delivered twelve lectures there, on social subjects, economic questions and literary themes. The discussions that followed were extremely interesting.

My last speech in Winnipeg was delivered on 1st May. There were several other speakers at that meeting, who spoke in English, German, Polish and Russian. During the meeting the weather changed. When we started, the sky was clear and sunny. Suddenly there was a snowstorm, and in a few minutes the streets were thick with snow, a foot high. Luckily my stay in Winnipeg had ended; I left the next day.

It was time to think of returning to London. I had been away three months, and Frumkin, who was editing the *Arbeter Fraint* during my absence had to go back to Paris, where he had things to do. So I refused a whole batch of invitations which came to me from Calgary, Edmonton, and lots of other places to lecture there. I only had to decide whether to return the way I came, or to go via Chicago and Detroit back to Toronto.

I went to Chicago. The journey took me about thirty hours. The train stopped two hours in Minneapolis, so that I had my first sight of the Mississipi. I must have expected too much, for between Minneapolis and St. Paul the mighty "father of waters" is fairly narrow, and nothing like so impressive as I had expected.

We reached Chicago late at night, and there was no one to meet me at the station. The comrades had expected me at another station, and I found afterwards that they were waiting there for me. But of course I didn't know that, and I made my way myself to the house of the comrade with whom I was to stay. I got there after midnight. Presently the comrades who had gone to meet me arrived there, wondering what had happened to me. They were delighted to find me there.

This group too included a number of old London friends; comrade Jaxon, whom I had met in London a year before, was a most remarkable man. He was a half-breed Indian. I shall have more to say about him later.

I couldn't stay in Chicago more than four days on this first visit. I had several lectures still arranged for me in Canada. The first thing I did after I arrived was to visit the big German cemetery at Waldheim, where the Chicago martyrs lie buried. The simple monument over their grave is most impressive, the figure of Liberty with the laurel wreath, and the year 1887. And these last words of August Spies on the pedestal: "The day will come when our silence will be more powerful than the voices you are throttling today."

For more than twenty years I had in various countries joined in the annual memorials held on 11th November for these men at whose grave I stood now. There is no question that they were condemned unjustly, that they were the victims of a judicial murder, put to death not for any crime, but for their beliefs, which they upheld courageously before their judges. There can be no doubt of it after the publication by Governor John P. Altgeld in 1896 of his "Reasons for Pardoning Fielden, Neebe and Schwab" when he ordered the release of the three men after they had been in prison for nearly twelve years. His pardon could not bring back to life the five who were executed.

I stood for a long time, thinking, silently, beside their grave. Near by there was a fresh grave, with grass and wild flowers growing over it. It was the resting place of Voltairine de Cleyre, who had died in Chicago on 6th June 1912, at the age of 46. A remarkable woman, a rare spirit. The Chicago martyrs played a strange part in her life. When the disturbances of May 1886 took place in Chicago and the anarchists were arrested, Voltairine was under 19. She was infected by the general fury roused against them by the press and others, and she shouted: "Hang them!" But before they set out on their road to the gallows she had undergone an amazing transformation. The course of the proceedings and the manner of their conviction opened her eyes. Soon she stood in the same camp as those men who had been sentenced without any proof for a crime with which they could not be shown to have had any connection; the true criminals were never traced. Voltairine could never forgive herself for having once in the general hysteria joined in the cry "Hang them!"

"I can never forgive myself," she wrote, "though I know that those dead men and all who were close to them in life would surely have forgiven me. But my own voice will always ring in my ears, reproachfully, shaming me, till the end of my days."

Voltairine afterwards dedicated some of her loveliest poems to the Chicago martyrs. *At the Grave in Waldheim* begins with these words:

> Quiet they lie in their shrouds of rest,
> Their lids kissed close 'neath the lips of peace;
> Over each pulseless and painless breast
> The hands lie folded and softly pressed,
> As a dead dove presses a broken nest;
> Ah, broken hearts were the price of these!

Now she lay beside them, joined with them in death. My heart was heavy thinking of the hours Milly and I had spent with her in London. I picked a few wild flowers from her grave, put them in an envelope and posted them to Milly.

The same evening the comrades gave me the customary reception and dinner. It was at the home of the Liefshitzes, which was a sort of headquarters of the Chicago anarchists. Voltairine de Cleyre had lived there in her last years. I met most of the Chicago comrades and again a good many among them with whom I had worked in London. It was a pleasant company, but the heat in Chicago was too much for me. It was a change from the severe cold of Canada, but I didn't like it. I hadn't a dry stitch of clothing on me.

Jaxon, the half-breed Indian, was my chief guide in Chicago. I found him extremely valuable in my expedition to the big Ethnological Museum, which has a wonderful collection illustrating the life of the Red Indians. Jaxon was of course at home there. He had their blood in his veins. He had lived as a young man with the Indians in Canada, and had taken a prominent part in their last big rising under Louis Riel in 1885. He had been sentenced to death with Riel. Riel was shot; Jaxon got away, escaped to the United States. Afterwards he found his way into the libertarian movement.

When I was in Chicago again twelve years later Jaxon had disappeared. Nobody knew where he was. The comrades thought he was dead. In 1935 I was speaking at a May Day celebration in New York when an old white-haired man came over and asked me if I remembered him. "Jaxon!" I cried. He was 88 then. He told me that he had been living for years in an Indian settlement in Maine, and had come to New York for a few days on some legal business for his people. He left New York the same evening.

My two meetings in Chicago were wonderfully attended, in spite of the terrible heat. I still wonder how people could have stood it in that heat in that densely packed hall. The sweat poured down my face, and my clothes were sticking to my body.

From Chicago I went to London, Ontario, and from there to Hamilton. I had one meeting in each of these two towns. I had two meetings in Toronto, and another in Ottawa. On 18th May I was back in Montreal. The whole eastern part of Canada now looked quite different. The snow had gone, the land was green, the trees were covered with foliage. Even the streets of Montreal looked different. I got to know some of the beautiful country round Montreal.

I stayed another ten days in Montreal, and addressed four more meetings. I thought of paying a short visit to New York, but London letters told me that Frumkin was getting worried; he had to get back to Paris. So I gave up my plan about going to New York this time.

On 29th May I took the train to Quebec, to board the "Empress of Ireland" for Liverpool. The Empress was a fine boat, about three times the size of the Corsican on which I had arrived.

Exactly a year later, on 29th May 1914, the Empress collided in the St. Lawrence, a few hours out of Quebec with a collier, and sank in a few minutes with most of her passengers; there was no time to save them. Milly and I spent some anxious hours when we heard the news in London; my son

Rudolf who had gone to Canada with me and had remained behind, was to have returned to England on the Empress. At the shipping office they could only tell us that many passengers had lost their lives, but they hadn't received the names of the survivors yet. When we came home from the shipping office there was a cable from Rudolf waiting for us to say that he had postponed his departure by a week. He had therefore not been on the Empress.

When I travelled on the Empress the weather was terrible until we neared the English coast. There were heavy seas and thick fog, and it was bitterly cold. We kept coming across huge icebergs. We reached Liverpool on 5th June. I took the train at once for London, and arrived there about midnight. I was terribly happy to be home again, with Milly and our small son Fermin.

Chapter 25

The War

The same month, on 28th June 1914, soon after my return to London, the heir to the Austrian throne was murdered with his wife in Sarajevo, and the world found itself on the brink of war. Even those who had till then refused to believe in the possibility of war were alarmed.

The first reports about the Sarajevo assassination were vague and confused. Same papers tried to suggest that it was the work of anarchists, though it must have been clear to anyone acquainted with the political conditions that it must have been done by a nationalist group.

The Federation of Jewish Anarchists had arranged, before the Sarajevo assassination, to hold a conference on 4th July, with Malatesta and myself as the speakers. The Conference took place, and was well attended. Malatesta referred in his speech to what had happened at Sarajevo, saying that he feared there would be very serious consequences. But he did not think there would be war. Events proved him wrong.

Two days later the Kaiser gave Germany's full support to Austria in any action that she would take against Serbia. On 23rd July the Austrian government sent a 48 hour ultimatum to Serbia. Russia mobilised on 25th July. Great Britain tried to prevent the war by proposing an international conference on the Serbian issue, but Germany rejected the proposal. On 28th July Austria declared war on Serbia. Then followed Germany's ultimatum to Belgium, to let her troops march through. On 1st August Germany declared war on Russia, and on 3rd August against France. The German invasion of Belgium brought Britain into the war.

An ominous feeling hung over London during those fateful days. People hoped against hope that Britain would keep out of the war. But as soon as the German armies marched into Belgium, as soon as Germany had torn up the scrap of paper guaranteeing Belgium's neutrality Britain was in the war.

Some people still believed that Britain could be kept out of it. There were socialists like Hyndman and Blatchford who were inciting to war. But Keir Hardie and the Independent Labour Party were against it. The liberal press favoured neutrality. There was a powerful peace movement in the country. The murder on 31st July of the French socialist leader Jean Jaures, who had called for a general strike of French and German workers to stop the war, intensified this British peace movement. On Sunday 2nd August, there was a big anti-war demonstration in Trafalgar Square called by the Independent Labour Party, with the support of a number of other bodies. Small noisy groups tried to break up the meeting, but they were ineffective against the overwhelming feeling of the mass of the people there. I was in Trafalgar Square for that demonstration. When it was over I met Tarrida and Tcherkesov. They both looked grave and feared the worst. We parted with heavy hearts. I had no doubt that Britain would go into the war. The day after the Trafalgar Square demonstration Germany declared war against France. The day after that, 4th August, Britain declared war on Germany.

A few days later Milly and I happened to pass Trafalgar Square. Just then the first contingent of British soldiers came marching by on their way to Waterloo to entrain for France. It was a long procession of fine well-built young men, setting out on their way to death. The streets were lined on both sides with silent crowds watching anxiously, serious-faced. Suddenly two open cars draped with Union Jacks came along from Charing Cross Road and drove to the Square. Eight or nine men climbed out of them, waving to the marching soldiers, and started singing *Rule Brittania*. There was no response from the silent crowds. The men realised that their gesture was out of place. They climbed back into their cars and drove off. The long line of soldiers marched on amid silence.

I went home feeling that the work we had carried on for so many years was doomed. The international socialist labour movement had failed to stop the mass slaughter. The speeches and the resolutions of the International Congresses had proved empty phrases. All the talk about the brotherhood of peoples and about international solidarity had been meaningless.

Few people believed that the war would last long. Everybody said that no nation could stand the strain more than a few months. Modern weapons and modern war methods would soon compel them to stop. The destruction would be too great. Their treasuries couldn't possibly find so much money. The national economies would break down. A few months, they said, and the war would be over. I didn't share their optimism. On 7th August 1914, I published an editorial in the *Arbeter Fraint* where I said: "The workers were the only class who could have prevented the horrible lapse into barbaric bloodshed. A tremendous demonstration by the international working class before the outbreak of the war, and their firm, unshakeable determination to use all the methods in the power of the working class to prevent the sinister plans of the imperialist blood-politicians could have saved the world from this tragedy. It is now too late. Europe is in the grip of the red madness, and the working classes of the nations at war will be scourged with whips and scorpions for their heedlessness, for their cowardly vacillation at the right moment, when everything could still have been saved.

"Let no one try to console himself with the illusion that this will be a short war. Its ramifications are too wide. There is too much at stake. This is a struggle for supremacy in Europe and in the world. It will have to be fought out to the end.

"We have entered a period of mass-murder such as the world has never known before. All the wars of the past will pale before this, will look like child's play against it. No one knows what awaits us. Those of us who will live to see the end of it will tell of experiences such as no human tongue has told of before."

Chapter 26

Arrested

Some weeks before the war began the British authorities started the registration of enemy aliens. The yellow press had been conducting a campaign which had forced the government to take this step. Dailies like the *Daily Mail, Evening News, Daily Express* and weeklies like *John Bull* dished up scare stories about anti-British activities by the Germans living in Britain, who were mostly innocent working-class people, as though they were all spies in the pay of the Kaiser, busy plotting against Britain. There were stories about German bakers putting arsenic into their bread, Germans dropping poison into the reservoirs which supplied London's drinking water, and there was one report that the police had discovered a vast store of arms in a German club. It turned out that this was supposed to be the club of the Second Section of the Communist Workers' Educational Alliance. The members of this club were political refugees who had fled from Germany when the anti-socialist laws were introduced there. It made no sense that they should now be storing arms to fight for Germany against England which had given them refuge. Such things could only be explained by the wave of hysteria which had swept the country.

But the story was enough to bring the police down on the club, to carry out a search. A couple of guns were in fact found, old flints which had no locks, and looked as though they had been last used in the Thirty Years War. They were props belonging to the club's amateur theatre. Even the police laughed at their find.

But the agitation went on. Feeling against the Germans rose until there was a real pogrom atmosphere. The cry became "Watch Your German Neighbour!" The government was forced to listen to "the voice of the people". It was clear that the registration of enemy aliens was a first step towards their arrest. I felt sure I would not be long left at liberty, and I made preparations for that event.

I was for years the Financial Secretary of the Anarchist Red Cross, an international body whose object was to send small sums of money and books for study to comrades in Russian prisons or in Siberia. There was a considerable sum lying in the bank in my name, which would be confiscated if I were arrested. So I transferred the money to Alexander Schapiro, who was the Secretary of our Relief Committee. My next concern was to arrange for the continued appearance of the *Arbeter Fraint*. All the comrades were determined on that. There was a wonderful feeling of solidarity among the comrades. Many who hadn't been active in the movement for years came back now to help us.

The outbreak of the war was followed by an industrial crisis, as we had expected, and the workers in the East End were badly hit. A lot of our comrades were unemployed, and in distress. We had to do something to help them.

It was worse in the West End; most of our German comrades were out of work. People were afraid to employ Germans. The yellow press would have been after them. The German and the French comrades got together and started a communist kitchen to help their unemployed. There were several cooks among them, and they took charge. The unemployed themselves peeled potatoes, prepared the vegetables, and washed dishes, pots and pans. Those comrades who were working supported the kitchen by coming there to have their meals and paying for them, even contributing small additional sums towards the upkeep. It was wonderful to see German and French workers engaged together in this common work of help, while over on the continent millions of German and French proletarians were killing each other on the orders of their governments.

We followed the example, and started a communal kitchen in the East End. We rented a house, knocked together a few tables and chairs, and borrowed pots and pans, crockery and cutlery from the homes of our comrades. The women bought food and prepared it. The unemployed comrades helped to fetch and carry. In a few days everything went swimmingly.

Kropotkin came to visit our kitchen and wrote about it in *Freedom*. We had no fixed price for a meal. Those who couldn't pay anything didn't. Those who worked gave as much as they could afford. Some who had left London to find work in the provinces sent us money by post. Even our married comrades who had their meals at home came once a week with their wives to eat in our communal kitchen.

We felt that there were hard times coming. We decided therefore to reduce the size of the *Arbeter Fraint* to save costs. We also sent a call to our comrades in America to help us. Our old friend Dr M.A. Cohn and his wife arrived in London just then. They had left America shortly before the war on a European tour, and they were in Vienna when the war started. As American citizens, they got away to Switzerland, and then came to London through Paris. They were thrilled by what we were doing, and took most of their meals with us in the communal kitchen. As an enemy alien I was not allowed to go beyond the five mile limit, so I couldn't accompany them on their visit to Kropotkin, who had gone to live in Brighton. Milly went with them. I took them to see Malatesta.

Malatesta viewed the situation very seriously, even though he held on to his belief that the war would end with a great revolutionary era. We discussed the question of the internment of Germans and Austrians. Malatesta clapped me on the back and said: "You're all right, Rudolf. Nobody will suspect you of spying for the Kaiser. They won't touch you!" I didn't share his optimism. A few days later the Cohns left London on their way home to America.

The agitation against the enemy aliens continued. In October mobs collected in the streets, in the Old Kent Road, in Deptford, Brixton, Poplar, and smashed and looted shops which they thought were occupied by

Germans. There were real pogroms. Some houses were set on fire, and the people who lived there had to fly for their lives over the roofs. The police were helpless. The troops had to be brought in before the outbreaks were put down. About forty people were arrested, and punished, but they were not the worst offenders. The yellow press which incited them kept up its campaign to force the government to intern all enemy aliens.

The government announced that it had decided to intern the enemy aliens "for their own protection". I felt sure that my turn would soon come. Linder, the manager of the *Arbeter Fraint*, was also an "enemy alien", and expected arrest. On 23rd October we published a call in the *Arbeter Fraint* to our comrades that they should see to it that the paper should continue to appear when we were no longer there. This issue had just come off the press when Linder was arrested. Several other Jewish comrades in the East End were arrested at the same time. In the West End the police came into the hall where our German comrades held their meetings, and arrested everybody there, about thirty people.

Most of those who had been arrested were entirely without means. So we started a fund to send them a little help to the internment camp. I published an appeal in the *Arbeter Fraint*; the comrades responded warmly, and a special relief committee was formed. As I expected arrest myself any moment I took no part in it, but Milly became secretary of the committee, till she was also arrested, eighteen months later.

The anarchist movement in England was in a great state of agitation at this time over Kropotkin's pro-war attitude. Those of us who stood close to him had known his attitude for a long time. But most of the comrades learned of it only now, when he made it public. He did this in the form of a letter to Professor Steffen, in Sweden. He sent me a copy of the letter, and I published it at once in the *Arbeter Fraint*. It was now impossible to avoid an open clash with him. The conflict with Kropotkin meant much more to me than most of my friends could realise. I owed a great deal to Kropotkin. His books had influenced my whole development, had shaped my whole life. I was also bound to him by ties of close personal friendship and affection. I admired him more than any man I had met in the whole of my life. My respect for him was unbounded. It was therefore not easy for me to oppose him. But this was a matter of conscience, and I had to take a firm stand. I had no doubt at all that he was absolutely convinced of every word he said. Much of it seemed to me thoroughly justified. But I could not follow him to his conclusions, which I feared must lead to dangerous consequences. Most comrades in England and in other countries felt as I did, though some attributed his attitude to a different cause. They thought it was because he was a Russian, and was prejudiced against Germans. I believe it was the result of his particular view of history.

The period with which Kropotkin was most occupied was that of the French Revolution. He judged every later development in Europe according to the experiences of those great events of 1789–1794 which had led to Napoleon and the new European nationalism. To him the rise of the German military state dominated by Prussia, and the annexation of Alsace and Lorraine, meant that the leadership on the continent had fallen into the hands of a military, reactionary, bureaucratic state, pursuing a policy of violence.

I believe those considerations influenced Kropotkin's attitude to the war against Germany. When the Germans marched into Belgium there was only one course left for him, to do everything he could to help to defeat Germany, whatever the cost. I could understand and respect Kropotkin's reasons for his attitude. But I could not agree with him. What he said seemed to me in absolute contradiction to everything we had fought for till then. I answered him in four articles which appeared in the *Arbeter Fraint* in October and November.

Kropotkin's stand in favour of the war started a heated controversy among our comrades everywhere. The Spanish movement was almost entirely against Kropotkin. Only Ricardo Mella and Frederico Urales (Juan Montsent) agreed with him. Tarrida's sympathies were with Kropotkin, though he took no part in the public discussions. It was much the same in Italy, where only a few anarchists of the individualist school sided with Kropotkin. In France alone there were a number of prominent comrades, like Jean Grave, Charles Malato, Christian Cornelissen, Charles Albert and others who vigorously supported Kropotkin. Malato and Cornelissen came from Paris to London to try to win over the English comrades. They found the great majority of the English movement against them, and they dropped the idea.

There was a meeting a few weeks later at the office of *Freedom*, attended by Malatesta, Tcherkesov, Keel, Parawitch, Schapiro, Schreiber and others. The discussion was a heated one. Tcherkesov shared Kropotkin's attitude. He went even further than Kropotkin. He said that if Germany won the war the entire free development of Europe would be ended. The labour movement would be dead. It would start a long period of reaction throughout Europe which would destroy all the achievements of the past hundred years. He was therefore convinced that we must take our stand with the allies. It was our duty as revolutionaries to prevent the victory of Prussian militarism.

Malatesta couldn't contain himself. He kept angrily interrupting Tcherkesov, who had been his intimate friend for many years. He said this war like every other war was being fought for the interests of the ruling classes, not of the nations. It would be different if the workers of France and Britain had fought for their countries, and had won, to introduce a new social order. Then it would be right to fight to repel a foreign invasion. But now it was different, and whichever side the workers fought on they were only cannon-fodder.

Malatesta agreed that a victory for Germany would lead to a general reaction in Europe, but he argued that a victory for the allies would have the same result. He thought that a French victory would bring a clericalist and royalist reaction which would overthrow the republic. He said that he too wanted a German defeat, but for different reasons than Kropotkin and Tcherkesov. A German defeat would start a revolution in Germany which would spread to other countries. The rest of the comrades expressed similar views. At this meeting Tcherkesov stood alone.

Then the action against enemy aliens was relaxed. The arrests stopped. Apparently there were not enough places prepared for so many people in the internment camps. Some who had been arrested were released, Linder among them. He must have had a bad time in the internment camp at Olympia. But we gathered that only from his appearance. He refused to say a word about what he had gone through.

Some people said now that Linder had been released I was no longer in any danger of being interned. I didn't share their optimism. Perhaps if I had kept my mouth shut and put away my pen I might have escaped. There were some Germans who were left at liberty all through the war. But I could not be silent. As I wrote my articles in answer to Kropotkin I felt that they would bring the police after me. I kept my small case packed ready. Indeed, my last article had just appeared in print when I was arrested.

Chapter 27

Olympia

They took me away on 2nd December at 7pm. I had been expecting it, so it didn't come as a surprise. Milly was very brave about it. My son Rudolf, Milly's sister Polly, and a few friends who were there pressed my hand silently. I said goodbye to my young son Fermin. He was only seven. The child burst into tears. The two plain clothes policemen were as much moved by his crying as we all were. We couldn't pacify him. He was still crying when I left under escort the home to which I never returned.

The hour was too late to take me to Olympia. So I spent the night in Leman Street Police Station. Milly and Rudolf came to visit me there at nine o'clock in the morning. They were allowed to spend some time with me in my cell, and we talked without being disturbed. The Police Inspector, who knew me, even allowed Linder to come to see me to discuss the future publication of the *Arbeter Fraint*.

Then a Scotland Yard man arrived to take me to the internment camp at Olympia. We got there just before noon. I was taken before an official who seemed annoyed, and wanted to know why they had brought me there. Didn't they know that the arrests had been stopped? My escort explained that I had been arrested by special order of the War Office. I was the only person arrested that day.

I was shown into a large comfortable room, the Camp Commandant's office. The Camp Commandant, Lord Lanesborough, a pleasant old gentleman, sat at a big table, with an officer at each side. The Scotland Yard man spoke to him quietly so that I couldn't hear what he said. But Lord Lanesborough kept looking across at me with visible interest. The detective must have been telling him about me. Presently Lord Lanesborough asked me in a very friendly way if I would like to stay in the Restaurant. When Linder saw me at the Police Station he had told me what he knew about the Olympia internment camp from his own stay there, and he had spoken of the "Restaurant" as the place where the *best people* lived. They had to pay a pound sterling per week, and they got better conditions than the rest of the camp. I couldn't think of buying my comfort by putting such a charge on my friends outside. I said, no. He nodded, and said "Camp 12".

A soldier led me away. I found myself in the camp proper, consisting of the two immense Olympia Exhibition halls. In the first, groups of prisoners were breaking stones, each group under guard of four soldiers with fixed bayonets. The whole place was filled with a fine dust. At the back of the hall were the offices of the administration, which was almost entirely in the hands of the internees themselves.

The people were very nice to me; after my particulars were taken I was given my number and was conducted to the second hall, which was used as

149

our living quarters. A soldier went through the belongings I had brought in my small case, and a sergeant watched him. It was time for the mid-day meal, and the internees were lining up for their rations.

When I got to Camp 12 the people were sitting down to their meal. Someone called my name. It was Karl Meuel, an old acquaintance, who belonged to the First Section of the Communist Workers' Educational Association. I wasn't a bit hungry, but the other internees urged me to take my rations. I did. But I couldn't eat. The man sitting next to me saw that and asked if he could have my food; without waiting for an answer he snatched my plate and ate greedily. I noticed others licking their plates or devouring the leavings on other plates, bits of fat or skin. Then I understood that these people were hungry.

Karl Meuel afterwards introduced me to my fellow internees. We spoke about all sorts of things. They were people of all classes and characters. I was very tired however, and I was glad when the day ended, and we retired to sleep. I wanted to lie down and rest. But I couldn't sleep. I kept thinking of my loved ones at home. I listened to all the sounds of the night, people coughing, snoring, groaning, and the measured tread of the sentries. My neighbour snored to waken the dead. It was a long miserable night. When the call to get up came I was still awake.

Milly came to visit me the next day. I would have been happier to be spared these visits. They were a torment to me. She and all the other visitors had to stand about for hours in the street in the cold and rain till their turn came. Many women had to go home without seeing their menfolk who were interned there, because by the time their turn came the visiting hours were over. Only three minutes were allowed for each visit. There was little time for more than a handshake and a word of greeting, and time was up. The sight of so many soldiers with fixed bayonets must also have struck fear into the poor women's hearts. An officer stood by to listen to the conversations, which had to be in English only. Milly had just time to tell me that everything was all right at home. The comrades were working to secure my release. They hoped I would be out soon. I thought that hope was a good medicine, but I wasn't at all sure that it would work this time.

Olympia was arranged in twelve camps, separated from each other by heavy ropes. Each camp had a hundred to a hundred and fifty internees. The rule was that the internees in one camp must not visit those in another, but this senseless regulation was soon dropped in practice.

The whole internment camp looked a sad and hopeless place. It was grey and drab and miserable. There was no drying room for our washing, and the damp clothes hung all over the place. Olympia hadn't been built for people to live in. The air was foul with the smell of human bodies crowded together day and night, and with the stink of the latrines, which were on top of us. There were only five of these, absurdly inadequate for twelve hundred people. It was the same with our washing facilities, only five basins for the lot of us. Of course, it meant that there were continually queues waiting outside the latrines, day and night, with the result that they were left always in a filthy state. Soldiers with fixed bayonets kept the queues moving. A liberal use of barrack room epithets and an occasional bayonet jab livened up the proceedings.

The worst of it was that we were never allowed out to breathe the open air. We went for walks every afternoon, but only inside the building, through the great hall where stone-breaking went on all day. We marched in companies, like soldiers. The fine dust from the stone breaking settled on us. And as there was no division between the two halls it penetrated into the living quarters, and found its way into our lungs.

Camp 12, where I lived, enjoyed certain privileges, and the other internees called it the House of Lords. We were treated better than the rest, The soldiers left us alone. We were released from forced labour, and we had our own straw sacks. To understand how much these privileges meant it is necessary to have an idea of the conditions in the rest of the camp. The treatment was rough. The soldiers used bad language. I saw them shoving people about with their rifle butts. The practice of making the internees break stones for several hours each day was contrary to the Geneva Convention, which released civilian prisoners from all forced labour. Those who refused to do it were put in chains, and had to stand for twelve hours facing a wall, with a soldier on guard at their side to see that they didn't move. All the internees except those in Camp 12 had to drag their straw sacks each morning to a particular spot where they were stacked, till they came to fetch them again at night. It meant sleeping on a different straw sack each night. I can't understand how the camp doctors allowed such an insanitary arrangement.

At 6.30am we each got a mug of some disgusting brew; we never found out what it was. I made two attempts to drink it, but the taste was so horrible that I wouldn't touch it any more. We also received three thin slices of bread with a smear of margarine that was almost invisible. The bread was grey and tasteless. The midday meal consisted of meat, vegetables and potatoes. It was very well cooked. The trouble was that there wasn't enough, and we got no second helpings. At 5pm we got a repetition of the morning meal. Those who didn't get extra food from outside went hungry all the time. The arrangement by which we got our meals seemed specially designed to humiliate and degrade us. We had to line up and file past to the serving point between two rows of soldiers whose bayonets almost grazed our faces. The catering was done by the big Lyons firm.

In winter the huge Olympia building was freezing cold. The halls were never heated. The wind whistled through the holes and crannies. The floor was asphalt, and the straw sacks lay on the asphalt, so that they couldn't keep the cold from us. Later we got wooden boards to put under the straw sacks, but they came round so slowly that when Olympia was closed as an internment camp many internees had not yet received their wooden boards.

Because of that most of the internees always had colds and coughs, and their sneezing and coughing kept us all awake at night. The indigestible bread made us constipated. There was only one doctor in the camp. His treatment was strong aperients. So half the internees were always constipated while the other half had diarrhoea. The thought that one might fall ill in this inferno was frightening.

There was a hospital in the camp; at least, that is what it was called. My hair stood on end the first time I saw it. It was in the same part of the camp where we had our living quarters, divided from the rest of the place only by a partition about five feet high. The entire furniture was an old bedstead and three wooden benches. The bedstead had only three legs, with some bricks to prop it up in place of the missing leg. It was enough to make one weep. There was no peace and quiet there. All the noises of the camp came in during the day. And all night the sneezing and coughing never stopped. It got on our nerves when we were well. What must it have been like for the sick people who lay there, with never a moment's quiet all day and all night? Of course they had the same foul air that filled the whole camp. I wondered what the doctor thought of it. I know that when he had a couple of serious cases he had them removed to a proper hospital.

Besides the so-called hospital we had a VD corner, separated from the rest of the camp only by a rope. The patients included in my time several advanced cases of syphilis, who used the same latrines and washbasins as all of us. Moreover, the patients in the VD corner were only such who had reported their condition themselves. There were many others who had VD who didn't report it. We never had to submit to a medical examination.

My friend John Turner came to visit me about the middle of December, he said steps were being taken to secure my release. James O'Grady MP and W.A. Appleton, the Secretary of the General Federation of Trades Unions, who both knew me, had offered to stand surety for me. Kropotkin had written a long letter to Appleton urging him to do everything he could to get me released. He had also put my case to a Liberal MP who was working on my behalf.

It was good to know that my friends were doing their best for me. I had never doubted it. But I had no faith in their ability to get me released. My reasons were that I had been arrested by a special order of the War Office at a time when all further arrests had stopped. The police could never have suspected me of supporting the Kaiser. They knew my political history quite well. I am still convinced that I would never have been arrested if I had come out in support of the allies. That I could not do. It was my firm belief that Germany bore most of the blame for the war. But that could not make me support the other side. I had explained my feeling in a number of articles, especially in my controversy with my old friend Kropotkin. I felt sure that this was the reason I was arrested. They wanted to keep my mouth shut. So I indulged in no false hopes about my being released. I didn't like being interned, especially under the conditions in the internment camp at Olympia. But there was nothing I could do about it. I couldn't change my attitude. I became resigned to being interned.

What struck me among the other internees in Olympia was the almost hysterical German patriotism of most of them. It was grotesque. I had never heard *Die Wacht am Rheinor* or *Deutschland, Deutschland ueber alles* sung with greater fervour. I couldn't understand it at first. German patriotism was the last thing I expected from Germans abroad. I soon discovered the reason. Most of the internees were working men or small shopkeepers who had lived quietly and law-abidingly in England for many years, had English wives and children, and had lost all contact and relationship with their native Germany. These poor devils had suddenly found themselves hunted like wild beasts, abused in the press, and attacked by the mob. Then they were arrested and flung into these miserable conditions in the internment camp at Olympia. It created in their minds that perverted, exaggerated German patriotism which had so puzzled me. They were being punished as Germans. Therefore they tried to justify themselves as Germans. It was their way of asserting their human dignity and pride against the humiliation to which they were subjected. It was the only thing they could do in their desperate state. I feel sure that if they had been left alone these people would have been no danger to Britain.

Chapter 28

The Royal Edward

Many years have passed since that grey December morning when we left Olympia, but I still shudder at the thought of it. They woke us at 4am. There was endless waiting, counting, registering, and waiting again. Then we were packed into two trains, with a heavy military escort, and sent off to Southend. After the monotony of Olympia even this short railway journey was a welcome change.

When we got to Southend we had to walk right through the heart of the town to the pier. It was about noon; the streets were crowded. We hadn't known there had been a German air raid over Southend that night, and that several people had been killed. If it hadn't been for our guard we would have been lynched. There were cat calls and wild threats, and several attempts were made to rush us. Some people, mostly women, spat in our faces.

I couldn't be angry with them. I just felt humiliated and ashamed. There was a steady thin drizzle coming down; by the time we reached the pier we were soaked to the skin. We were kept hanging about while the police cleared the pier for us. Then we were herded into the small pier train that took us in a few minutes to the end of the mile and half long pier; a tender was waiting there to take us to the "Royal Edward", which was to be our floating prison. It was a terribly slow business. It took hours to get us all on the tender, and then off again on to the Royal Edward. We had to stand in the rain, waiting our turn. I hadn't a dry stitch on me. My eyes and my head were swimming. I could hardly see what was going on. I knew that only half of us would go on the Royal Edward. The rest would be put on the "Saxonia". I wanted desperately to be on the Royal Edward, where I had my brother-in-law, Ernst Simmerling, and a number of my friends and comrades. Suddenly, when I had got to within a few steps of the gangway an order was shouted down from the ship to put the rest of us on the Saxonia. The soldiers were already pushing us back, when a second order came to send another 21 on board. I was one of the 21. With a feeling of intense relief I climbed slowly with my pack up the gangway.

On board the Royal Edward our packs were searched again. Then we were led to a big room, with 106 beds in it, arranged in twos. Karl and I deposited our packs on two adjoining beds, and went on deck. We met a number of old friends there. It was good to know they were there, but I was feeling quite numb, and at that moment I would have given a great deal to be left alone for an hour or two. I hardly heard what my friends were saying. I was glad when they ordered us to bed.

It was a long, a terribly long night. The air was thick with the breathing of all these people. I couldn't sleep. I couldn't think. I heard the watch pacing over my head, and the water lapping the sides. My body was like lead. I sank like a heavy weight. The next thing I knew was hearing the call to get up. I washed and dressed and made my way to the dining-room. I wasn't a bit hungry. But I greedily gulped down the nameless brew we were served for breakfast. It made me feel better.

I hated the idea of going back to the big, stiffling dormitory. Karl found out that there were still a few unoccupied two-berth cabins; he managed to get one for us. Cabin 106 was tiny; there wasn't enough room for more than one of us to stand up. The other had to lie on the bed while he was undressing. There was no porthole; the light had to be kept burning all day. But it was paradise compared to the place where we had spent our first night.

It took me a long time to get used to my new surroundings. Though I had Ernst there, and a number of old friends I felt strange in this place. I can't say why, because the conditions were better than in Olympia. Perhaps it was the continual counting, to make sure that we were all there. Twice every day we all had to assemble on deck to be counted. It always took a drearily long time, over two hours. Such things can hurt more than physical cruelty. It was torture to me. I was prepared to put up with the discomfort, the cramped quarters, the bad and insufficient food. But this everlasting counting was maddening. I have no idea why they did it. We lay two miles out at sea, and it would have been lunacy for anyone to attempt to escape then, in mid-winter. It gave the crew something to do, and it kept us in our place.

The Second Officer of the Royal Edward addressed us a few days later. He spoke very decently. He said he was sorry that the war had made our internment necessary. The war was a terrible thing, but we couldn't do anything about it. Everybody had to make the best of it. The great thing was not to lose courage. He promised us that if we obeyed orders we would be treated fairly and justly. But he also warned us that we were there under military law, and we would all have to answer for the disobedience of any one of us. Then he pointed to the Saxonia riding at anchor about a mile away, and said that conditions there were not as good as on the Royal Edward. He meant it as a threat.

I had been about a week on the Royal Edward. There was a severe storm at sea. The ship pitched and rolled. Many of the internees were seasick. I was sitting in a corner with Ernst, talking about home. Since I left London I hadn't received a word from home. The post was very slow at that time. I heard my name called. A soldier was looking for me. The Adjutant had sent him to fetch me. He said he had a message for me. I followed him to the Adjutant, who was on deck with a group of officers, all holding fast to the rail, and staring down into the storm-tossed sea. The Adjutant told me in the most friendly way that my wife was here to see me. I followed his gaze, and saw a cockleshell of a boat trying to come alongside, with Milly in it. The high waves hurled the boat away. I saw Milly's lips move. She called out to me, but the wind drowned the sound. The boat made at least a dozen unsuccessful attempts to tie up. Each time the waves lifted it up and carried it way. Once it almost turned turtle. At last the boatman skillfully caught the rope and made fast. I was stunned by what I had seen. It was wonderful to catch a glimpse of Milly again, but I couldn't forget the risk she had run to get to me. I was sick with fear for her.

And we didn't even meet. The weather was too stormy for her to climb up to the ship. She stood up in the boat; she was absolutely wet through. But her eyes were shining. We exchanged a few words, but half of them never reached us. The wind picked them up and hurled them into the sea. Then the boat made its way back to the shore. I watched it with beating heart, tossing up and down, until I saw it, with thankful relief, reach land at last.

I learned afterwards that Milly came to Olympia to see me there the same day we had left for Southend. She saw the Commandant, who told her where we had gone. She had then written to the Commander on the Royal Edward to ask for permission to visit me. As soon as she got permission she went to Southend, and though she was warned not to attempt it in that storm, she insisted on having the boat try to reach us.

* * *

As Christmas came near, the weather grew icy cold, and there were storms all the time. Yet we still had to spend three hours every morning, from eight till eleven, on open deck, with no consideration at all for even our older people, who were in no fit state to stand such treatment. We realised of course that we couldn't stay below while the cabins and the halls and passages were being cleaned. But that took only about an hour. There was no reason except that we were prisoners for keeping us for three and often four whole hours on the open deck while the rain and wind and storm beat down on us.

We had a small smoking room on board, where about 25 of us used to come each evening to smoke a pipe of tobacco for a couple of hours before turning in. Most of them were German sailors who had been taken off their ships as soon as the war broke out. I sat silent among them at first, listening to their conversation, making up my mind about the kind of people they were. The talk was usually about the war, and how long it dragged. Their feeling was about the same as that of the internees in Olympia. They were pro-German more as a protest against their imprisonment by the British than out of any real German patriotism. They had come from different camps before they were sent to the Royal Edward. They used to speak about their camp experiences. From all I heard the camp at York must have been about the best of the lot. Not that the conditions were any better there than in Olympia. The food and the sanitation were about the same. But the Camp Commandant was a gentleman, and he treated the internees like human beings. He tried to make things tolerable for them. He was always ready to listen to their complaints and to help them wherever possible. People who suffer, blame those in charge, and often unjustly. But I never heard a word from anyone who had been interned in York against the York Commandant. That was because he had treated them as human beings; whatever their hardships they had not felt humiliated.

I watched and studied my fellow-internees. I grew to have a great liking for the seamen among them. They were rough, weather-beaten, open-hearted, kindly people. They certainly didn't mince their words, but they were forthright and honest. They said straight out what they meant. And they did my heart good with their constant good humour. One evening a man I hadn't noticed in the smoking room before launched into a patriotic German harangue. I listened for a while. But I couldn't keep quiet for long. I interrupted him, and said what I thought about the war and its causes. There was a complete hush in the room. I had touched a delicate question. I had brought a new note into the discussions. Everybody listened to me attentively. When I finished they overwhelmed me with questions. I tried to answer as many of them as I could. But the call for us to retire cut me short. I could see several making their way to their sleeping quarters lost in deep thought. I began to feel that I had sown seed in fertile ground.

Christmas Eve was celebrated very noisily in the great hall. I wasn't there. I stayed in my cabin alone. The sounds of revelry reached me from afar, but I was deep in my thoughts. It was the first time I was alone since I had been snatched away from my home and my dear ones. I have never been a hermit. I am by nature a social being. But the worst thing about my internment was this having to be all the time with other people, to have no moment of privacy and solitude. I hadn't looked all the time at the few books I had brought with me. Now I took them out. I picked up *Faust*. The light fell on the pages. The poetry entered my heart. I was transported. I have never been carried away by poetry so much as on that Christmas Eve alone in my cabin on the Royal Edward. I was recalled to reality by heavy footsteps past my door. The Christmas Eve festivities had ended; the people were off to their beds.

On Christmas Day we had an alarming experience. I was on deck talking to a couple of my friends. It was near time for our midday meal. Most of the others had already gone down to the dining-room. Suddenly there was a boom of cannon from the direction of Sheerness. Shots fell in the water only about fifty yards from us. The entire ship's company came rushing on deck. They were looking up at the sky. They took aim and fired. I spotted an aeroplane flying high overhead. Then an officer noticed us and ordered us below.

When we came into the dining-room everybody crowded round us. What was happening? Who was shooting at us? A German aeroplane had taken a chance on Christmas Day to slip over to the British coast.

By this time I had more or less acclimatised myself. Conditions on the Royal Edward were incomparably better than in Olympia. We never got any of the coarse insults and actual blows that had been our common lot in Olympia. We had more washing facilities than in Olympia. But still not enough for 1,300 prisoners. We always had to wait in queues till we got a wash-basin free. A great boon were the two bathrooms on board, where hot seawater baths could be taken at any time of the day. Two bathrooms for such a lot of us weren't much. But in Olympia there had been no bathrooms at all.

We got three meals a day, as in Olympia. A pound of bread each, which was handed out at breakfast. The bread was baked on board, and was much more tasty than the bread we had in Olympia. The trouble was it wasn't baked well enough. It was doughy. It was often impossible to eat any of it except the crust. The midday meal was prepared at first by the English cooks on the ship. The portions were bigger than in Olympia, but the food was tasteless. At 6pm we each received a pat of margarine or a bit of cheese, that with some of the bread constituted our third meal. It was not enough for a grown man. We went about hungry all the time.

Organisation was simple. We were divided into hundreds; each hundred had its own captain, who was responsible to the Adjutant.

Our postal service was run by the prisoners themselves under the supervision of the English censor. It worked splendidly. Parcels that came for us were opened under the eye of the censor or of another officer, always in the presence of the prisoners to whom they were addressed. Plenty of parcels still went astray, but it was nothing like what we had in Olympia. One would have thought that people suffering a like fate as prisoners on board the Royal Edward would have a certain sense of solidarity, of sticking together. There was nothing like that. Class distinctions prevailed to a disgusting extent. When the prisoners were first brought on board the English made no distinction between us. We were all treated alike. Cabins and sleeping quarters went in turn, first come first served. It was pure luck who got a second class and who got a third class cabin.

But there were some among us who had more of the world's goods, who didn't like this equality at all. They went to the Commandant and wanted him to give them separate quarters, away from the common herd. The Commandant couldn't understand it at first. He said he would consider it. They offered him payment for better accommodation. The leader of this group was a certain Baron von Nettelheim. Their behaviour was so much worse because these were the people who were always proclaiming their German patriotism. Every German was supposed to be their comrade. Now they told the English that they regarded the great mass of their fellow-Germans on the boat with such contempt that they would pay for the privilege of not having to mix with them. I don't know what the English Commandant thought of them. But he agreed. Why shouldn't he? It could only make his job easier if the Germans under his charge split into hostile camps.

There was an attempt made to justify it by saying that the money went to improve the conditions of the poorer prisoners. I know of no such thing happening all the time I was on the Royal Edward.

The worst of it was that this clique assumed an air of protection over the rest of us, for which nobody had ever given them any authority. But they established such a relationship with the Commandant that we were powerless to resist. A few who stood out got themselves denounced as trouble-makers and were deported to the Saxonia. That broke the back of the opposition.

I was sure that I wouldn't be able to stand it for long. I wasn't attracted by the Saxonia. But it was more than I could do to take it lying down.

I was in the smoking room one evening; we were discussing all sorts of things. An elderly gentleman objected that something I said was in conflict with the attitude of my own friends in Germany, who had ranged themselves solidly behind the Kaiser in support of the war. I asked him whom he meant by my friends. "Why, the social democrats, of course," he said. I told him I completely disagreed with the social democrats not only in their attitude to the war, but on almost every point of their entire ideology. I said I was an anarchist. That seemed to puzzle everybody in the room. They flung questions at me. They wanted me to tell them more about my beliefs. I explained the basic principles of anarchism. They were interested. I began to feel that my internment might not be altogether fruitless. A new field had been opened to me, that was waiting for the plough, and might produce a harvest.

Milly visited me a few days later. We were given a quarter of an hour together, with an English officer and a sergeant present in the room. She told me that everybody was well. The comrades were trying hard to get me released. They were sure that I would soon be back at home. I had my doubts, but I kept them to myself. It was good to hear that the *Arbeter Fraint* still appeared, and that the comrades were working hard to keep it going. Our quarter of an hour flew by. I had so much more to ask and to tell Milly. But her visit had set my mind at ease about a number of things that had been worrying me.

The Baron and his clique were continuing their efforts to withdraw from all contact with us. Previously they had eaten in the same dining-room, at a separate table which was reserved for them. Now they were given a saloon to themselves. They each paid six shillings and sixpence a day for the privilege. In return they had better food, and they were served by waiters. We didn't mind that. None of us missed them.

But then something happened that made us all furious. The ship's decks had been open to all the prisoners for our daily walks. Now we were suddenly ordered to keep to the lower deck, which was not so spacious. We were all on top of each other. We couldn't move. We couldn't walk about freely as before. While the Baron and his clique had the whole spacious upper deck to themselves. Now they really did avoid all chance of being contaminated by contact with us of the common herd.

Shortly before Christmas our numbers on the Royal Edward were increased by a few hundred people who had been interned in Gibraltar. We got half the total number. The other half went to the Saxonia. They belonged to different classes, from aristocrats to ordinary seamen. But there was a closer solidarity between them than we had known in Olympia or on the Royal Edward. They were mostly young people, who had lived abroad, in the Argentine, Brazil, Chile and other parts. When the war broke out they had tried to make their way back to Germany to join the forces. Few got there. The British navy took them off the neutral ships on which they travelled and interned them in Gibraltar. There were some adventurous spirits among them, quite unlike the Germans who had lived in England for years with their families and had become passive and cautious, influenced by all the different considerations which arose out of their life and contacts in England. The Gibraltar contingent had no such considerations. Few of them if any had ever been in England. They had no family there, no friends, no connections. The British in Gibraltar had treated them decently, and therefore they found the restrictions on the Royal Edward oppressive.

They were all great German patriots. Each wore a black, white and red badge in his button hole, and hated the British on principle. Of course I wasn't attracted by their patriotism, but I liked the way they stood up for their rights. It was so much preferable to the meek submissiveness of many of the others, who seemed ready to accept any humiliation.

There was bound to be a clash. The Adjutant always went mad when he heard anyone singing German patriotic songs. I don't know why, because in Olympia no one had ever objected to that. When the men from Gibraltar heard that it was not allowed on the Royal Edward they all got together in the dining-room and struck up the *Watch on the Rhine* at the top of their voices. They hadn't got through the first verse when the door was flung open and the censor rushed in bellowing furiously that they should stop. No one took the blindest notice. He went off to tell the Adjutant, who arrived in a couple of minutes with a company of soldiers. The crowd was still singing lustily. He shouted and they went on singing. *The Watch on the Rhine* was sung to the end. Then there was complete silence. The Adjutant withdrew with his soldiers, and he must have felt as he walked out that he had cut a ridiculous figure.

Since Christmas Eve I hadn't had a book in my hand. Our cabin was too small for both of us to undress at the same time. On deck I never could find a corner to myself. So I wasted my time and found my own company getting intolerable. I couldn't even express my annoyance, because it would only have upset the others. I managed to spend a couple of pleasant hours each evening in the smoking room. I had managed to form a small group there, the regulars, who came every time, and took part in all discussions. Among those who had joined the Royal Edward after my arrival were several members of the Second Section of the Communist Workers' Educational Association. We had some very interesting discussions.

I made friends there with Father Heck, a powerfully built man with a lot of natural intelligence. He was not educated, but what he said was always sound and to the point. He had worked for thirty years at the Hotel Metropole in London. It had been a happy uneventful life, except that his wife had been very ill the last few years. When the war broke out and the anti-German agitation started, old Heck had lost his job. A few weeks later he was arrested and interned in Olympia. His wife was in hospital, waiting for a serious operation. He wasn't allowed to go to see her and he didn't know for weeks whether the operation had been successful. Six weeks later they told him the operation had been successful, but she would never be really well. He had an inextinguishable good humour. Sometimes when he was depressed I would say to him: "Cheer up, Father Heck! There'll be better times coming." "Yes, you're right," he would answer bravely, his eyes shining.

160

Another friend of mine was August, a young Hercules of 27. He was a really jolly fellow. Nothing ever upset him. Everybody of course liked him. He had read a lot and understood what he read. He was one of the first Germans whom the British arrested. He had lived in Hamburg and just before the war had gone out with a small fishing fleet to the Scottish coast. They had no idea that the war had started. They were asleep in their bunks at night when they heard shooting. They all rushed on deck to find themselves surrounded by British war vessels. They were ordered to their boats, and it was only when they were on the British warships that they heard for the first time that there was a war on. The British sunk their fishing boats without giving them a chance to take away their personal belongings. The British had been under the impression that they were mine-laying.

Conrad was another young seaman among my friends in the smoking room, a quick, wiry fellow with mischievous eyes and an adventurous little pointed beard. He was a born rebel. I found him very likable. He was an active member of his seamen's union, and a socialist; the socialism he knew was social democracy. But when I had spoken to him several times about the anarchist ideas it was like a revelation to him.

I liked the seamen. They were a splendid crowd. Most of them made good use of our little library, which some philanthropic body had sent us. They were great readers, but they read anything they could get hold of, good books, poor books, trash. They had no literary taste. The story, the plot was what they wanted, something thrilling and exciting to hold their attention. There was Roehm, an elderly sailor who once tried to tell me the story of a book he had read. I soon realised it was Goethe's *Werther*. He didn't remember the name Goethe. He never bothered about authors' names, he said. He hadn't cared for the book. He had thrown it aside twice, but when he had nothing else to read he had gone back to it. I wanted to know why he hadn't liked it. "Too much talk," he said. "The stupid fool drove himself mad over a silly woman." Lotte had only been playing with Werther, he said. If she had loved him she wouldn't have led him such a dance. He had no feeling at all for the complicated problem of the soul with which Goethe was concerned.

I once found him absorbed in a book by Dumas Pere. "You like this book better than Werther?" I said. "Naturally," he answered. "It's full of exciting things happening all the time." "But don't you see that it has nothing to do with real life?" I pointed out. "That's just what I like about it," he said. "All the stories of real life are so boring. What do I want them for? I know all about the things that happen in real life. I don't need to read about them. I want to read about adventure, about things we don't know in real life. I read to pass the time; I want entertainment in my books. I know what's in the book isn't real, but I want to get away from reality."

Peter, another seaman, was only 26. He was born in Holstein, and had been on the high seas with a sailing boat out of Chile when the war started; they were stopped by a British cruiser, and everybody on board was interned. I liked Peter. He was quiet and dreamy. He took little part in the discussions in the smoking room. He sat and listened. He was a great reader. I rarely saw him without a book. One day I found him reading very intently Gottfried Keller's *Der gruene Heinrich*. I asked him if he liked it and he surprised me by saying that he had read it a number of times and always wanted to read it again. It roused feelings in him that uplifted him, as when he was at sea at night alone on watch, with the stars overhead and the deep water all round. Peter was sparing of words. This was one of the longest speeches I ever heard from him. He was sensitive and reticent. He was a strikingly handsome man, tall and straight, with flaxen hair and big blue eyes.

Our discussions every evening in the smoking room were always well attended. Sometimes there wasn't enough room for everybody, and some had to stand in the passage, at the open door, to listen. So the idea came to several people that we should have a lecture once a week. We felt sure that the Adjutant wouldn't permit any lectures. So it would have to be done behind the backs of the British. Yet such an attendance as we expected, fifty to a hundred people, couldn't pass unnoticed for long. There was also the question of a suitable room in which to meet. The sailors suggested the smaller dormitory, which had forty beds. It seemed just what we wanted, but there was an English soldier on guard near the doorway, and he might wonder what brought so many people to this dormitory. It worried me, not so much because of myself. A few weeks under arrest in a cell didn't frighten me. But I had a responsibility to the other people who would come to the lectures. I had no right to expose them to the anger of the authorities. The Adjutant would probably punish the lot of us. On the other hand the lectures would be a change from the dull routine on the ship. I decided to chance it. If we were discovered I would take the blame.

The people were happy when I told them I agreed to give the lectures. For my first lecture I chose a literary theme, "Six Characters in World Literature". About eighty people came. For a secret meeting it was a success. Some of the beds had been folded away to make more room, and there was some sort of primitive seating arrangement. The room was full. Only a few dim lights were on, and it looked very mysterious and conspiratorial. I spoke for an hour and a half. Everyone sat spell-bound. No one moved. It seemed that no one breathed. They hung on every word. I had finished; but they still sat, enthralled. It took them a little while to come back to reality. Then one by one they rose and walked out, silently.

In the middle of February I was called to the censor's office. He was very polite and friendly. Then he produced a letter, and asked me to read it. It was my own letter written home four weeks before. I knew how they looked forward to my letters, so I felt sick when I saw it still in the censor's office.

"I can't think there was anything I shouldn't have said in this letter," I ventured.

"I didn't keep it back," he assured me, speaking very affably. It was returned by the chief censor at Salisbury House in London."

"But why?"

"You said that except for two kinds of tobacco and cigarettes there is nothing one can buy in the canteen."

"Isn't that true ?"

"Yes. But it might be misunderstood. People might think our prisoners are treated badly."

"Would you say that we are having a pleasant time here?"

He dropped his jovial manner. "I am not going to discuss that question with you. Being a prisoner is never pleasant. You know I can't alter these things. But I can make them a little easier for you. That's what I called you for. Would you let me have a list of foods and other things the people want most, and I'll try to get them for the canteen."

I promised to prepare a list; I was already on my way out, when I remembered my letter. "My people at home will be anxious," I said.

"I understand," he answered. "Write another letter, and I'll forward it at once."

I had meant the remark about the canteen in my letter as a hint to Milly. The food we got on the ship had been terrible lately; it was uneatable even when you were ravenously hungry. I hadn't touched the meat for weeks. The only vegetables we got were boiled turnips, put in the pot uncleaned, so that the grit got into our teeth. Milly was Secretary of the Aid Committee for the Arrested German Comrades, and I had wanted her to know it was useless sending us money because there wasn't anything to buy in the canteen and they should send us food instead.

I wrote another letter, I made out the list, and I took them both to the censor. He read the letter and his face dropped. He said: "I can't forward this."

I was completely taken aback. I couldn't think of anything I had said to which he could object. He continued brusquely: "You don't expect me to help you with your pan-German ideas."

I stared at him. What could he mean? "What pan-German ideas do you accuse me of? I had to leave Germany because of my anti-nationalist, anti-militarist views. I have lived in England for twenty years as a political refugee."

He put his finger on a passage in my letter: "Then how do you explain this?" I read the passage out aloud: "Please give my regards to all the comrades. Tell them my heart is with them and with our great cause, fighting for a higher social culture and the brotherhood of all nations, in spite of everything."

"Do you really consider this pan-German ideas?" I asked. "Have you heard pan-Germans speak of the brotherhood of all nations?"

"But you speak of a higher social *Kultur. Kultur* is the favourite word of the pan-Germans."

"Maybe," I said, "but it is no monopoly of the pan-Germans."

"Tell me, then, what you mean by a higher *Kultur*."

"I mean a system of society under which the great majority of people will no longer be degraded to the state of beasts of burden and objects of exploitation by small privileged minorities, and where such horrible crimes as this present mass slaughter of nations will be a thing of the past."

He considered this. Then he said: "I see. You are a follower of Tolstoy."

"In many respects, yes," I declared. "I certainly subscribe to everything Tolstoy has written about war and the part played by governments."

"Who are the comrades you speak of in your letter?"

"Anarchists."

He looked at me. "I was wrong," he confessed. "I misunderstood. It is all clear to me now. I shall forward your letter immediately."

About the end of February we were told that we could now receive newspapers. I have no idea what decided the War Office to lift the prohibition. But we still couldn't choose what newspaper we could have, The notice on the blackboard said that no socialist papers would be allowed. The list on the board didn't include even the liberal papers, and when some of us asked for the *Manchester Guardian*, or the *Daily News*, we were told we couldn't have them. All the papers we could get were Conservative, including the *Daily Mail* and the *Daily Express*, which led the agitation against "enemy aliens".

Then rumours spread that we were going to be removed from the Royal Edward and the Saxonia. There was nothing official, but the rumours persisted. We couldn't feel sorry even if it was true. We were crowded together on the ship like cattle. There was no room to move. The food was getting worse than ever. We were allowed visits once a month, twenty minutes. But most of our people couldn't afford the journey from London to Southend and back. It cost five shillings. No provision was made for visitors to get to the ship. They had to hire a boatsman to take them out, and the charge was five shillings to the Royal Edward and ten shillings to the Saxonia, which lay further out.

One day the censor called me to his office. One of our men had written to his wife that he would rather she didn't come to visit him any more and she should have to go short afterwards at home, because the visits worked out too expensive. The censor wanted to know how that was. I told him what my wife had to pay. He questioned a number of other prisoners. They all told him the same thing. After that the tariff for the boatsmen was fixed at one shilling. The trouble was that many of the boatsmen refused to take passengers at that price.

It was only the little clique of superior gentlemen grouped round Baron von Nettelheim who regretted the possibility of a change. In return for their six shillings and sixpence a day they had comfortable quarters, first-class accommodation, with a fine saloon, and the whole upper deck to themselves for a promenade, and much better food. The Baron asked the Adjutant if there was any truth in the rumours. The Adjutant replied that he couldn't give him any information, but it was not unlikely. Thereupon the six and sixers, as we called them, drew up a petition to the War Office, and expected us all to sign it. It said that everyone was absolutely satisfied with the conditions and the treatment on the Royal Edward and begged to be allowed to stay. If we had signed that we should have made it impossible to complain about our really lamentable conditions, to try to get them improved. This little clique weren't concerned with our conditions. They only wanted to keep their own privileges.

When the clique found their plan miscarried, and their petition would have only a few signatures on it they started a rumour that those who didn't sign would be sent to the internment camp on the Isle of Man. The Isle of Man had a very bad reputation among the internees. The weaker among us were frightened by that story into giving their signatures.

The Adjutant forwarded the petition to the War Office. It didn't change the decision to remove us from the ship. But it gave a chance to papers like the *Daily Mail* and *John Bull* to start a campaign that the "enemy aliens" were living in luxury.

The Royal Edward became a floating hotel. We were supposed to be having a grand time. To make things worse some idiot among us scratched the words, *Gott strafe England* on a latrine door. When the Adjutant saw it he demanded that we should hand over the culprit. Of course we didn't. I don't think anyone knew who he was. But we all got punished for it. We were allowed no more visits and no more post.

Most likely the culprit was one of the Gibraltar men; they had nobody in England and they were therefore not affected; they never had any visitors and they never had any post. Another punishment was that all the doors were locked at night. If one of us had to go to the latrine he had to ring a bell which brought the guard. The soldiers on guard didn't like it either. One morning the Adjutant found that somebody had smashed down one of the doors. He tried to find out who had done it, without success.

To stop all our post was a cruel and a stupid thing to do. We couldn't all be blamed for the idiotic behaviour of some hyperpatriotic fool who wouldn't own up. It meant that thousands of innocent people spent anxious days and weeks without knowing what was happening to their menfolk on board our boat. My experience with the Adjutant was that he was not a bad sort himself. But these things are part of a system. It isn't personal ill will. It is bureaucratic insensitiveness.

It was at this period when we were not allowed to receive post or visitors that I had a surprise visit from Milly, and we were able to talk quite freely, with no guard to listen to what we were saying. Milly had arrived in Southend to visit some comrades interned on the Saxonia. The Commandant of the Saxonia happened to be an shore, and Milly saw him getting into his boat to return to his ship. She asked him if he would be good enough to take her to the Saxonia with him. He was very nice about it and agreed. She was surprised when instead of going straight to the Saxonia he stopped by the Royal Edward and went on board. Milly stayed in the boat. One of my friends had his cabin just where the boat was made fast, and saw Milly. He ran off to fetch me; for nearly an hour we talked to each other freely through the porthole of the cabin. I had such an opportunity to talk to Milly so freely only once again; that was in the Houses of Parliament two years later, and then we were both prisoners.

At the end of February it was announced that three hundred of our number were being transferred to the Isle of Man. My brother-in-law Ernst Simmerling and other friends and comrades were among them.

We thought at first that the three hundred were being removed because the ship was overcrowded. But a fortnight later we got a fresh batch of 380 in their place, so that we were more crowded than before. The worst of it was that we got some ugly customers in that lot. Most of them were ordinary decent folk, that we could get on with easily, but the people who set the tone were very unpleasant. They came from Portsmouth where they had been interned on the "Canada", lying there at anchor. The War Office had ordered the ship to be cleared; some were brought to the Royal Edward, the rest went to the Saxonia. They were all terrible German patriots, and many wore the black, white and red emblem in their buttonhole, like those who had come from Gibraltar. The Gibraltar men did have a strong sense of solidarity, while these were terrible snobs, arrogant, university men and army reserve officers, who looked down on other people as a lesser breed.

The majority of the three hundred who had gone to the Isle of Man had been sleeping in the two big dormitories. So the new batch from the Canada were naturally quartered there. They didn't like it. I don't blame them. I had been terribly unhappy there myself when I had first come on board. But it was the only way. These people demanded that we should be turned out of our cabins, and that they should have them instead of us, because they were university men and reserve officers, and therefore had more right to them. The British authorities took no notice of course. Their next step was to put their demand to the German captains, some of whom ordered people to give up their cabins to the newcomers. About a dozen weaklings did that.

Then they discovered that the Baron and his clique had the ear of the Adjutant. They got together. The same day an order was issued that there would now be a charge of a shilling for each cabin, and that those who couldn't pay would have to go to the dormitory. Everybody knew that this was the work of the German superpatriots, who came immediately after with their baggage to take possession of the cabins. Many occupants refused to leave, and had to be thrown out by British soldiers, while the new arrivals stood there and laughed.

The Adjutant must have realised what a storm of indignation this was creating. The order was withdrawn. No further steps were taken to clear us out of our cabins. We would have taught the crowd from the Canada a lesson they wouldn't forget in a hurry.

I was continuing my lectures. It was surprising that we hadn't been discovered. Once indeed during my third lecture, dealing with the nature and development of nationalism, an English corporal walked in. He was a friendly old chap, whom everybody called Dad. One of our comrades explained to him that it was a Bible meeting, and he went away satisfied. I was now delivering a series of lectures on the different tendencies and movements in socialism. Our meetings were always well attended. I had been able to get a few books from friends outside by Kropotkin, Reclus,

Landauer and others. They went the rounds of our circle and served a very useful purpose.

About the end of April Karl Meuel, who was the German captain in charge of the dining-room, told me that the German captain-in-chief, a man named Razier, had informed him that the Adjutant, while discussing matters of administration with him had asked what he knew of a prisoner named Rocker. Razier said he knew me only by sight. He had never spoken to me. He knew nothing bad about me. I was held in very high regard by many of the prisoners.

The Adjutant asked him if he knew I had been delivering a regular course of lectures for the last few months. Razier said he didn't know. What he knew was that several of us met every evening in the smoking room to discuss various questions, but he wouldn't call that a course of lectures. Then the Adjutant handed him a note, and said, "read that".

It was the work of an informer, unsigned of course. It told the military authorities that I was holding secret meetings, and conducting anarchist propaganda. The Adjutant said this wasn't the first note he had received, about it. There had been six or seven before. All were anonymous. The informers hadn't the courage to sign their names. The Adjutant said that he knew I was an anarchist; he had spoken to me about it, and I had never tried to conceal it. He said he thought the informers were a lot of skunks.

I wasn't surprised. There were a lot of nasty people among our fellow prisoners, and we couldn't stop them coming into the room where the lectures were held. It was nice of the Adjutant to refuse to pay attention to anonymous notes. But now that he knew about the lectures should we continue them? I decided we should. Indeed, the best way to deal with the informers would be for us to come out into the open. We decided to show ourselves on 1st May with our colours. Hundreds of prisoners on that day wore the red ribbon in their buttonhole. We held a meeting in the afternoon. We had songs and recitations, and I spoke about the meaning of May Day. I infuriated the German patriots who wandered in to see what was going on with my denunciation of the warmongers who had started this mass slaughter which was decimating Europe.

While I spoke my friends noticed a prisoner named Korn sitting in a corner taking notes of what I said. Korn was one of those who had come to us from the Canada. He was a sort of Sunday preacher on board. If ever I met a sanctimonious hypocrite it was Korn. He had devoted several of his Sunday sermons to my wicked activity. He couldn't understand why the English authorities didn't put a stop to this "professional revolutionary, who had no respect for any of the human obligations."

A few days later one of my friends told me there was a notice on the blackboard forbidding all meetings, lectures and the like under severe penalties. I sat down at once and wrote a note to the Adjutant, according to the regulations, asking for an interview. He gave me an appointment. I told him I had come about the notice prohibiting meetings and lectures. I confessed that I had been delivering lectures for several months to a group of prisoners. I hadn't notified him, because I hadn't been told that it was necessary. My lectures had all been about literature and social philosophy. The group of prisoners who attended the lectures looked forward to them. They found them an intellectual stimulus. Would he permit the lectures to continue?

"Of course," he said, "I know about your lectures. Your own people saw to it that I should be informed." He went on: "I didn't see anything to suggest that your lectures caused any trouble on board, so I let them go on. I have no objection to letting them go on now, provided you take complete responsibility for any consequences that may follow."

I said I would do that gladly.

"Very well. See the censor, and tell him that I have given my consent for your lectures."

I thanked him, and was leaving the room when he said: "What is the Rocker Release Committee?"

I told him it was a body composed of representatives of trades unions and various political parties who were trying to secure my release.

"Do you think you'll be released?"

"I don't. But my friends outside do."

"If you don't think so, you won't be disappointed. I asked you because two gentlemen of the committee want to visit you. I shall send them permits."

I went along to the censor, to tell him that the Adjutant had given his consent for my lectures being continued. I thought the attendance would fall off after this. On the contrary, there were more people at the next lecture, some of whom, including Korn, came angry and indignant, to see what the "Reds" were up to. I have no doubt they expected British soldiers to invade the place and carry me off to punishment.

I spoke on "Kropotkin and Social Darwinism". When I had finished I added: "I have something to say that will interest you. You will have seen the announcement on the blackboard prohibiting meetings and lectures. I know that this announcement made some of you feel very happy. In fact it was through anonymous letters that some of you here sent that the command was informed about these lectures. The result is that these lectures which were held till now in secret are now being held openly. The Adjutant has given his consent to them. Thank you."

Chapter 29

The Rocker Release Committee

My friends outside had not given up trying to secure my release. I have already mentioned W.A. Appleton, the Secretary of the General Federation of Trades Unions, and James O'Grady MP, a leading member of the Labour Party, who knowing me personally, wrote to the Home Secretary asking for my release and offering to stand security for me. Peter Kropotkin and John Turner, who was General Secretary of the National Union of Shop Assistants, Warehousemen and Clerks also worked hard on my behalf. It was not for want of trying by all these friends of mine that the movement to get me released failed. The application made to the Home Secretary by Appleton and O'Grady received the following reply addressed on 11th December 1914 to "James O'Grady, Esq. MP":

Dear Sir,

I am desired by the Home Secretary to acknowledge the receipt of the letter signed by yourself and Mr. Appleton in regard to the case of Rudolf Rocker, and to say that he will make enquiry in the matter. If Mr. Rocker has been interned as a prisoner of war, the decision as to his release rests with the military authorities, but Mr. McKenna will consider whether this case is one in which he can make a recommendation to them.

Yours faithfully

L.N.A. Finlay

Over a month later, on 28th January 1915, the Home Secretary, Mr. Reginald McKenna, wrote to Appleton himself:

Dear Mr Appleton,

I have made enquiry about Mr Rudolf Rocker and I am informed that after careful consideration the military authorities regret that they are unable to authorise his release from internment.

I wasn't surprised. I had expected it. The police knew all about me, all about my past activities. There was no question of suspecting me as an agent of the Kaiser and of the German military machine. But they knew I was strongly opposed to the war, so I had no illusions about being released before the war was over. But my friends outside were more hopeful, and they did not slacken their efforts. Twenty-four East End trades unions and representatives of all shades of socialist opinion met and formed the Rocker Release Committee, and this body launched a mass petition to the government for my release. I was widely known through the work I had been doing, and the petition soon had many thousands of signatures. Nothing happened. The committee decided to hold a protest meeting. It was ill-starred. They naturally wanted it in the East End. But all the large halls there were engaged for months ahead.

When the committee finally got the Mile End Empire for 4th April, the only date available for a long time ahead, it left only eight days for preparing the meeting. It gave no time for getting speakers or publicity. Keir Hardie and Ramsay MacDonald had agreed to speak, but they were booked to speak that particular night in Norwich. They wrote pledging complete support to the committee, and asked that their messages should be read out to the meeting. Several other speakers who had promised to come were also engaged elsewhere that evening. So the committee decided to postpone the meeting. Before a new date could be fixed the sinking of the Lusitania by a German submarine on 7th May roused such anti-German feeling that it would have been useless to hold the meeting.

About twenty people prominent in all sections of the British trade union and socialist movement had been approached to speak. With one exception they all agreed to come if they were free on the date arranged, and they sent messages of support. The one exception was Hyndman, the leader of the Social Democratic Party, the outstanding Marxist in the country. He wrote the following:

9 Queen Anne's Gate, Westminster. 25th March, 1915.

Rocker Release Conference,
Dear Sir,
I cannot see my way to take any part in the Rocker Release Conference without much more information than you give me in your letter. Already I know of more than one case where sureties have been deceived. Kropotkin can know little of the circumstances, and I doubt if Messrs. Appleton and O'Grady are ready to go quite so far as you suggest. Perhaps you can give me more facts?

Yours truly,

H.M. Hyndman.

Hyndman knew me personally. I had often met him at the time of the Montjuich Affair, and had supplied him with material that was sent to me from Madrid. He knew I had left Germany for political reasons and was a political refugee in England. He knew all about my many years of activity in the East End, so that the tone of his letter was really strange. I shrugged my shoulders when I read it. But my friends outside were indignant. Why had he thrown doubt on their knowledge of the case? Why did he impute to me the possibility of having deceived them? Why had he suggested that Kropotkin and Appleton and O'Grady might not be ready to go so far as they had already undertaken in their communications to the Home Secretary?

Alexander Shapiro, who was the Secretary of the Rocker Release Conference, wrote to Hyndman:

Dear Sir,

Your card of 25th March to hand. I am ready to give you more information about the Rocker case; but I have to tell you that I cannot understand the meaning of your card. We never asked you to be surety for our friend, and therefore your remark that you "already know more than one case where sureties have been deceived" is out of place. The same applies to your other remarks that "Kropotkin can know little of the circumstances" and that you "doubt if Messrs. Appleton and O'Grady are ready to go quite so far as you suggest."

I would never have believed it possible that so many insinuations could be brought in a few lines. I would never have mentioned that Messrs. Appleton and O'Grady were to be sureties had this not been a fact. It would have been much better to make enquiries whether the facts stated in my letter were correct before throwing doubts on them. As a matter of fact Messrs. Appleton and O'Grady not only wanted to be sureties for Rocker, but they have also approached the Home Secretary with reference to his possible release. Both know our friend Rocker personally, and they know that he is a man who can be trusted.

As stated in my first letter, Rocker has lived in England for the last twenty years, and has taken an active part in the labour movement. He is known not only among the Jewish workers, but also in the English labour movement. In Germany he worked in the Social Democratic Party, but afterwards he joined the antimilitarist and anarchist movement, and he is internationally known in this world, as you are known in the social democratic world.

This conference, which is working for his release, is a body of all the East End trades unions, workers' circles, anarchist groups and also the Jewish Social Democratic Party. The whole conference is ready to be sureties for him. As to Kropotkin — *he does know the circumstances*, as he is a personal friend of Rocker for the past nineteen years. From the moment Rocker was arrested Kropotkin has worked hard to get him released. He wrote to Mr. Massingham, the editor of the *Nation*, who approached the Home Secretary. He also wrote to Josiah Wedgwood MP, Cunninghame Graham, Ben Tillet and others. Even now when he is seriously ill in bed Kropotkin has written to me to send him all the letters inviting speakers to the 4th April meeting, so that he may append his signature. As you see Kropotkin therefore knows *all the circumstances*, and your remark that he can know little of them is very far fetched.

I could mention to you a score of other well-known people in the general labour and socialist movement who have taken an active part in the movement to secure Rocker's release. They have failed because the political police are against Rocker as they are against all revolutionaries. If the authorities would have arrested him for his revolutionary propaganda we should not have been surprised. We are protesting against his internment as an enemy alien.

If the authorities would ask for twenty British-born responsible sureties we could obtain them, for Rocker has many friends in the English labour movement. You have yourself spoken more than once from the same platform as Rocker, and I have seen you listen to him attentively. I am writing all this to you not to try to persuade you to come to our meeting as one of the speakers, but to show you that you have been in error in the hasty reply you made to us.

Hyndman never answered this letter. He was not a small man, and he rendered much service to the socialist movement in many ways. But he was so carried away, as many others were at that time by the war emotion that he could not judge fairly. The sinking of the Lusitania had set off a new wave of anti-German feeling in the country and the yellow press did not hesitate to stir it up to fever-heat. Germans who were still at liberty were attacked and assaulted. There were mob riots and violence. Men like Horatio Bottomley worked up the passions of the mob. In one of his articles in *John Bull*, of which he was editor, he called for "A New Vendetta — Blood Revenge", the title of his article, against all Germans living in Great Britain. Some time after the war this superpatriot was exposed in the law courts as a common rogue and swindler, and was sent to prison. He exemplified Dr Johnsan's dictum that "Patriotism is the last refuge of a scoundrel". But at this time he was a powerful demagogue, and many honest people whose only crime was that they were born in Germany had to suffer because of incitement by people like him. He wasn't the only one. There were others of the same kind busily at work doing the same mischief in all the warring countries.

The Lusitania disaster also hit us on the Royal Edward. Our super-German patriots who instead of saying "Good morning" greeted each other with *Gott strafe England*, to which those of their kind gave the accepted response, *Gott strafe es*, went mad with joy. A few idiots even demonstrated their joy to the English soldiers on board, and it led to fights. One of the worst of these people was Korn, who rushed about among his friends like a lunatic, shaking hands and repeating, "Congratulations". This snivelling hypocrite who was always talking about the love of the Saviour and about forgiveness and mercy to all people hadn't a moment's thought for all the innocent women and children who lost their lives on the Lusitania.

I don't say that the sinking of the Lusitania was worse than the hellish air raids by both sides, in which many defenceless people, including women and children, were killed. There is no "civilised warfare". But to go about rejoicing over the sinking of a big ship with women and children on board seemed to me barbarous.

The Adjutant took action against our idiots by tightening the discipline on board in such a way that we all suffered from it. Every day new punitive regulations were issued, whose only purpose was to make everybody miserable. Stopping our post was an inhuman thing to do at a time when we knew there were anti-German riots in London, and many of our people were worried about their families there.

On the night of 12th May we were wakened from our sleep by heavy firing. We looked up from the narrow passage next to our cabin and saw searchlights and, caught in them, two Zeppelins flying very high. The guns of Southend and Sheerness were firing at them. We read in the papers next day that the Zeppelins had been over London, doing much damage. We had seen them flying back to Germany. A week later we were again wakened at night by heavy firing and by what sounded like the dropping of explosives.

In the morning we heard that the Germans had been over Southend and had dropped bombs.

On 27th May, round about noon, I was standing with a friend against the ship's rail, looking as I often did down into the sea. Suddenly a huge pillar of fire rose from the direction of Sheerness. We heard a dull roar. Then there came a pillar of smoke that stood like a giant palm in the sky all the rest of that day. We felt that something horrible had happened. Then we read in the papers that the "Princess Irene" had blown up. The ship had been loaded with explosives. It was a terrible tragedy. Over 300 people had lost their lives.

About that time, in the last week of May, we were informed that both the Royal Edward and the Saxonia were to be cleared. We didn't know where we were to be transferred. Two days later we were told to pack our things, and then we learned that on 1st June we would go to Alexandra Palace, in North London. I could hardly sleep that night. I was on deck very early. The weather was glorious. At 11am a tender came to take us off. We walked off the Southend Pier to be met by a sullen crowd, who stared at us angrily. But no attempt was made to rush us or to insult us as when we had come to Southend. There were no threats and no abuse. We were met by dead silence.

When we came to the railway station our train was already waiting for us and it soon moved off. It did my eyes good to see fields and trees again after such a long time imprisoned on a ship.

The sight of the familiar crowded London streets when we arrived there moved me tremendously. We soon reached Wood Green, and got out. We marched slowly up the hill that is topped by the building known as Alexandra Palace. This was our new internment camp.

Chapter 30

Alexandra Palace

I didn't get a happy impression of our new home. We arrived at Alexandra Palace tired out and hungry, but before we were marched into the grand central hall of the palace we were lined up on the terrace that runs all round the palace building, and after being kept waiting endlessly we were counted all over again to see if we were all there. Inside we had to stand up to listen to an address by the Commandant of the Camp, Lt. Colonel R.S. Frowd-Walker, a grey-haired old gentleman, with the unmistakable bearing of the regular soldier. He stood in the middle of the Hall with his officers round him, and ran his eye quickly and appraisingly over us. He spoke quietly and deliberately, emphasising his points with his cane. He said that if we obeyed orders and behaved ourselves we would have no cause to complain. He seemed to have made a good impression on most of my fellow-prisoners, but I am afraid not on me. He looked too much the military man to have any understanding for civilian prisoners. After his talk we were numbered off in companies, and each was given his place in the camp, and a number. I was Number 4040, in Company 4 in which I had a number of my old friends. We were quartered in the vast grand central hall.

Alexandra Palace, a big building covering over seven acres, is situated in Alexandra Park, a huge space of over 200 acres in North London, just beyond Highgate it runs from Muswell Hill to Wood Green. It was built as the cultural and entertainment centre for North London. The grand central hall had been used as a concert hall. It will give an idea of its size to remember that it seated 12,000 people, besides the orchestra of 2,000. It was immensely high, with a semi-circular roof supported on four rows of columns. Along both sides stood the statues of the Kings and Queens of England, from William the Conqueror to Queen Victoria, and Oliver Cromwell among them, placed right next to Charles I. There was a statue of Shakespeare at the entrance.

Behind rose the huge balcony which had accommodated the orchestra and choir, and the gigantic grand organ. On the left a lot of doors led to a part of the building that was always kept locked and was shut off in addition by a big railing. On the right, glass doors led to a bare space called the Italian garden. It had been used in peace time for the exhibition of tropical plants. The doors could be opened, but there were gates just beyond them which barred us from going further. The orchestra was also shut off from the rest of the central hall by a grille. There was a roughly constructed platform behind it from which the whole great hall could be observed. Day and night there was an armed sentry pacing heavily up and down that platform, with fixed bayonet. There was a similar platform at the entrance to the hall, with another armed sentry.

The left section of the hall was used as our dining-room. The rest of it was occupied by low plank beds, all crowded together. Each prisoner had a straw pallet, a straw-filled bolster, and three horse-blankets. The different companies were divided off from each other by a grille three feet high.

I was absolutely tired out, but I couldn't sleep a wink. Karl who lay next to me also kept tossing on his bed. I lay awake, thinking that this was really a wasted existence. For the first time since my arrest I began to think of escape. Then I must have dozed off. I was wakened by the whistle which was the signal to get up.

Breakfast over, we all had to stand by our beds, to be counted. There was an officer in charge, but the counting was done by the soldiers, and their figures usually didn't tally, so that we had to be counted two or three times over before the officer was satisfied. Then we lined up in twos by the doors, waiting till they were opened. A military escort then marched us to the compound, a big space overgrown with grass and fenced off all round with barbed wire. There were sentry-boxes on three sides, so placed that nothing could be done in the compound which escaped notice by the sentries. We were kept under strict watch.

But the feel of the ground and the grass under our feet after all the months we had been cooped up on the Royal Edward put us all in a good mood. Some of our people rolled in the grass like children, overjoyed. At 9am the Sergeant-Major arrived, and we formed into companies. We stood at attention for about an hour till the commandant came with his attending officers and wished us good morning. He spoke with our company leaders, and then went off with his staff. When we found that this farce was to be repeated every day, our spirits fell.

At 12.30 we lined up again in twos, and marched with our military escort up the terrace. Half-way up we were ordered to halt. At one o'clock the Commandant appeared on the terrace with a group of ladies and gentlemen who wanted to have a look at "the Huns". We were counted all over again, and then we went in to lunch. The same thing was repeated in the afternoon, and we were marched back from the compound into the camp at 6.30pm. We had supper, and were counted for the third time. I felt thoroughly sick of it. Surely it was enough that we were kept as prisoners, under strict watch and guard, without all this military marching and counting and discipline. We were not soldiers who had been captured in battle. We were civilians. Most of us had never worn uniform in our lives. And this was in England, which had been so free from militarism.

A few days after our arrival a wave of excitement swept through the camp. We were going to have elections for a new camp administration, and for what was called our battalion leader. Our German patriots who had managed to get separate quarters for themselves on the Royal Edward now lived like the rest of us, only they had their own separate companies. They were determined to capture the camp administration, and to have their man elected battalion leader. Their candidate was Marschthaler, a Swabian nobleman; they launched a big campaign for him in the camp. But it turned out that the Commandant hadn't meant us to have real elections. He just appointed our old captains from the Royal Edward to be the new camp administration, and he asked them to elect one of their number as battalion leader.

The whole camp at Alexandra Palace was divided into three battalions. To our left was Battalion A. To our right Battalion C. We in the middle were Battalion B, the largest in number of the three. Each battalion was organised in companies. Our battalion had thirteen companies. Each company consisted of 80 to 100 men, and each had a company leader or captain, who was responsible for keeping order and for cleanliness; he received requests and petitions for the Commandant, which he passed on through the battalion leader. There were also the sanitary companies consisting of ten men each, headed by a captain, who did the daily cleaning — basins, baths and latrines. They were paid a small sum for that out of the battalion funds, for they released the other prisoners from those duties. The rest of us were only required to keep our sleeping and eating places clean. There was a Mess leader, also with the rank of captain, who was responsible for keeping order at meal times and for the serving of the meals. Each battalion therefore had fifteen captains, all under the battalion leader.

The captains at their meeting elected a man named Kollin as the battalion leader. The group of German patriots who had put up Marschthaler as their candidate were furious. They disputed Kollin's authority, and demanded that the whole battalion should elect the battalion leader. The Commandant stopped that by announcing two days later at our morning parade in the compound that he had given his approval to Kollin's election, and he wanted it to be considered final. I had no relations with either of the two men, but it seemed to me that Kollin, who had lived in England for many years was better equipped for the job than Marschthaler. I wasn't sure though that Kollin would be able to assert his authority against so much vehement opposition. It wasn't easy to get on with the Commandant, and on the other side our group of German patriots could make things very difficult for him. Kollin wasn't the man to put up a fight.

All the internees were in a bad mood, thoroughly fed up, full of complaints and grievances. We were all upset over some of the stupid regulations that were imposed with no other purpose, it seemed, than to be irritating and to make us feel small and humiliated. One puts up with all sorts of unpleasant things that appear to be necessary. But there was no excuse for these petty annoyances. They may not have been intended as such, but that is the impression they left with us. We saw no reason for the daily parades in the compound, and for being counted over and over again. Sometimes we had to stand for hours in the hot sun till the Commandant appeared, to wish us good morning. Some of the older people dropped off their feet. More than one fainted and collapsed. Counting us three times a day took an intolerable time, and almost always there had to be several recounts.

There were no latrines in the compound; we had to ask the sentry for permission to go back to the camp. As a rule he kept us waiting till there were four or five of us who had to make the journey. Then he called out the guard, and one soldier with fixed bayonet led the procession, and another marched behind. Up the slope of the terrace we went, and the two guards posted themselves at the door till we were all ready to march down again. There was no reason at all for this, because the barbed wire entanglements all round, with armed soldiers at every point, made any attempt to escape impossible.

The three armed sentries in the grand hall who paced heavily up and down all night kept everybody awake. The sentries were changed every two hours, and then there was a lot of stamping, presenting arms, and shouted orders of command. Those who had fallen asleep were wakened by it. The fact that all these things were afterwards done away with, shows that they were never necessary.

After our first month at Alexandra Palace we were told to our very great delight that we could now have one visitor a month, for twenty minutes each visit. Our joy didn't last long. Our visitors were shown into a room with two long tables in it, each of them three feet wide, and with a partition fifteen inches high fixed to the middle of the table to prevent any contact between the prisoner and his visitor. The prisoner sat on one side of the table and his visitor on the other, with a soldier between every two visitors. We were not allowed to shake hands, not even with wife or child. There was an officer present to watch everything we did.

I couldn't believe it, till I experienced it myself. At Olympia we had been permitted to embrace wife and child. On the Royal Edward husband and wife could sit together and hold hands.

Then Milly came to see me, with our small son Fermin. When I saw the partition I told the officer in charge that I didn't want the visit. He was a middle-aged man, who was always decent to us, and he was taken aback. I explained to him that I thought too much of my wife to expose her to such a humiliating performance.

"But it's the Commandant's orders," he said.

"I know," I told him. "I am not complaining about you."

"But don't you realise what you're doing?" he argued. "Your wife and child have been waiting for weeks for their turn to visit you. Now you want to send them away without seeing them. I'll do what I can to make it as easy as possible for you. Please take your seat at the table."

Of course he was right. It would have been a shame for Milly and the boy to go back home without having a word with me.

"Very well," I said. "But I'll tell them never to visit me again under these conditions."

The other prisoners who were waiting in the room for their visitors hung on to every word of this conversation. I could see from their faces that I was giving expression to their own feelings. Our visitors were shown in. Milly and the boy rushed towards me; but a soldier stopped them, and showed them where they had to sit. The officer in charge called the soldier over, and after he had spoken to him the soldier stopped where he was, standing by the side of the officer. Milly saw that I was agitated. I told her what had happened, and then I had to give my attention to young Fermin, who kept asking me questions. He wanted to know when I would be coming home.

It happened to be our day for writing letters. I was still very much worked up over this business, and I couldn't help referring to it in my letter to Milly. I wrote that I would much rather she didn't come to visit me any more under these humiliating conditions. I knew the censor would never pass such a letter. He would probably give it to the Commandant, and I would be summoned to his presence, and I might be punished for it. But I had to have this thing out with the Commandant, even if it meant punishment. A week later my Company leader told me I was wanted in the orderly room. That was where the Commandant sat every other day from 10am to 11:30am to listen to complaints and to receive requests. Interviews with the Commandant were not considered a pleasant way of spending our time. The experience of most of the prisoners was that he was generally in a bad mood, angry and irritable. He wasn't a young man any longer, and he was in very bad health. If he had a fairly good day he was very decent, and if somebody was lucky enough to put his request to him on a good day he would probably agree to it readily. But if he was in pain and bad tempered you couldn't talk to him.

I was sure it was my letter he wanted to see me about. My Company leader took me to the pagoda, a small wooden building which had been used as a refreshment room for visitors to Alexandra Palace. It was now used as the orderly room. About a dozen other prisoners were waiting there when we arrived, men belonging to all three battalions.

The censor and several other officers sat at a long table. Suddenly officers and soldiers jumped to attention: "The Commandant!" A sergeant opened the door, and saluted. The old man came in, waved his hand, and the officers sat down again. The censor laid the first case before him. Plainly he was in a bad mood. He was terribly impatient. He couldn't be bothered to pay attention to us. He got rid of us as quickly as he could, with a laconic yes or no.

Then my turn came. I went up to the table, and saw that the Commandant was reading my letter. He read it through, leaned back in his chair, and looked me up and down. Then he said: "Did you write this letter?"

"Yes," I answered. He stared at me grimly. Then he banged his fist on the table and roared:

"It's a damned insulting letter! What on earth made you write such impertinence!"

I bit my lip, to keep back the words on my tongue. I said: "I wrote what I felt. I feel the same about it now. And I would write the same thing now."

The censor and the other officers looked at me strangely. Nobody had ever spoken to the Commandant like that before. He lost his temper with me.

"You dare to say in your letter that this is nothing else but cruelty. What do you mean by that? Are you accusing me of being cruel?"

"I didn't say that you personally were cruel, I meant the system."

"What is there cruel about it?"

"Don't you call it cruel if my wife and child come to see me and I mustn't hold their hand? I call that cruel. We were allowed to do it at Olympia, and on the Royal Edward."

"Damn Olympia! Damn the Royal Edward!" he stormed. "My job is to see that nobody smuggles anything into this place or out of it. Your letter is a piece of damned impertinence! Do you know that I can have you severely punished for it!"

I said: "Yes, I know that you can have me punished. I am here at your mercy. But your punishing me won't change the way I feel about it. If you were in my place you would feel just the same as I do."

The officers looked at me with interest. The sergeant stood impassive, as though he hadn't heard. The old man stared at me, and said nothing. Then he spoke, very quietly:

"You shouldn't have written this letter. You should have sent your request to me. I'll see to it that next time your wife comes to visit you she can hold your hand, and you may hold your child in your arms."

I thanked him, and the censor called the next case. The other prisoners who had been waiting their turn in the orderly room and had heard my talk with the Commandant soon spread the news through the camp, and wherever I went people looked at me with gratitude in their eyes.

A few days later somebody who had received visitors told me that the partitions had been taken away from the tables and that the prisoners had been allowed to embrace their wives and children.

A good many people who had been on the Royal Edward with me now begged me to start another series of lectures. I was willing to do that, but I didn't see where we could meet. Then we discovered that there was a large theatre in the Palace. We formed a lecture committee, on whose behalf my friends Papenberg and Karl Meuel addressed an application to the Commandant for permission to use the theatre. They had to go to see him; they found him in a very good mood. After he had put several questions to them he gave permission for us to have our lectures once a week in the theatre, on the understanding that we would not discuss present-day politics, and that the lectures would not start any disturbances in the camp. Prisoners in all the three battalions could attend the lectures.

We decided to keep to literature. I suggested a series on "Tolstoy as Artist and Social Philosopher". Some who had heard my lecture on the Royal Edward on "Six Figures in World Literature" asked me to repeat that lecture. I agreed to do so. As soon as our patriotic clique heard what we were doing they set up a howl. They threatened that they would break up our meeting. They told Kollin that it was his duty as battalion leader to go to the Commandant at once and to tell him that I was an anarchist, and make him cancel the lectures. Kollin refused to do that.

My first lecture was arranged for 21st June. The day before, Kollin came to tell me that some of our patriots had been to the Commandant and had said that if I spoke there would be disturbances in the camp. The Commandant didn't want any trouble and had withdrawn his permission.

That started a riot in our battalion. The great majority of the men were on our side, and they made it quite clear to the members of this small clique how they felt about it. The clique hadn't expected this sort of reaction; they sent one of their members to ask me to use my influence to calm my friends, and to say that they would sign a petition to the Commandant to let me deliver my lectures. What could I say to them? I told him that I didn't want to have anything to do with him or his friends.

A petition did go to the Commandant, with 679 signatures on it, and he renewed his permission.

The theatre was packed for my first lecture, on 12th July. Some of the members of the clique came along, no doubt expecting to hear a fiery revolutionary tirade. Of course there was no such thing; I imagine they must have sat there feeling rather silly. It was their doing that so much interest had been stirred up in my lectures, and that so many people had come to hear me.

* * *

The Bishop of London paid us a visit in the middle of July, and addressed us in the theatre. He wasn't very profound. He repeated the old story that God had sent the war as a punishment for our sins, so that we should repent and be better people. We had visits from all sorts of missionaries and religious cranks, who tried to win our souls. One distributed printed postcards addressed to "Christ who saves from sin", which we were to sign and send to the headquarters of some missionary society in London. We were flooded with religious tracts, even from Germany. One day returning from the compound we found a German tract on each bed — "Three letters. An open word and an earnest greeting to our fellow-countrymen in the British prison camps." The three letters were from a German clergyman, a German woman and a German doctor; their purpose was to warn us against sexual perversion. I wish the lady had heard some of the remarks our men made about her well-intentioned but very stupid exhortations.

The whole atmosphere in the camp was becoming unbearable. Petty annoyances and red tape regulations were heaped upon us, sometimes quite senseless, as when we found a notice on the board one day telling us to inform our correspondents that they must keep their letters brief, and that beginning a fortnight from the date of the announcement no letters would be delivered to us if they exceeded the stipulated length. Now the censor knew that there was no chance of passing this information to our people in time; he usually kept our letters for a fortnight before he forwarded them. Besides, many of us got letters from abroad which took longer than a fortnight in transmission. Max Grohe, who was in my company, used to live in the Argentine. He had a small business there. He fell ill, and decided to go to Berlin for an operation. He sailed in July 1914; the war broke out while he was on the boat. The British stopped his ship, and he found himself interned. Three weeks after the announcement had been made he was informed that three letters had arrived from his wife in the Argentine, but he couldn't have them because they were too long. Grohe pointed out that even in peacetime it took three weeks for a letter to reach London from the Argentine, so that his wife couldn't have had his warning in time. It was useless. Orders were orders. Grohe didn't get his letters. Anyone who has any idea what letters from home meant to us, what they must mean to anyone in our position, will understand how this arbitrary action affected us. Repeated acts of this kind roused the indignation of the prisoners to boiling point, and an explosion seemed imminent.

I felt sick of it all; I began to consider the possibility of escape. It didn't seem difficult to get out of Alexandra Palace. The difficulty was to find a hiding place outside. The police wouldn't rest, of course, till they got hold of me again. I didn't like the idea of being cooped up in some hole for the duration of the war, and endangering my friends who would agree to risk giving me shelter. What I wanted was to find out if there was any chance to get out of England into a neutral country. If there was, I could work out a plan of escape.

I would have to talk it over with some of my comrades outside. How? It wasn't possible during visits. I couldn't even hint at it. I could try smuggling a letter out. But suppose it was intercepted? It would cause a lot of trouble to anyone to whom I addressed it. Somebody would have to slip out of the Palace at night, meet my friends, and return to the camp with his information the same night, before we had to get up, before we were counted. I couldn't go myself, because people in the East End knew me too well, and I was afraid of being recognised.

I spoke to August Ludolf Arndt, a young Hamburger whom I had got to know at Olympia. I had found him devoted to our cause. He was intelligent and educated, calm and self-possessed, brave and daring, and I could trust him to the death. He begged me to let him make the attempt. He said he had been contemplating escape himself. He had discovered some loose floor-boards in the washroom. He took them up one night and found a hollow space in which a man could move about comfortably. He hadn't explored further; he was afraid to do so unless he had someone there to stand by to warn him if anyone was coming.

We went to look at the place. We had to take a candle to light our way. We found there was a passage under the flooring that led straight to the underground railway. Before the war Alexandra Palace had its own underground station, for the crowds coming to the exhibition. Since it was turned into an internment camp the trains had stopped running. We explored further another night, and found the passage led into the disused railway tunnel, and that we could make our way out from there to Wood Green Station. From Wood Green Station we could easily get into the street through the air shaft. Things were more promising than we had expected.

Arndt knew little English. I made him repeat my home address until he knew it by heart. Then I explained to him very carefully how to get there from Wood Green without having to ask the way.

He left Alexandra Palace at 10pm on the night of 14th July. I reckoned he should reach my home before midnight. He should be there for about an hour. He need only communicate what I had in mind. If they hit on a plan, my friends would find a way to get in touch with me. It was very important that Arndt should be back in the camp before daybreak, in time for the counting.

I lay awake all night waiting for him. He didn't come. The signal to get up sounded. We would soon be counted and his absence would be discovered. Suppose he had been delayed? He couldn't get into the palace by day. He would have to hang around somewhere and try to come back at night. We must somehow prevent his absence being noticed. It could be done. During the counting one of us who had already been counted could slip round among those who were still being counted, to make up the number. We did manage it.

We repeated the trick in the evening. The trouble was that our company leader had noticed it. He hadn't said anything in the morning, nor in the evening, but he was worried that the authorities would find out and he would get the blame. About an hour after the counting he reported that Arndt was missing. The Commandant wasn't in the building at the time. When he returned and was told the whole place was in an uproar.

It was just after 10pm. Most of us were asleep; the rule was bed at 9. Keys rattled, doors banged, cries of command were shouted, all the lights went on. The Commandant came with some of his officers and a company of soldiers and called for the battalion leader. They proceeded to Company 4. Our Company leader who had reported the missing man stood trembling. The Commandant raved at him. How had it happened! Where had the man got to! Why hadn't he seen him and stopped him! The Commandant slashed his cane about furiously across Arndt's bed, like a madman.

The whole enormous place with over a thousand people rudely wakened from their sleep was like a madhouse. Everybody wanted to know what was going on. Only our Company knew that Arndt was missing. Some of the men made nasty remarks about the Commandant's behaviour. It made him madder still. He ordered some of the men to be put in the guard room for insubordination. That made things worse. It was past eleven before the Commandant left us muttering wild threats of what he was going to do to us.

In the morning it started all over again. We were not allowed to leave the hall. The compound was out of bounds. An hour later an announcement was made that we would be confined to battalion quarters for three days. Visits and letters were being stopped for three weeks.

That brought things to a climax. The prisoners had been feeling sullen and resentful for a long time. Now they were in open revolt.

I discussed the situation with my friends, and it was decided that all Company leaders should resign; the Commandant should be told that they could not under such conditions take responsibility for keeping order among the prisoners. Some of the Company leaders didn't like it, but the feeling in the whole camp was so strong that they could not resist it.

Just before midday a detachment of soldiers marched into the hall with loaded rifles. The Commandant strode behind them, took up his position and tried to speak to us. But there was such a roar of protest that it drowned his voice completely. I felt this was getting dangerous. It was a good thing to show the Commandant that there was a limit to what we would put up with, but we didn't want any shooting. Some of us tried to restore order, and we succeeded.

The old man looked at the angry mob unmoved, without the flicker of an eyelash. When we got quiet restored, he addressed us quietly, emphasising every word. It was clear from his first words that he was in a conciliatory mood. Instead of repeating his threats of the night before he spoke to us like a human being.

I could hardly believe it was the same man. He said he had ordered this punishment not as a collective penalty for Arndt's escape, but because we had insulted his officers. He had full power to enforce his orders. But he had no intention of using it against defenceless people if there was any chance of achieving the same result through an understanding.

His speech made a good impression on us all. When he finished he asked if we had any complaints. He looked at one man who was facing him. He fixed him with his eye and said: "Have you any complaint?"

Luckily the man he had picked on, Munding, was not a fool and he was not afraid to speak. He told him straight out that we were not soldiers but civilians, and that was what we wanted to be treated like. He said we were not satisfied with the internal administration and wanted a new election of our captains. About Arndt he said it was impossible to punish a thousand people who hadn't any idea of what he was doing, for the act of one man. We were not supposed to be guards there.

When Munding had finished the Commandant said the British government considered us war prisoners because we had all done army service We made it clear at once that hundreds of us had never worn uniform or handled a gun. That surprised him.

In the end the Commandant cancelled all punishments, and ordered fresh elections for our administration, to be held that same afternoon. He said he would discuss the other questions with our battalion leader.

He was cheered as he left the hall with his officers and soldiers. Everybody was delighted. We sat down to our midday meal feeling much happier. Immediately after the meal we started preparations for the new elections. My friends urged me to let my name go forward as battalion leader. It was not the thing I wanted. But I couldn't get out of standing as candidate for Company leader. The whole company insisted that I should. They said that if there was to be a reorganisation of our administration I must be in it to help to reorganise it. When the votes were counted I had polled 96 votes out of the total 98.

Kollin felt that he stood no chance of being confirmed in his post as battalion leader, and he refused to stand. Munding was elected by a big majority. Half the old captains were re-elected. There were six new Company leaders. Munding informed the Commandant of the result, and we held our first meeting of the captains immediately after.

Just before bedtime an English corporal told us that Arndt had been arrested that afternoon near Alexandra Palace, and was in the guard room now. I had been thinking about him all the time, wondering why he hadn't come back. I had never doubted his intention to return as we had arranged. I was sure that whatever had happened it was not his fault.

In the morning I was notified that Arndt would get his meals from our battalion kitchen, and that as he belonged to my Company I would have to attend to that. I was glad because it might give me a chance to have a word with him. I took his breakfast to the guard room. The soldiers on guard were sitting round a table busy with some game they were playing. Arndt sat on his plank bed in the corner. I gave him my hand. He had no idea of course that I had been elected Company leader, and he was surprised to see me there. We couldn't say much just then, but as I had to attend him three times a day I felt sure that I would find an opportunity sooner or later. Bit by bit I managed to piece together his story.

When he had got out of Alexandra Palace and found himself safely in the street he had in spite of my detailed instructions lost his way. We had forgotten the blackout. He didn't arrive therefore till 2am. Milly was wakened out of her sleep by his knock. She wondered who it could be at that time of night. She opened the door and was surprised to find a strange young man. He told her he had a message from me. She let him in, and he explained what had brought him. By then day was breaking, and he could not have got back into Alexandra Palace. He stayed in the room all day. At ten o'clock at night Milly and one of our comrades got on a bus with Arndt and took him to Wood Green. There he disappeared.

Arndt had actually got into Alexandra Palace. But when he came to the place where the loose boards in the wash room were and was lifting one of them to make his way in he heard the alarm. It was just when the Commandant had arrived and was told that Arndt was missing. He waited in his hiding place for a while, but when the alarm did not subside he slipped out of the Palace again, thinking he would return the following night. Somehow he managed to escape detection all day. When he returned at night the passage had been discovered and blocked up. He made his way back into the street, and walked about openly near the Palace, in order to get himself arrested.

* * *

Things were running more smoothly in the camp. The men had confidence in their new captains and in their battalion leader. The question was how the new battalion leader and the captains would get on with the Commandant. He was an old soldier, who had served in India for years, a typical peppery Colonel, who had contracted a lot of illness in India and took it out of us when he was in pain.

The day after our elections, the Commandant came with his officers to see the new Company leaders. He stopped in front of me and asked my name. He must have remembered my interview with him in the orderly room. When I told him he said: "I hope you will help me to keep order in the battalion." I answered: "I'll do my best." He went away. Then he turned back, and asked me what my next lecture in the theatre would be about. I said there would be a series about Tolstoy. Was I a follower of Tolstoy? I said that I looked up to Tolstoy as one of the great men of our time, but I didn't accept everything he said. He nodded, and asked me to submit to him a short synopsis in English of each lecture.

The next morning I had to appear in the orderly room with one of the men in my Company. He had received a parcel from his family in Germany, which among other things included a jar of honey. There was a note in the honey, with a few intimate words of the kind that people don't like to trust to a letter which has to pass the censor. It was not unusual for such notes to be found in parcels. Generally the parcel was confiscated. The Commandant addressed the man sternly: "We found a note hidden in a jar of honey in your parcel. What is it all about? What secret messages are passing between you? How do you explain it?"

The man said he knew nothing at all about it. It was the first parcel he had received. The Commandant cried angrily: "Your parcel is confiscated. And I am going to have you punished. We must teach your people not to do such things!"

Then he turned to me, and went on: "I am only doing my duty. Would you do any different in my position?" I hadn't expected that question. I answered: "I wouldn't have confiscated his parcel. I would have got him to write to his family to explain that such things get him into trouble, and they shouldn't do it again. You heard the man say this is his first parcel from home. He couldn't have known about the note. You have shown him how efficiently parcels are examined here. If the note hadn't been found the man wouldn't be in front of you now."

The old man smiled. Plainly he was in a good mood. "Very well," he said, "you can have your parcel this time, and I won't punish you for it. But write to your family at once and tell them not to try such tricks again. You won't get away with it so easily next time."

This experience proved to me once more that it was better to stand up to the old man and tell him what you thought. He didn't like people who cringed. When he was in a tolerable mood he was reasonable, and fair. But one needed tact to deal with him. I am not sure how tactful our new battalion leader Munding was in his dealings with the Commandant. I doubt whether he was. He was a straightforward man, an honest man, a man of character. But he had never lived in England, and knew nothing of English ways and of the English mind. He was also a German nationalist, which made him misunderstand the Commandant's motives, and created mutual mistrust. I must say that though Munding and I were at different ends of the pole politically, we respected each other, and our personal relations were most friendly.

Arndt appeared before a court martial on 20th July. I had been seeing him and speaking to him every day. He told me the Commandant had visited him and had been very kind. The soldiers were very decent to him. The court martial was composed of several officers of our camp and a representative of the War Office. His defence counsel was Major Mott, who was the good angel of Alexandra Palace. With the exception of a few fanatical German patriots everybody in the Camp loved and respected Major Mott. He always had a kind word for everyone.

Of course Arndt gave no hint of my part in his escape, or of his visit to Milly. He said he had a sick mother in Hamburg, and he had received news that both his brothers in the German army were missing. He had wanted to break out of confinement. He had no plan of escape; all he wanted was to be outside alone for a while.

The proceedings lasted less than an hour. The court's decision was to be announced later. Major Mott had made a passionate and very human plea on his behalf. We hoped the sentence would not be severe. On the morning of 28th July all the captains of all three battalions were summoned to the pagoda. Arndt was brought in under armed escort, and the Commandant read out the sentence. 168 days imprisonment with hard labour. Then Arndt was taken away. I spoke to him afterwards when I took in his food. He said he didn't mind; he rather welcomed being alone for a few months in a quiet cell. We shook hands and said goodbye. He was taken to prison the same day.

We hadn't expected Arndt to get such a severe sentence. It may have been because the day he appeared before the court martial three other prisoners in Battalion C had escaped. They were caught six days later in an old barn seventeen miles from London, and were brought back to the camp. Arndt did not serve his full sentence. He left prison three months later for another internment camp.

My office as captain brought me in touch with people in a different way than when I was one of the rank and file. Our Company 4 was a happy company. The whole camp called us the Red Company. The fanatical German patriots hated us, but many in other companies envied us, and said they wished they could join us. Sometimes one of the other captains asked me if I would take one of his men with whom he couldn't get on. I never refused such a request. And I was never sorry for it. I found some excellent men among these transfers. A thousand people living together in one place can't help getting on each other's nerves, especially when they are prisoners, and can never get out of the place.

One day I accepted a new man in my Company. It was the same Max Grohe who had been refused his wife's letter from Buenos Aires because it was too long. He had since then wandered into three other companies, and had quarrelled with each of his Company leaders. Then he came back to us. Grohe who was born in Berlin was a man who couldn't keep his mouth shut. When he was in a good mood he was a fine fellow. He had a sense of fun, and used to keep us in roars of laughter. But when he was in low spirits or his illness got him down he was unbearable. I gave him the plank bed next to mine. For a few days he was all right. Then he got obstinate. He was on duty that day with another man, and their job was to scrub the floor. We had a rota for two men in each company to do that in turn. Grohe had often done it before. This time he flatly refused. The other man begged him to get on with it. He swore at him, till the man lost his temper and flung down his scrubbing brush and went away to complain to me. He said he wouldn't pick the brush up if Grohe didn't do his share.

I found Grohe sitting on his bed. "Why don't you get on with your job?" I asked him. "Tell the old man to get one of his soldiers to do the scrubbing! I'm fed up."

"My dear Grohe," I said. "You know very well that the old man will do nothing of the kind. If we all behaved like you we'd be up to our knees in dirt. Don't act the fool. Do what everybody else must do."

He didn't move. "Nothing doing," he snapped.

"Very well," I said. "If you won't do it I will." Then I took off my coat, rolled up my sleeves, picked up the scrubbing brush and got down to work. He hadn't expected that. He jumped up, snatched the brush from my hand and cried: "I won't let you do it!" "But if you won't do it, and you won't let me do it, who is going to do it?" "All right, I'll do it," he said. I never had any more trouble with Grohe.

There was an engineer named Hoffmann in our Company. He was a Rhinelander, and a very hard nut to crack. He had embittered the lives of several Company leaders before he came to me. His job had been building bridges in Siam before the war. He was on his way to Europe for an operation for hernia when he was captured on the ship by the British. I liked the man. He had brought away several cases of interesting objects from Siam, and when he was in a generous mood, which was often, he presented some of them to people in the camp. He told us many stories about his life in Siam. He was a very good chap. His close friend was Stemmler, an adventurous character, who had been in Buenos Aires when the war broke out. He was romantically patriotic; so he immediately decided to make his way to Germany to fight. His ship was stopped at Gibraltar and he was interned. Both Hoffmann and Stemmler attended my lectures regularly and discussed them with me afterwards. They were impulsive, headstrong, active men, who found the enforced idleness of the camp intolerable. They often got up to some trick or other to put a little excitement into this monotonous existence.

One day they wrote a letter to the Commandant that he should release them or have them shot, because they couldn't stand this inactive life any longer. Max Grohe couldn't resist adding his signature to such a letter. Hoffman gave it to me to pass on to the Commandant. I didn't know what was in the letter. I gave it to the battalion leader Munding, who afterwards told me laughingly what it contained. He treated it as a joke. He said he had no intention of placing it before the Commandant, but somehow it had got mixed up with a batch of papers that Munding handed to the Commandant's secretary. As the Commandant wasn't there at the time it came into Major Mott's hands. In the afternoon Major Mott asked me to let him see Hoffman, Stemmler and Grohe. I immediately thought of the letter. None of the three knew a word of English, so I had to act as their interpreter. Major Mott spoke to them kindly and patiently, as he always did to everybody. He pleaded with them to be calm, to wait, the war wouldn't last for ever. When he had finished he asked me to go with him to his room. He told me that he was very worried. He didn't want the three men to do anything foolish or desperate. Did I know their financial position? I said that Hoff'mann and Stemmler had a little money; Grohe had nothing. He gave me a large packet of cigarettes and half a crown each for them. The three were waiting for me anxiously. The Major's words had affected them very much, and when I produced the cigarettes and the three half crowns they didn't know what to say. They accepted the cigarettes, but they wouldn't take the money. When I wanted to return it to the Major he said he would rather I distributed it among some others who needed it. That is what I did.

The Major must have discussed the matter with the Commandant. One day I was ordered to bring the three men to the Commandant's office. He asked me if I knew what had made them write a letter like that. I told him their story. How Grohe had been on his way to Germany for an operation, which he had never had because of the war, and he was therefore in constant pain. How Hoffmann also was going to Europe for an operation when his ship was stopped and he was interned. He had contracted malaria in Siam, and he often had severe attacks in the camp. He had asked for an extra blanket, which the doctor had refused.

The Commandant listened to me carefully. Then he addressed the three. He exhorted them not to lose their courage, to accept their fate like brave men. He could not give them their freedom. That was not in his power. But he would try to make things a little easier for them. Hoffmann declared dramatically that if he couldn't have his freedom he demanded that he should be shot.

I was afraid the Commandant would take it badly. He didn't. But I was very much relieved when we left his room at last. The same day Hoffmann received two extra blankets, and a few days later Grohe was sent to the German hospital in London, where he was operated on successfully. In five weeks he was back in the camp, quite well.

On 5th August, the English papers reported the fall of Warsaw. The German patriots in the camp went mad with joy. The fools thought the war had been decided by that, and that Germany could now dictate peace terms to the world. It made me very sad. I would have preferred the isolation of a prison cell to those scenes in the camp. On top of that I read Maeterlinck's hysterical call for a crusade against everything German. And then Hauptmann's answer to Maeterlinck's outburst, praising German *Kultur* and saying that German soldiers were going into battle with copies of *Faust* and *Zarathustra* in their knapsacks. How utterly stupid it all was. I seemed to have been born out of my time.

* * *

When we had come to Alexandra Palace, many of us had hoped that we would be given a chance to do some useful work, which lack of space had made impossible on the Royal Edward. But when the opportunity came it caused trouble between the Commandant and our battalion leader Munding, and nearly started a riot in the camp. The War Office sent an instruction to draw up a list of mechanics and iron workers among the prisoners who would be prepared to work at their craft outside the camp. We were quite sure that it meant war work. When the Commandant asked the three battalion leaders to prepare such a list, Munding said that his conscience wouldn't allow it. He was the only one who refused, The Commandant lost his temper and told Munding that if he didn't cooperate he couldn't remain as battalion leader. Thereupon Munding took off his armband, and said that he was quitting.

When the news got round the battalion things looked ugly. We were afraid of an open mutiny. In the end the Commandant decided to drop the whole idea. He sent for Munding and told him he didn't want him to do anything that conflicted with his conscience, and he asked him to return to his post as battalion leader. Munding agreed.

The first week in September there was fresh trouble. One of our men, Schmiedt, escaped from the camp. He had for years been Captain of a Dutch boat between Holland and England. He had been given permission to go to the German hospital in Dalston with another prisoner to have his eyes treated. He disappeared on the way.

The Captain of Company 3 to which Schmiedt belonged was a clergyman also named Schmidt, a good, decent man, who had before the war been in charge of a small German church in England. I liked the man, and spent a good deal of time with him. He came to all my lectures. He was a convinced pacifist, a Christian in the Tolstoyan sense. He was one of the most honest men I knew. Certainly he could have known nothing about Schmiedt's escape. But he was supposed as his Company leader to report immediately that he was missing. He hadn't done that. He said he didn't like acting the informer. When the Commandant heard about it he came storming into the battalion and swore at Pastor Schmidt.

"Why didn't you report to me at once?"

"Because I don't feel it is part of my duty to act as a policeman." The next morning Major Mott sent for me and asked me to go for a walk with him round the terrace. He wanted to know what I thought about the recent incidents, meaning Munding and Pastor Schmidt. I said I thought both men had been right. The job of the battalion leader and of the Company leaders was to attend to the internal administration. They were not supposed to be informers.

"How would you have acted," I asked him, "if you found yourself in the same position in a German camp for British prisoners of war?"

He admitted that he would have acted as they had. Then he asked me if I thought that people who were placed as we were had a right to try to escape. "Most certainly we have," I said.

It so happened that a few weeks before two English civilian prisoners had escaped from the German internment camp for British prisoners at Ruheleben. They crossed Germany on foot and got into Holland. The English press had praised their daring. I asked Major Mott if there was any difference between them and Captain Schmiedt. He didn't answer for a while. Then he said that the Commandant couldn't be expected to take no notice of the escapes, and that he had to do something to stop them. I

189

pointed out that there were few places from which people couldn't escape if they tried. People had escaped from the Bastille, and from the leads of Venice. Why shouldn't it be possible from Alexandra Palace?

Major Mott looked me straight in the face, and said: "Yes, but the Commandant is worried about something else. You and the other Company captains can move about more freely than the other prisoners. You can get to places where they can't go. It would be easier for you to plan an escape. Would you abuse the trust placed in you to escape?"

I answered: "I can speak only for myself. It has never been my way to misuse the trust placed in me. If I wanted to escape I would first surrender my position."

"That's what I wanted to know," he said. "It's what I expected from you."

I immediately told Munding about the conversation.

The Commandant was a very sick man at this time. He was in constant pain, and therefore very irritable. I felt sorry for the old man, but it was wrong to keep a whole camp of three thousand people subjected to the whims and caprices of a man plagued by illness and pain.

Munding had a clash with him almost every day. Until finally he said he couldn't stand it any longer, and he resigned. Very soon after a batch of our people were sent to the internment camp on the Isle of Man. Munding was one of them; so was Pastor Schmidt. The Commandant hadn't forgiven the Pastor for Captain Schmiedt's escape.

* * *

When Munding resigned I was again besieged from every side to become battalion leader. I was most unwilling to take a position where I would probably find myself in daily conflict with the Commandant. If he had been a man like Major Mott, I would have accepted gladly. I told the men in my battalion that it was impossible. What I could do in the internal administration as Company leader I would do, but that was all. They elected a man named Trepte as battalion leader.

The batch of prisoners who had been sent to the Isle of Man included some of my best friends, and I missed them very much. Were it not for the fact that Milly and Fermin and all my dear ones were in London I would have asked to be sent to the Isle of Man to join them. My only satisfaction was that I could go on delivering my lectures. I had kept them to purely literary subjects, and I had met with no difficulties from the authorities. Sometimes, not often, one of the censors would come in to listen to what I said. That was all. I had just started a new series on the Romantic School in Germany. Suddenly a new censor named Welton started raising objections. He was a hypocrite and a bigot, who kept us supplied with religious tracts by some of his pet societies. He kept poking his nose into all our affairs, and worrying the men to tell him about their private lives, and about their families.

Welton's first clash with me was over a parcel of books I had been sent. He refused to give them to me; he said they were all socialist books, which couldn't be allowed in the camp. I told him I would appeal to the Commandant; then he gave me the books at once. After that he had his knife into me. One of the men in my Company complained to me a few days later that Welton had confiscated his copy of Zola's *Germinal*, saying that it was an immoral book. I went to Welton and asked him to return the book. He refused. I got the owner of the book to write a complaint to the Commandant, and the book was returned immediately.

Then Welton tried to stop one of my lectures. I had announced my subject as E. Th. A. Hoffmann. Welton drew the Commandant's attention to a new War Office regulation that no lectures on modern German literature could be given in the camps. It was a reprisal for a German order forbidding lectures on modern English literature in the German POW camps. The Commandant called me to his office and showed me the War Office regulation. I asked if Hoffmann, who died in 1822, belonged to modern German literature. The Commandant threw an angry look at Welton, and said that I could deliver the lecture.

More of our people were being transferred to the Isle of Man, and new internees were brought to our camp at Alexandra Palace, to take their place. They were mostly Germans who had lived in England and had been exposed for a long time to the continued insults and humiliations of the anti-German propaganda. They had been intimidated by their experiences outside, and were fearful and anxious. They nearly all had families in London, and were terribly afraid of being sent to the Isle of Man, where their families could not visit them. The military authorities naturally took advantage of their fears by tightening the discipline and transporting anyone who started trouble to the Isle of Man.

Owing to the continued transports to the Isle of Man the composition of our camp kept changing the whole time. We always had new people to deal with. The battalion leader's job was therefore not enviable. Our new battalion leader Trepte was not big enough for the job. He was always getting into hot water with the Commandant and the other officers and with our own people. He kept coming to me to help him out of his difficulties.

Welton was particularly nasty. It was he who was responsible for the wholesale deportations to the Isle of Man. Whole Companies were sent there with no attempt at selection. Previously special consideration had been given to those with families in London. Now that no longer mattered. They were sent to the Isle of Man like the rest. It often happened that their wives came to visit them at Alexandra Palace only to be told that they had been shipped to the Isle of Man that morning or the day before.

Winter started early that year; the central heating in our battalion quarters wasn't working, and we froze in that vast space. The men lay about all day on their plank beds with their blankets over them. Many went down with bronchitis and lung trouble; there was no room in the sick bays, so they had to stay in the battalion quarters. It was terrible at night; the coughing and groaning kept us all awake.

The camp began preparing for our second Christmas celebration. We decided to give the men at least a good dinner, and we started collecting the money for it among ourselves. Some of our well-to-do people contributed, and we arranged several special performances by our concert group to help to raise more money. There were a great many good German musicians in London before the war. Nearly all were interned; those at Alexandra Palace had formed themselves into a very fine orchestra. The Commandant was a music lover and helped the orchestra all he could. He himself never missed a performance.

But our men felt depressed. They were worried about their families, and about the future. We spent a most unhappy Christmas. New Year's Day came. The Commandant had given us permission to stay up till half an hour after midnight, to have a small New Year's party.

I was feeling quite happy that day. I had just received a number of letters from Kropotkin, Keel, Emma Goldman and other friends. And I had Milly and Malatesta to visit me on New Year's Day.

Malatesta was sure that the war wouldn't last very long now. He said Germany couldn't stand the blockade much longer. Germany's defeat would mean the collapse of the old regime, it would mean revolution. There would be revolutions in other countries. All Europe would be exhausted by the war. There could be no question of victors and defeated.

He was careful to add that if America came into the war things would turn out differently. Then Germany's defeat would be overwhelming. She would be crushed. The Allies would emerge triumphant. France would have a nationalist-clericalist revival, which would last at least five or ten years; it would hold back the whole European revolution for a long time.

At our New Year's party the men insisted that I must speak. My letters and my talk with Malatesta had put me in a good humour, and I spoke to them hopefully; I tried with some success to stir these poor people out of their dejection.

The first day of the New Year was a sad one in the camp. One of our men, Michaelis, a fisherman, received a letter from his wife that their four sons had been killed in battle, all in the same week. The wife of one of his sons had gone mad when she heard the news and she was in a lunatic asylum. The man didn't say a word. He just sat dumb. It cast a heavy cloud over the whole camp.

More people arrived at Alexandra Palace. After each new German air raid on England, more Germans were arrested and interned. I found that several of my old German comrades had come into our battalion.

They arrested not only Germans and Austrians. There were Spaniards, Argentinians, Russians and Americans in these new contingents, even an Englishman, who was born in Birmingham.

They had all been taken off neutral boats. Their papers had not satisfied the authorities. It was very easy to get oneself into an internment camp. It was harder to get out again. We had an Argentinian four months in the camp, a Dutchman five months and a Russian seven months before their consuls in London got them released. The Englishman, who had been on his way back to England from America, took his internment philosophically. He said he didn't mind it. He was quite willing to wait till they decided to release him. It might be better, he said, to be a live Englishman in an internment camp with Germans than a dead Englishman buried in Flanders.

In February the Commandant was very ill, and spent whole weeks in bed. Major Mott was in charge. Everything went smoothly under him. We had no trouble at all.

One day they told me that the Commandant wanted to see me. I went to his home. The doctor was there, and there was a nurse. The doctor said that I mustn't tire him; he asked me not to stay more than ten minutes. The nurse showed me into the sick room. The old man smiled faintly when he saw me. He looked very ill. He was not the same man who used to storm and rave, and despite his age walked quickly, with a firm, springy step, through the whole camp.

I asked how he felt and said I hoped he would soon be better. He shook his head and said it was not likely at his age. He asked me how things were going in my battalion. I told him that nothing had happened since he was away. He smiled. He told me that he had been thinking a great deal about us while he was lying ill in bed. Then suddenly he said:

"I always tried to do my best for you. Not many of you understood that. Of course, I could not satisfy everybody. I wish I could. My hands are tied. I can't always do what I would like. I am sorry for you people. I know what it means to be torn away from your families, and your normal life. It is hardest for the older ones. We must do all we can to save them from falling into despair."

I was amazed. Had he called me here only to tell me that? Or was there something else he still wanted to say to me? I was moved by the very human way he spoke about us.

I told him that there were many of us who knew that he meant well, but he could hardly blame us if people who found themselves shut up like convicts for no fault of their own sometimes lost patience. That seemed to please him; he smiled. Then the nurse came back, and said I must go now. He nodded, and gave me his hand, something he had never done before.

He was up and about again in a couple of weeks. For the first few days the nurse walked with him round the terrace. Then he came into the camp to have a look at us. His illness seemed to have softened him. But not for long. As soon as he was himself again he was the same martinet as before. He swore and cursed, and it was impossible to please him.

Our battalion leader Trepte was having a lot of trouble. The men blamed him for everything that went wrong in the camp. The War Office had cut our rations, as in all the other camps. He became the scapegoat. But many of the other complaints about him had a sounder basis, since he was not the kind of man who would stand up to anyone. Welton walked over him. There was constant friction, and in the end Trepte decided to chuck it.

As soon as the news got round that the Commandant had accepted Trepte's resignation everybody came to try to persuade me to take the job.

I felt I had no right to refuse again. The election was held the same day. I got 898 votes, with 87 against, and 13 abstentions. I wasn't as happy about it as my electorate was. I was too much aware of the responsibility I had assumed. And I wondered how long, with all the continuing difficulties in the camp I could expect to count on their support. As it happened I remained battalion leader for two whole years, the duration of my stay in the camp and in England.

After my election I went to see the Commandant. He said he was very happy indeed to have me in that position; he hoped that we would manage between us to establish a pleasant friendly atmosphere in the camp.

I thought it was my duty to make it quite clear to him that first of all I was the representative of the men in my battalion, and that I had to look after their interests, and to retain their confidence. I said I would never bother him with anything that I could settle myself. But in matters requiring his consent I would need some cooperation. I would not assume my duties unless I could count on that. My candour seemed to please him. He told me that as soon as he had been informed of my election he had telephoned Scotland Yard for my record. "Of course, I knew your political opinions," he explained, "but I thought I ought to know what Scotland Yard had to say about you." He paused. "They said Rocker has been for years one of the most active anarchists in the country, but we know nothing to his personal discredit. That was all I wanted to know. Your political beliefs are not my concern. What matters to me is your personal character."

I asked for a new election of all the Company leaders, so that we should know whether they still had the confidence of those who elected them. Almost all were re-elected.

Our first business was to see if we could do anything to improve our food situation. The size of our rations was fixed by the British government, we couldn't do anything about that. The United States Embassy still represented the interests of the Germans and Austrians in England. But sending complaints to them proved futile. However, if we got no increase in our rations, it would be something to make sure that we got our full rations. We knew that much of the food never got to us. There were some among our own people in every internment camp who had no compunction about abusing the confidence of their fellow prisoners, and robbed them of some of their food consignments for their own personal profit. It was one of the blackest and most shameful chapters in the story of our internment.

I suggested that we should elect someone who knew the food trade — we had a number of these in our camp — who would receive our government rations and check them to see that they were correct in quantity and quality. They would be immediately weighed on our kitchen scales; as a further safeguard we would have a daily rota of two men from each Company to keep watch in the kitchen. That would make it fairly certain that all the rations we got would come to us.

We had now been at Alexandra Palace for ten months, and we still had four armed sentries always on guard in our quarters. The guard was changed every two hours, with much stamping and clanging, which woke us from our sleep at night. We had made several unsuccessful attempts to get the Commandant to withdraw the sentries; I got him finally to agree.

About the middle of May our battalion received a fresh batch of prisoners, 206 priests and monks and missionaries who had been arrested in India, and after a long period of internment there had been transported to England, to be exchanged for English prisoners in Germany. Most of them wore long flowing beards, and with their monastic habits gave an altogether different appearance to the camp. There were several renowned scholars among them, men who besides their religious duties had been doing valuable ethnological and sociological research work in India. I found them extraordinarily interesting. It so happened that I was giving a series of lectures in the theatre on French socialism in the first half of the 19th century, and was dealing with the ideas of Buchez, Lamennais and Leroux. Naturally these Catholic socialist thinkers interested them. They followed me closely, and I saw some of them taking copious notes. Father Gebhard, a Jesuit, afterwards came to my small office to make my personal acquaintance. I felt attracted to the man. He had a fine intelligent face, a high forehead, long bushy beard, and wise eyes. He spent a lot of time with me, and talked about all sorts of things except religion, which he carefully avoided. He was a man of wide reading, completely at home in the field of socialism. He was extremely good company. His judgment of people and affairs was shrewd and to the point, and he had wit and humour. He had lived in India for many years, and knew all about the life there. There were not many people in the camp like him, and when he had to leave us I missed him terribly. His world was so utterly different from mine, yet we both felt a strong bond of understanding between us.

On 26th May the English press carried a long report of a speech by Lord Newton in parliament about the terrible conditions of the English civilian prisoners of war in the camp at Ruheleben, near Berlin; it alarmed the British public. I never doubted that the Germans treated their British prisoners badly. But the whole system of interning civilians for no other reason than their birth in an enemy country was wrong. Lord Newton said that a number of British civilian prisoners who had been released in exchange for German civilian prisoners in England had lost their reason. We had such cases too. It would be futile to record every one of them. Just before Lord Newton spoke, one of them, a man named Machner, had in a fit of madness, cut his throat with a razor. We had dozens of people in the camp who went mad and were put in lunatic asylums. There was Kaufmann, a ship's captain in Battalion A, who came to us a perfectly normal man. After a few months he started talking nonsense. He was quite insane, but the doctor refused to send him to a hospital. When he began to masturbate in public they finally put him in a lunatic asylum, and he died there. I remember Bonsel, an intelligent working man who had been a social democrat for years. He came to my lectures regularly, and we often discussed various subjects. Later, he became subject to fits of depression. One evening he came to me in a state of great agitation to tell me that his wife was having an affair with an English officer in our camp. When his wife came to visit him a few days later I made it my business to see her. She was such a faded poverty-stricken little thing, the most unlikely person to indulge in illicit love affairs. He reproached her because she came late. "It isn't my fault," she sobbed. "The fare is fourpence to come here. And I can't afford it. I have to walk part of the way." I was touched by the poor woman's plight, and tried to reason with Bonsel. In vain, his hallucinations became wilder. One morning Bonsel was missing at the count. We found him crouching in a corner. The next day he was raving mad. He was sent to a lunatic asylum and he died there.

I am no psychologist, but it seems to me that there is something quite wrong about the whole idea of imprisoning people who have done nothing themselves to deserve such punishment. After all, a criminal expects to be caught some time, and when he is sentenced he knows more or less when he will go free. We had no idea how long the war would last, and keep us imprisoned. The conditions of our internment were such that we were never free from anxiety, about ourselves, and about our families. It was all mad. But half the world had gone mad then, and we were only some of the victims of this world-wide madness.

Chapter 31

Milly is Arrested

On 29th June 1916, I was informed that our friend Thomas Keel, who published the English anarchist paper *Freedom*, had been sent to prison for three months under the Defence of the Realm Act, because of an article of his. It made me fear for the future of the *Arbeter Fraint*, which had been appearing regularly since my arrest, without changing its anti-war policy.

On 24th July, Milly came to see me with her youngest sister Rose, and told me that Shapiro, Linder and Lenoble had been arrested because of an article in the *Arbeter Fraint*. I was afraid Milly might be drawn into the affair. When we parted, I had a feeling that we wouldn't meet again for a long time.

On 28th July Shapiro, Linder and Lenoble, as editor, publisher and compositor of the *Arbeter Fraint*, appeared at Thames Police Court. Shapiro was Russian, Linder Austrian and Lenoble Romanian. There was also a charge against Edward Ryde, who printed the *Arbeter Fraint*; he was not connected with the movement; he was a commercial printer. Police Inspector MacGrath said Shapiro, Linder and Lenoble were known anarchists, and it was impossible to count on their loyalty to the country. The only witness for the defence was Professor Waller, Director of the Physiological Laboratory of London University, whose private secretary Shapiro had been for a number of years. He gave him an excellent personal character.

Shapiro got six months, Linder three and Lenoble one month. Ryde was fined £50. The police took away the *Arbeter Fraint's* type, and sealed the offices of the paper.

On 29th July, Milly was to have visited me. Instead our Dutch comrade Staamer came to tell me that Milly had been arrested at our home the previous day. My son Rudolf had also been arrested the same day at his place of work, and was in the internment camp at Stratford. I was worried about our young son Fermin, who was only eight then.

I had been expecting this to happen, yet when it did happen it was a terrible blow to me. It was worse because I was myself a prisoner and couldn't lift a finger to do anything.

The evening papers carried the report of Milly's arrest, so that the whole camp soon knew about it. People who meant well, came to try to comfort me, and it only made me feel worse. I wanted to get away from everybody, to be left alone, and as my duties permitted me to go to parts of the Alexandra Park grounds beyond the barbed wire entanglements, I spent hours on end in the Chestnut Avenue, where I was not disturbed.

I was in despair. My work for years past seemed to have been destroyed. Milly was arrested, my son was interned, my friends were prisoners. I thought bitterly of the German super-patriots in the camp who had accused me of being in the pay of the British government to conduct anti-German propaganda.

I asked the Commandant if there was any chance of having my son transferred from Stratford to Alexandra Palace. He said he couldn't do anything himself, but if I sent a request to the War Office he would support it. It went off the same day.

The *Herald*, edited by George Lansbury, which later became the *Daily Herald*, said in its report about Milly's arrest: "The authorities have suppressed the *Arbeter Freint*. Milly Rocker who was connected with the paper was arrested and taken to Vine Street Police Station. So far as is known no definite charge has been made against her. Many of her friends fear she may be interned without any trial or any charge being brought against her. The East End trade unionists who know the work her husband and she have done for trade unionism must do their utmost to secure her a fair and open trial. We suggest that local Members of Parliament be asked to put questions relative to her case to the Home Secretary and Prime Minister."

On 26th August, the *Herald* again wrote about "The Case of Milly Witcop": "We are asked to call public attention to the arrest and detention of Milly Witcop, who as readers know, was arrested on 29th July and taken to Vine Street Police Station, where neither her friends nor solicitor were allowed to interview her until special permission was obtained from Scotland Yard. Apparently she was kept at Vine Street Police Station for six whole days, and then removed to Holloway. We are informed that no charge has been brought against her, and that her friends have been told that no charge will be brought against her. We hope her East End friends particularly will write not only to their Members of Parliament but to the Home Secretary and ask that some definite charge shall be brought against her if she is to be detained in prison any longer. We ask this because there is a grave suspicion abroad that she has been put under lock and key because of her socialist activities and her appeals on behalf of Russian refugees."

On 5th August, I received a letter from Milly dated from Vine Street Police Station. There wasn't much in the letter, but it was wonderful to hear from her. Then I was told that she had been transferred to Holloway Prison. The same afternoon my son Rudolf arrived at Alexandra Palace. We were both very happy to be together.

My friends outside were doing all they could to get a public trial for Milly, which was after all only what Shapiro, Linder and Lenoble had been given. Kropotkin had intervened for her. He sent me, on 4th September, a long friendly letter about his efforts for Milly, and assured me that though we differed so much in our views about the war he still considered me among his dearest friends.

On 23rd August Mr Joseph King, a Liberal MP, asked the Home Secretary, Herbert Samuel (later Lord Samuel) in the House of Commons if he was aware that Milly Witcop-Rocker had been arrested on 29th July, and was in Holloway Prison, treated as a criminal without any charge having been made against her. The Home Secretary's answer was that Milly Witcop-Rocker was arrested in the interests of public security under the Defence of the Realm Act.

Our friends put the case in the hands of a solicitor, who saw Milly at Holloway. He found that she was accused on three counts, her relations with the enemy alien Rocker, her relations with the enemy alien Linder, and her efforts to prevent Russian nationals joining the British Army. The solicitor's statement contained some glaring untruths, among them that Milly had never worked for the *Arbeter Fraint*. Milly was outraged when she saw it and was determined to repudiate it.

On 28th August, Milly appeared at Westminster before the Advisory Committee appointed to hear such cases.

She was asked: "Do you know Rudolf Rocker?" "Of course," she said, "he is my husband for the last sixteen years." "Where is he?" "Under arrest." "Do you know S. Linder?" "Yes, he is my comrade." "What do you mean by comrade?" "He belongs to the same anarchist group as I do." "Where is he now?" "Under arrest." "Do you know Mr Shapiro?" "Yes. He is my comrade." "And where is Mr Shapiro?" "Under arrest." "You know Mr Lenoble?" "Yes." "Where is Mr Lenoble?" "Under arrest." "I think you also know Thomas Keel and Lilian Woolfe." "Of course." "Where are they both now?" "As far as I know under arrest." "Do you know Guy Aldred?" "Yes. He is my brother-in-law." "Where is Guy Aldred?" "He is in prison, a conscientious objector." "Strange, isn't it, that all your friends are in prison? Why is that?" "Because they are against militarism and war." "You said you belong to an anarchist group. What do you understand by anarchism?" "I understand by anarchism a social system where economic exploitation and political oppression of the masses of the people by privileged minorities is impossible. A form of society where the producers themselves own and control the means of production and social wealth, so that there can be no masters and no economic monopoly. Anarchism is a system of society where there is economic equality with political and spiritual liberty, where the largest measure of social responsibility is accompanied by the greatest degree of personal individuality."

"Have you been a frequent speaker at public meetings or put your views forward in writing?" "I have never been a professional speaker or writer, but when I had anything to say I expressed my views at meetings or in writing."

"You said your comrade Shapiro is in prison. Do you know why?" "Yes. Because of his article in the *Arbeter Fraint*." "Do you agree with that article?" "Yes." "Do you know of a leaflet circulated in the East End that would hinder recruiting?" "Yes." "Do you agree with the ideas in that leaflet?" "Yes." "All right. That will be all for today. The committee thanks you for your information and will consider your case. You will be informed later of our decision."

Two weeks after that hearing Milly was transferred to the Women's Prison at Aylesbury.

Our third Christmas under arrest was approaching. I had a talk with my colleagues in charge of Battalions A and C, and we decided to ask the Commandant to let the men's relatives visit them, in turn, for four hours during the holidays, without military supervision, leaving the control to our own Company captains. We further asked for permission to use the theatre, where our orchestra would play during the four hours visiting time. The old man raised several objections, but finally agreed; only he said that if there was any smuggling discovered he would stop the whole thing at once.

The news made everybody in the camp very happy. The poor devils couldn't have wished for anything better. I begged them not to do anything silly that would upset the Commandant and make him withdraw the privilege. One stupid fool could spoil the whole thing for everybody.

I must say that all the men were on their best behaviour. Then suddenly, the whole atmosphere changed. A week before Christmas a new list was posted up of people in our camp who were to be transferred before Christmas to the Isle of Man. It came like a bombshell. We knew it wasn't the old man's doing. He couldn't help it. The order came from the War Office.

We went to the old man and spoke to him, and he made a personal request to the War Office. The result was that the order was suspended till after Christmas. But the damage was done. It didn't lift the cloud from the camp. Those poor devils who had seen their names on the list couldn't shake off the thought that immediately after Christmas they would be packed off to the dreaded Isle.

Yet when visiting day came everybody was happy. It was the first time for more than two years that most of the men were able to speak freely with their wives and children. The Commandant kept his word. The soldiers didn't come near us during the visiting hours. The Commandant afterwards thanked us all for having kept everything going smoothly. There had been no trouble at all. The only disturbing note was introduced by the women and children who were in tears all the time, saying goodbye to their men who were being sent to the Isle of Man, where they would not be able to visit them.

When I saw the Commandant after Christmas and he complimented me on our successful experiment, I took my courage in my hands and asked him if we couldn't repeat the experiment at all our future visits. He wouldn't hear of it. It wasn't possible. Out of the question.

But the following day he called me to his apartment; he said he had been thinking it over, and he believed it could be done. When our next visiting day came there were no soldiers present, and it was left to our own Company captains to keep order. In addition, where visits had previously been limited to fifteen minutes once a month we were now allowed two whole hours once a week. It was the most important concession we had gained during the whole period of our internment; and we had gained it all ourselves. We had asked the United States Embassy previously to intervene to get our visiting hours extended to one hour every two weeks, and we had been told it was impossible because there were not enough soldiers at Alexandra Palace to keep order if the visiting periods were longer. The whole camp went mad with joy when they heard the news.

But we had other troubles, like our food problem, that we could do nothing about, because these things were not in the Commandant's power. They depended on direct War Office orders. On 7th February, a new order was issued that we could no longer receive parcels from our people in England containing meat, fats, flour, bread, etc. We could only get food parcels from abroad. We couldn't obtain these foodstuffs any longer even at our canteen. On top of that our daily rations were considerably cut by a new War Office order issued on 28th February. Our food situation became desperate.

The English press was printing at the time statements by Dr A.D. Waller, Dr S. Russell Wells, Dr J.B. Leathers and Dr E.J. Spriggs, Home Office experts, that the minimum daily need of an individual was 3,000 to 3,200 calories. We got only 1,489 calories, and allowing for 12% uneatable stuff only 1,311 calories. We were issued for instance in March 1917 with smelts that had been preserved in saltpetre for goodness knows how long. Our cooks tried all they could, but it was uneatable. The Commandant making his rounds while the stuff was being served said: "It looks like chunks of Lot's wife."

The Commandant and the camp doctor made repeated representations to the War Office, but with no success. The doctor told the cooks to keep the fish soaking in running cold water for 24 hours to get the saltpetre out, but at the end of the time the fish stank and had to be thrown away.

Seventy-five per cent of the internees fell ill, and had to be treated in the camp hospital for stomach and bowel trouble. There were an enormous number of ruptures due to constipation. I was told one day that over a period of ten months we had brought 500 rupture belts into the camp. Naturally it spread depression over the whole camp. The men were irritable and quarrelsome. There was hardly a meal time without a row. There were frequent thefts. Some of the men found their memory failing. The whole atmosphere was unhealthy.

People say that hunger is a spur, that it makes us keener and more enterprising. That was not my experience. Chronic starvation makes people cowardly and mean; they lose all social sense, and become brutalised. They lose hope, and become insensible to the things of the mind and spirit. That was my experience among my fellow-internees during those years of hunger and privation.

Chapter 32

The Russian Revolution

The first reports of the revolution in Russia appeared in the English press on 19th March 1917. Czarism was overthrown, the flag of the revolution flew over Moscow and Petrograd! I couldn't believe my eyes. I read the news over and over again till I was convinced that it had really happened. I felt a tremendous surge of elation and excitement. Surely the revolution would bring this mad war to an end, and give the peoples peace at last! I couldn't rest. The revolution for which we had hoped and worked had come, was here! What would it mean to the world? Would it be confined to Russia or would it spread to other lands as well? I thought of Germany and my heart sank. The military juggernaut of Prussia might crush the revolution before it developed. Or was something happening in Germany? Something had to happen. I could hear the bells ringing in the era of peace and brotherhood, the nations gripping hands, all joining in singing the International.

When I read the report of Bonar Law's statement that an agreement had been reached between the governments of Russia and Britain that all Russians of military age must join the British forces or go to Russia, I was stunned. How differently things had turned out. I could see all my comrades in the East End rushing off to go to Russia! The revolution had opened their native land to them! They would not hesitate one moment to give their services to the revolution! They would kiss the Russian earth from which Czarist despotism had exiled them! I thought of Milly. It was maddening that we had to stay here, imprisoned, useless, rusting, when we could both be working there to help the cause.

The news about Russia excited the whole camp. Everyone felt sure that the war would now soon be over, and we would be free. Every bit of red cloth that our battalion could get hold of was turned into a red flag and flown from our beds. I read the news from Russia in the papers with feverish impatience. I still feared that the revolution might have a set-back. But when I heard that Miliukoff's government had fallen, I was sure that the old regime would not return. I had a letter from Milly. She was as unhappy as I was at being a captive here while a new world was taking shape in the East.

On 7th April the press announced that America had declared war against Germany. A little while before it would have plunged us in despair, we would have taken it as a sign that the war was entering on a new stage, and that there was no end to it in sight. Now after the Russian Revolution it could not shake our conviction that the war must soon end. How wrong we were! The war went on as savagely as before for eighteen more months.

I received a letter from Kropotkin, telling me that the new situation had encouraged him to take a fresh step towards securing Milly's release and he had reason to hope that this time he would succeed. He went on to speak of the wonderful things that were happening in Russia, and said that he would have liked to take the first ship to Russia, only the doctors warned him that his lungs and his heart would not stand the journey now, and that he must wait for better weather. I could understand his impatience. It was wonderful that Kropotkin had lived to see the revolution victorious, and that in his 70s he would have the great joy of returning home to liberated Russia.

May Day this year was Russian Revolution Day. I had asked the Commandant for the use of the theatre for our May Day meeting. He wanted to know if there would be any demonstration and disorder. I told him I took full responsibility that everything would be quiet. On that assurance he gave us the permission for which I asked.

The large theatre was packed. Every seat was occupied, and crowds of people stood in the gangways and in front of the stage. I spoke about the revolution in Russia. Since the observance of May Day had begun, in 1890, I had spoken every year at some May Day meeting somewhere. But never had I been able to express by feelings as on this May Day 1917 in the internment camp at Alexandra Palace. We were prisoners, but we felt that the hour of liberation had now come not only for us, but for the whole world.

Soon after May Day the old man fell seriously ill, and had to go on leave. He had been ailing all the time since he had returned to his duties after Christmas, and as always, when he was in pain, he was extremely difficult to get on with. We all breathed more freely when he was away, not only the internees, but the officers and the soldiers as well. We did not realise then that he was at death's door. He died on 18th May.

Neither the soldiers nor the prisoners seemed a bit moved by his death. He had made himself thoroughly disliked in the last few months. Few knew him except as an angry railing disciplinarian whom they never saw except on his inspection rounds. Yet he had his moments, with a lot of human sympathy and understanding. His long illness had made him irritable and unpleasant. But difficult as he was, one could always depend on him. He was a man of integrity. He was a gentleman. How much that meant we were to learn very soon. We had hoped that the old man's successor would be Colonel Gordon Cumming or Major Mott, who had both deputised for him. We knew them, and we liked them. Alas, the authorities had other ideas.

I had special visits about that time almost every day from friends and comrades who wanted to say goodbye to me before they left for Russia. They came jubilant and hopeful. They said they had only one regret, that I wasn't going with them. I shared that regret with all my heart. I was sad also to see so many of my old friends and close comrades leaving me; I began to feel terribly alone. I wished that I could somehow get permission to go to Russia as well. Alexander and Tanya Shapiro came to say goodbye. Shapiro had served his time in prison, and was now going to Russia, full of hope. He told me a lot of things about the Russian Revolution that had not appeared in the London press. He told me that Malatesta had decided to go to Russia, if the British government would allow him to leave England.

Who could have known that six years later we would have to start a big protest movement everywhere to try to save Alexander Shapiro from the claws of the Communist dictatorship, which gave him no choice between imprisonment and exile?

Later Alexandrowitsch came to say goodbye to me. When he returned to Russia he flung himself with enthusiasm into the struggle, and perished at the hands of Denikin's White armies. Many who had said goodbye to me before they went to Russia shared that fate. Yet they were lucky, for they died with glowing hearts, still believing in the revolution, spared the dreadful disillusionment of those who remained alive and saw the new despotism rise in Russia, and every vestige of freedom disappear.

Kropotkin and his wife Sophie went to Russia in June. He sent me a farewell note, expressing the hope that I would soon be free to follow him, and that we would meet in Russia. I felt the world was becoming empty round me. So many who had been close to my heart had gone away. Now I had lost Peter Kropotkin, who meant so much in my life. He was a sick old man. There was little chance of our meeting again, unless it were in Russia. Even this hope was unfulfilled.

Malatesta came to see me. The Russian Revolution had given the old rebel new courage and hope. He was straining at the leash to go to Russia to serve the revolution. The British government had refused permission for him to leave the country. But he hoped to get out some other way. There was an International Socialist Congress being organised in Stockholm. He expected that he would be sent there as a delegate, and then he would try to make his way to Russia from Sweden. He was sure that the war wouldn't last till the winter. It all depended, he said, on Russia. If the Russians could hold the Germans back long enough there would be revolutions in Germany and Austria. If that didn't happen then the arrival of the American armies in France would end the war before the spring.

* * *

In the last week of May we heard that the internment camp at Stratford would be closed and that some of the internees would be sent to Alexandra Palace. What was worse was that the Commandant at Stratford and his staff would take over the camp at Alexandra Palace. The Stratford Camp and its Commandant had a dreadful reputation among the internees. News had spread of terrible things happening there. It was not always the fault of the British military administration. The German internal administration was as much to blame, particularly for a great deal of corruption that existed there. The head of the internal administration was a man named Weber, who seemed by all accounts to be a sadist, and did his best to make life in the camp impossible. We were told about a Sergeant Trinneman at Stratford, who was the Commandant's right hand and practically ran the camp. He was said to be a brute. So we felt very depressed about the coming changes.

The new Commandant took over on 4th June. He appeared at inspection with Major Mott, who introduced me to him as the battalion leader. He made no good impression on me. He didn't look the ogre that those who had been in his camp had painted. They said he had been the Governor of a prison in Dublin, and that he treated the internees like convicts. He was very nice to me, and complimented me on the cleanliness and tidiness of our battalion. What worried me was the man's apparent lack of intelligence. He was a colossus of a man, tall and big and corpulent, a mountain of flesh and fat. He looked as though he suffered from fatty degeneration. His eyes were dull and expressionless. I couldn't think how a man with such eyes could ever understand me. I was afraid we were in for a lot of trouble.

Weeks passed, and nothing happened. It began to look as though our fears had been unfounded. The Commandant seemed friendly and easy-going, and camp life went on without any friction. Sergeant Trinneman too gave us no trouble. If anything he was too friendly, so much so, especially to me, that I became suspicious. I was very polite, but distant, and strictly businesslike in official matters. I tried to avoid meeting him except on questions of administration. Gradually our people became less anxious and worried, and the spirit in the camp improved.

On 20th June we had a celebration. I had delivered my hundredth lecture. Without a word to me about it my friends had arranged a kind of commemoration. Karl Meuel took the chair for me as usual. When he had finished and I was rising to begin my lecture, Wuertz of Battalion C got up and asked the chairman for permission to say a word. Wuertz was an old social democrat. He said that he had got up in order to express to me on behalf of all who had attended my lectures their gratitude for having kept alive their interest in literature and thought and the things of the spirit. Then he handed me a picture painted for the occasion by a Hungarian artist who was in our Camp, inscribed: "To Rocker, for his hundredth lecture. From his grateful hearers. Alexandra Palace 1915–1916–1917."

Our first clash with the new Commandant came at the end of June. We had been sent a consignment of herring that the cooks found unuseable. We therefore refused to accept it, though we knew that we would get nothing in exchange. We were all summoned to the Commandant, Lutz, Hutt and I, the three battalion leaders, and the cooks of all the three battalions. The Commandant was furious. He called our action rank insubordination. His orders were that we must take the herring and eat it. The cooks tried to make him understand that the stuff was uneatable. He refused to listen. He said the government had sent us the food, so it must be good. I told him that the government had sent us food before which the camp doctor had certified as unfit for human consumption. And it had been replaced.

The Commandant looked at me balefully. Then suddenly he smiled and said in a conciliatory tone that if we insisted that we wouldn't eat the stuff he wouldn't force us to. But he couldn't give us anything else in place of it. And he would put the whole matter to the War Office.

The sudden change made me suspicious. I was sure he was going to ask the War Office to send me to the Isle of Man. The old Commandant had stormed and raved, but there was nothing two-faced about him. This man smiled and spoke soft words, but in his heart there was deceit. When he was most friendly we could trust him least. Dealing with him was a most

205

disagreeable business. In the end I announced my resignation as battalion leader.

New elections were held. 937 votes were cast for me, and eleven against. It showed the Commandant that the men were behind me. He pretended to be friendly. But I could sense that something very unpleasant was brewing. The following morning we found a notice on the board that we would parade every Wednesday in the compound. The whole camp was in an uproar.

My colleagues of Battalions A and C and I went to see the Commandant. We told him that his predecessor had abolished the parades because they served no purpose. We were neither soldiers nor convicts. The new ruling had already created a lot of resentment. He glared at us. But finally he said the notice was withdrawn. By the time we came back to the camp it had disappeared from the board. Sergeant Trinneman was the evil spirit behind the Commandant. He re-introduced searches during our visiting hours, "to prevent smuggling". The women visitors felt terribly humiliated by these searches. If one was found smuggling in a piece of chocolate or cake for her husband it was confiscated, and she was sent home without seeing him.

In July a list of names appeared on the board of internees at Alexandra Palace who were to be sent to the Isle of Man. It included four men in my battalion who had English wives. Under War Office regulations such men should not have been sent to the Isle of Man. Two were key men in our internal camp administration. Trinks, who was an Austrian, had represented his comrades in their relations with the Swedish Embassy, which looked after the interests of Austrian internees. He was an honest, straightforward man, who attended to his duties conscientiously, and was therefore regarded as *persona non grata* by the Commandant. The other was Dr Michaels, who was the heart and soul of our educational work in the camp. He and Dr Simonis organised all the trained teachers who were interned in our camp and had created a sort of High School. He gave his whole attention every day to this work. I couldn't understand why he should have been selected to be packed off to the Isle of Man unless the Commandant meant to show his contempt for our whole adult school system.

When I saw the names of the four men on the list I was furious. I decided that now or never I must resist. I asked my son to pack our belongings, for it was quite possible that the Commandant resenting my interference would have me and probably my son too, added to the Isle of Man transport.

I went to see the Commandant. I tried to master my agitation as I spoke. His answer was that his hands were tied. The list had been drawn up by the War Office. I was sure that he had drawn up the list himself.

"Then I must resign as battalion leader," I said. "It looks as if every decent man is being sent away and only those allowed to remain who will submit to insults and indignities. I have only one more request. Put my name on the list as well."

With that I left the room.

I went to my quiet corner in the Chestnut Avenue, where I could relax and think. Presently a soldier found me there and said he had been sent by

Major Mott to tell me that he would like to speak to me. Major Mott was waiting for me on the terrace. He suggested that we should go for a walk, so that we could talk without being disturbed.

I made no bones about how I felt, and enumerated all the indignities the new administration had inflicted on us. This latest move meant that anyone the Commandant didn't like would face deportation to the Isle of Man. Instead of waiting for my turn I preferred to go now. The worst of it was that nobody in the camp believed that the Commandant was doing all this. It was Sergeant Trinneman.

"Listen to me, Rocker," Major Mott said. "You must stay as battalion leader. The other people need you. We know that you have their confidence. Nobody wants to send you away. I shall bear in mind all that you said. We'll talk about it later."

"I can't stay," I answered. "Not as long as things go on like this. If Trinks, Michaels, Hermes and Hank remain on the list I cannot carry out my duties. Those senseless restrictions will have to be removed."

"I'll talk to the Commandant," he promised. "But you must help me. You must tell him that you resigned in the heat of the moment, and that you will return to your duties."

"I can't, Major. You know that I can't. I can't go to him and say that. If he wants me he must send for me."

"Very well. I'll tell him that. Go back to your office and wait there till he sends for you."

When I came back to the camp all the people crowded round me. They were ready for mutiny. The word had spread that I was being sent to the Isle of Man. All the Captains wanted to resign their posts. The entire camp was with me, anarchists, socialists, German patriots, all without exception. Luckily a few men had seen me talking quietly with Major Mott; that helped to calm the others. But the atmosphere remained tense.

The Commandant must have been aware of the feeling in the camp. A mutiny was the last thing he could have wanted. The War Office would have had something to say to him about it. The old Commandant had been there for two years without any serious trouble. And he had only just arrived.

About ten minutes later I was called to the Commandant's office. He had Major Mott with him. He was suddenly very amiable. He said there had been a misunderstanding; it had all been cleared up now. All the restrictions would be withdrawn. The old visiting hours would be restored. I must return to my duties as battalion leader.

"What about the four men?" I asked.

"I shall ask the War Office to remove their names from the list. I'll make it my business to see that they stay here."

There was a feeling of relief and joy in the camp when the news got round. But my heart was still heavy. I was afraid of what Sergeant Trinneman might be up to next.

On 14th July I received a very strange letter from Milly. A Scotland Yard man had been to see her in prison and had told her that she might be released very soon. He said that the Russian Revolution had changed the whole situation in her favour. He had then asked her if she would sign an undertaking that when she was released she would not engage in any propaganda against the war. She answered that she would do no such thing. She had been arrested and she was being kept in custody without any charge having been brought against her, without trial. If she was to be released it must be without conditions. That was the end of the conversation. She had no idea, she said, what would happen now.

At the end of July rumours went round the camp that Alexandra Palace was being closed and that we would all be sent to the Isle of Man. We had heard such rumours before. But this time it seemed serious. I had heard our English officers discussing it. Very soon the Swiss Embassy confirmed it.

Most of the men took it badly. The one thing that had sustained them all the time was looking forward to visits from their wives and children, and that would not be possible in the Isle of Man.

We were now in the fourth year of the war, and we were showing signs of our long imprisonment. Our visiting hours were tragic with partings and farewells. We had lost all hope of a speedy end of the war as a result of the Russian Revolution. Many revolutionaries had come to realise that a separate peace with the Kaiser's Germany might mean the overthrow of the whole revolution. If the Germans could withdraw their troops from the East and hurl them against the Allies in the West, Germany might still win the war. Then the victorious Germans could throw their weight into Russia on the side of the counter-revolution, and might even put the Czars back in power. I wouldn't have said that these fears were groundless.

Dr Vischer, from the Swiss Embassy, visited us on 9th August to tell us that a representative of his government had discussed the matter with Lord Newton, and it now looked as if the British government had abandoned the plan to close our camp. I must say that both the Swiss and the Swedish Embassy had done everything possible to help us in this matter.

A few days later something very serious indeed happened in Battalion C. All three battalions had bought our potatoes and vegetables for a long time from a farmer named Davis. He bought back from us the potato peelings and the vegetable refuse for his pigs. He came to the camp with his cart two or three times a week. That day Sergeant Trinneman stopped him and had his cart searched; among the kitchen refuse he found two hundredweight of rice. Davis said that John Immer of C Battalion had given him the rice for his pigs. Davis and Immer were arrested and handed over to the police.

The camp was in an uproar. Immer was Battalion C's chief cook, and the impression spread that he had been cheating on the battalion's rations and selling the rice to Davis to make money for himself. Trinneman strutted round like a peacock. The next development was that Hutt, the C Battalion leader, was ordered to pack his belongings, for immediate transfer to Wakefield Camp.

The Captains of C Battalion called an emergency meeting, and invited me to it. Hutt and all the C Battalion captains said that they would vouch for Immer's honesty. It was impossible that he had cheated on the rations.

Then the facts emerged. C Battalion had the largest number of well-to-do prisoners in the camp, people who received a lot of food parcels from their relatives and friends, and therefore did not claim their rice and certain other rations. Immer saved this food till he had a hundredweight or two, and he exchanged it with Davis for more potatoes and vegetables, No money passed between them, and Immer had never kept anything for himself. It all went into the battalion's stores.

The old Commandant would never have called in the police. Whatever it was he would have dealt with the matter himself. Now we saw nothing that could be done for Hutt or Immer. Particularly as Hutt begged us not to make any trouble for ourselves by starting a demonstration on his behalf. Battalion C elected a new battalion leader, Fritz Poppe, a well-to-do man, with a good, open, manly, bearing; everyone respected him. I couldn't have wished for a better colleague. Politically we were miles apart, but our personal relations were excellent.

On 8th October, Immer was sentenced to twelve months hard labour. The charge against him was that he had misused government rations. The food had been delivered for use in the camp, and he had disposed of it outside.

Feeling in the camp rose against Sergeant Trinneman. I must say that he was an ugly customer. The British soldiers in the camp couldn't stand him. The officers detested him. One officer told me that they were all furious because the Immer affair had been taken out of the camp, to the police court. "It's all that Sergeant Trinneman's doing. You must get rid of him. I wish that we could help you. But our hands are tied. You have the whole camp behind you. Do what you can to send the blighter packing. We shall all be very thankful to you."

On 20th September, I had another letter from Milly, that her case would be coming up again before the Advisory Committee. A few days later Milly's sisters Polly and Rose came to visit me; they said that Milly had already appeared before the Advisory Committee. Rose had been in Parliament, where the committee met, and she had seen Milly and had spoken to her.

The Chairman had asked Milly if she wanted to go to Russia. She had answered, yes. He then said it was his duty to warn her that conditions in Russia were developing unfavourably. She said that the conditions in Russia didn't frighten her. What she did want was that I and my two sons should go to Russia with her.

The Chairman said this was impossible. I was a German, and Russia was at war with Germany. Milly argued that Russia would nevertheless admit me. They knew my name and they knew my work.

The Chairman then consulted the other members. He said:

"Your older son is of military age. Can't you see that it's impossible for us to send him to Russia?"

"I can't see it," Milly answered. Then she continued: "I want to say something else. You have kept me in prison for fifteen months without trial. Why do you treat me differently from my comrades Shapiro, Linder and Lenoble? Why shouldn't we all be allowed to go to Russia? You know that I was arrested because of my political views. Yet I was put in prison with criminals, with prostitutes, with women suffering from disease, with whom I have to share toilet, bath and crockery."

The members of the Advisory Committee looked at each other; they were taken aback.

"Mrs. Rocker," the Chairman tried to assure her, "you must be exaggerating."

"I am not exaggerating. If you want the facts I can give them to you. I have mentioned this only because I don't want it to be said afterwards that I was here and that I didn't tell you about it."

"Do you mean to speak about these things when you are free?"

"Most certainly. I don't know when I shall be free. But when I am I shall certainly speak of these things."

The chairman consulted his colleagues again, and said: "We really can't agree to let your older son go to Russia."

"Will you let me talk it over with my husband?"

The members of the committee put their heads together; then the chairman announced that they had agreed to let her meet me and talk it over. They fixed our meeting for 4th October. That concluded the hearing, and Milly was taken back to Aylesbury. I could hardly believe that in a few weeks I would see Milly again, and would talk to her. It made me feel very happy. I had no idea what might come of our meeting, but it was enough for me that we would meet.

I was up very early on 4th October. I had hardly slept a wink all night. I waited to be called. I thought we would be leaving at about ten o'clock. But the morning passed and nothing happened. The afternoon came and went, and I was not even told that I was not going. I thought of Milly waiting in the same way, and nothing happening, and I felt very bitter. Eight days passed, and I was neither called nor told why I wasn't being called; I began to think the whole thing had been dropped.

On 12th October, I had a letter from Milly, dated 8th October. "I feel like a criminal," she wrote, "to have raised your hopes about our meeting. How could I have doubted these men when they gave me their word? They may say that it was no obligation of theirs, but I always thought that if you said something you had to keep your word."

The letter had of course been seen by the censor, who had added a note to me: "Mrs. Rocker seems to be under a misapprehension. Your meeting with her has been fixed for 17th October." It was very considerate of the censor to add that note, and I felt grateful. I wondered if Milly had really misunderstood about the date, but it no longer mattered. We were going to meet after all. Here was the date in black and white.

17th October was a nasty rainy autumn day. It was pouring when a plain clothes man came to fetch me at 10.30am. We went to the Houses of Parliament by bus. I was introduced to Mr Brodrick, the Secretary of the Advisory Committee. I asked him if my wife had arrived. "No," he said, "we expect her any minute."

He was most polite, and I must say that he treated me with every consideration. He took me into one of the rooms, where he said I would have to wait. I looked out of the window at the rain. A quarter of an hour passed; then the door opened and a woman came in, with Milly behind her. Mr Brodrick nodded to my plain clothes man and to the woman who had come with Milly, and we were left alone. We looked at each other dumbly. It was a long time before our tongues loosened, and we could talk.

Milly said she thought they would let us go to Russia, but not my older son. I had already spoken to Rudolf about this possibility, and he had begged me not to let our opportunity slip because of him. We therefore decided that if Rudolf couldn't go with us we would not insist on his going.

We were left alone for about an hour. Then Mr Brodrick came and said that the committee were waiting to see Milly.

"Are you still determined to go to Russia, Mrs. Rocker?" the Chairman asked her.

"Of course. On condition that my husband goes with me."

"Naturally. But we can't let your older son go with you. I want to make it quite clear that we are not ordering you to leave this country." As Milly didn't say anything, he repeated: "You understand, Mrs. Rocker, that we are not forcing you to go to Russia."

"I understand," Milly said.

The chairman asked her if we still had a home in London. Milly said we had, and that there were some things there, our library and a few other belongings that we would like to take with us. The chairman thought this might not be possible under the existing conditions. He suggested that she might ask me what I thought about it. Then they took her back to the room where I was waiting. It was now my turn to appear before the committee.

They took me to a large room where seven gentlemen sat round a long table. The chairman asked me to sit down.

"Do you want to go to Russia, Mr. Rocker?"

"Yes, if I am given the opportunity."

"Have you any friends in Russia?"

"A great many."

"I understand that Prince Kropotkin is one of your friends."

"Yes. For the last twenty years."

"Your wife spoke to us about your library. You realise that you couldn't take it with you."

"I never thought I could. But if we are allowed to go home for a couple of days we could arrange to dispose of it."

"I don't think that should be difficult. The Advisory Committee has agreed to treat your case as an exception, and to recommend that you may go to Russia with your wife and your younger son, provided the Russian government will admit you."

That concluded the hearing. When I came back to the room where I had left Milly waiting I found her sister Rose and our friend Milly Sabelinsky with her, and also our young son Fermin, whom they had brought with them. The boy was beside himself with joy; he danced about and jumped about, running up first to me, then to his mother, and then back to me again. We spent about an hour together. Then Mr Brodrick came in to tell us that there was a meal ready for Milly and me.

So we took leave of Fermin and Rose and our friend Milly Sabelinsky, and we followed Mr Brodrick to the House of Commons dining-room, where we found a small table laid for us. After the hardships of the last years this was certainly a change. It was wonderful to be treated with a little attention again, like ordinary human beings, not prisoners.

After the meal we were left alone together again till 5pm. We took that as a good omen that we would soon be free and on our way to Russia. How could we have known that a whole year would pass before we would see each other again?

It poured all the way when my escort and I made our journey back to the camp. But my heart was singing. I found my comrades in the camp waiting impatiently for me to return. The news soon went round all the three battalions that I was back, and that I was going to Russia. They all said they were very happy for my sake, but they were sorry for themselves that they would be losing me. I too felt sorry for them, knowing the plight in which I would be leaving them.

In the morning some of the English officers came to ask me what the result had been of my interview with the Advisory Committee, The *Globe*, which was still appearing at that time, had a short report about me: "Mr. Rudolf Rocker, the leader of the internees in Alexandra Palace, is going to Russia."

Lieutenant Martin informed me officially as battalion leader of an incident that had occurred during my absence. My colleagues had already told me about it. Major Mott had taken the inspection instead of the Commandant. As soon as he had appeared with Sergeant Trinneman at his heels, somebody had started a derisive whistle, which was taken up immediately on all sides. Trinneman knew that the demonstration was against him. He turned to Major Mott and said spitefully: "All that man Rocker's doing. That's the way he teaches his battalion to behave."

I told Lieutenant Martin that when the Commandant called me to his office I would disclaim all responsibility for what had happened. I hadn't been in the camp at the time. Sergeant Trinneman was the culprit. His intrigues had undermined my authority and destroyed the discipline of the camp. Lieutenant Martin who was one of the oldest officers there, knew that such things had never happened in the camp before.

Two days later, on Saturday, 20th October, just after visiting hours, the news went round the camp that Trinneman had physically assaulted a man named Mueller in Battalion C, and had locked him into a cell. The men were aroused as never before.

When the time for the count came Battalions B and C refused to line up. Poppe, the leader of Battalion C to which Mueller belonged went to report this to the Commandant. As usual he was not to be found when there was trouble. Then Poppe went to Major Mott, and told him the only way to restore discipline, was to send Mueller back to his battalion at once. Major

Mott ordered Mueller to be released from the cell and sent back to the battalion. After that the count went off quietly.

As soon as the count was over, Poppe told me what had happened. Mueller's wife had come to visit him. The signal had just gone for all visitors to leave, when his wife turned to kiss him goodbye. Trinneman had rushed up, swearing and cursing, and had told her to clear out at once. He said she had no business to be in the building after the signal had gone. The poor woman didn't say a word. She walked towards the exit. Then Trinneman while she was still on her way out turned on Mueller and shouted at him: "Get in, you bugger!"

When Mueller protested against such language Trinneman got hold of him and with the help of one of the soldiers flung him into the cell. He ripped his coat off him, shouting and cursing the whole time. "One more word out of you," he said, "and I'll have the skin off you as well as your coat!"

We decided that this sort of thing had to be stopped. We sent letters the same day to the Swedish and Swiss Embassies reporting the incident, and asking them to intervene with the War Office. I realised that this would probably take weeks. So I tried to think of a way to hasten the matter.

The next day was Sunday, and we had no inspection. Trinneman didn't show himself all that day. I was afraid though of what might happen on the Monday, if Trinneman appeared at the inspection with the Commandant. Something had to be done to prevent that. I consulted my two colleagues of Battalions A and C, and we decided to see the Commandant, and to tell him that if Trinneman appeared at the inspection we and all the Company leaders in the camp would resign our posts immediately.

We all three went to the Commandant's office. He wasn't there; we found Major Mott and Lieutenant Martin in the office. I told them what we had come about. Major Mott made no comment. He told us very quietly that he would convey what we had said to the Commandant.

There was no inspection on the Monday. On Monday afternoon Mueller appeared before a court martial. We warned him not to yield to threats or blandishments and promised to back him up. Poppe who was present as his battalion leader told us afterwards that Mueller had behaved splendidly. He refused to be intimidated, and stuck to his story. Trinneman had denied everything; he said that he would swear on oath that nothing of the kind had happened. Even when the soldier whom he had ordered to help him to bring Mueller into the cell had confirmed Mueller's story in every detail, Trinneman still stood by his denial. Mueller's innocence was clearly established, and the court had to acquit him.

That was the end of Trinneman. The Commandant must have seen that it was now impossible to keep Trinneman in the camp. He made one more attempt to save him. He called the three battalion leaders, Poppe, Luti and me to his office, and in the presence of Major Mott and Lieutenant Martin read us a lecture about undermining discipline in the camp.

"I am sorry," I interrupted. "If there has been any undermining of discipline it is Trinneman's doing, not ours. He got together with the lowest

213

scum in the camp, and used them to make life as miserable here as possible. We were elected by the great majority, and this man did everything he could to undermine our position. It had to come to a clash. Who can blame the men for losing their patience when they saw this beast attack one of their own men? It is bad enough that we are confined here for years through no fault of ours. We won't put up with physical maltreatment as well. Such things never happened when the old Commandant was in charge."

I spoke with some heat. I saw the Commandant's face go white, and then red. When I called Trinneman a beast he winced. I had thrown caution to the wind. Let him do what he liked! I was past caring.

Then Poppe spoke. He was also very blunt. He gave me his complete support. Suddenly the Commandant became all acquiescence and smiles. He had never suspected that things were like that. He said that he would do everything he could to win back the confidence of the camp. The only thing he wanted was to have the camp run smoothly and pleasantly.

We went back feeling quite sure that Trinneman was going to be sent packing. We didn't see him again till we heard on 28th October that he was leaving. It so happened that I had business that day in the staff office. When I came in, I saw Trinneman sitting there in a corner. Nobody took any notice of him. He looked deflated. He winced when he saw me.

The Chief Clerk winked at me, and said: "Lovely day, isn't it?" It was pouring cats and dogs, but I knew what he meant.

"Yes," I answered. "It is a lovely day."

"And are you going to the Isle of Man, Mr Rocker?" he went on.

"No," I said. "I am going to Russia."

When I came back to my battalion office my secretary told me that Mr Minister, the censor, wanted to see me. I found all the censors of the camp and several officers round a table, celebrating with a bottle of whisky. They were all in high spirits, and greeted me boisterously. I had to join them in a drink.

"It's a great occasion," Minister said. "We are celebrating a birthday."

"Whose birthday?" I asked.

"He isn't with us, you know. He is leaving the camp today, for good. So we are celebrating the occasion."

* * *

A whole month had now passed since our appearance before the Advisory Committee, and we hadn't heard anything about our going to Russia. My friends had sent a telegram to Kropotkin asking him to get the Russian government to inform the British government that I would be admitted to Russia. We didn't know whether anything had been done about it. The Kerensky government had fallen in October, and the Bolsheviks were now in power.

On 27th November I received a letter from Milly that the Home Secretary had notified her that she could not be released for the time being. I had no doubt that this was the result of the new upheaval in Russia. Milly wrote to me that she still hoped we would be sent to Russia as soon as conditions there had become more settled. But when the news came in December that Bolshevik Russia had concluded an armistice with Germany I knew that there was no more hope for us.

Christmas drew near, my fourth Christmas in captivity. Nobody felt like celebrating this time. We were all sick at heart, hopeless, resigned. There was no end to the war in sight. Another year in the internment camp and we would all be fit for the lunatic asylum.

Just before Christmas we got a new batch of internees sent to Alexandra Palace from the Isle of Man. They told me that my old friend Otto Schreiber had died in the Isle of Man of a heart attack. I had known Schreiber for twenty years. He had been active in our German movement. A lifelong anti-militarist, who had carried on a relentless war against the Kaiser regime, and had to live in exile because of it, he died in a German prisoners of war camp as though he had been one of the Kaiser's own men! And the British Press spoke of this as a war of democracy against Prussian militarism!

In the middle of January, Milly wrote to me that she had received another communication from the Home Office that she could go to Russia with our young son, but that no permission could be given to me. Milly had replied that she would not leave England without me.

On 21st January, Mr Joseph King, a Liberal MP, asked a question about us in Parliament. The Home Secretary's answer was not encouraging. *The Herald* took up our case and published an article demanding our release. Then an official Russian note came to the British Foreign Secretary to say that Russia would admit me. It didn't help. The British government seemed to have made up its mind that I must not go to Russia.

On 11th February, 1918, the British press reported that Russia had made a separate peace with Germany. My heart almost stopped when I read the shameful conditions to which Russia had agreed. General Hoffman crashing his fist down on the table at Brest-Litovsk during the peace treaty talks was Prussian militarism beating its mailed fist in the face of the world. It was irony indeed when this reactionary gang waxed indignant over the injustices of Versailles after they had done so much to precipitate the war and then imposed the terms of Brest-Litovsk on Russia. Most of my fellow internees failed to appreciate the significance of this peace treaty. Their only concern was to be free again, and they thought their hope was now to come true.

Chapter 33

Farewell to England

The camp was now terribly overcrowded, due to the endless negotiations going on at this time between the German and British governments about the exchange of civilian prisoners. The negotiations had gone on for fourteen months with no result. During the whole of this time people had been sent to us from all the camps throughout the country, in the expectation that in a few weeks they would be going to Germany. The negotiations dragged, and all these people remained stuck in our camp. We had nowhere to put them. Protests to the Swedish and Swiss Embassies didn't help. Our school rooms were taken away from us for sleeping quarters. It killed the whole of our educational work.

In the summer, when the men could go out into the compound things were bearable. But in winter when we all had to stay indoors it was hell. Everybody was ill. The infirmary was filled to suffocation. We had a great many cases of insanity. In the end the British and German governments agreed that those whose mental or physical state required it would meanwhile be interned in neutral countries, where they would enjoy better conditions.

At the end of January, 1918, a notice appeared on the board that prisoners who believed they ought to be for health reasons interned in Holland should put their names down for medical examination. The first examination would be by the Camp doctor. There would be a second examination by the Home Office doctor, and he would decide who was to go on the list for Holland.

I was ill myself at that time. I had developed chronic stomach trouble, and spent a couple of weeks in the infirmary. I couldn't keep my food down. Not even milk and water. Dr Dove did all he could to help me. After three weeks I returned to my duties as battalion leader. But I was no longer the robust man I had been. In fact I had to have an operation afterwards in Amsterdam.

Worse than my physical illness was my mental depression. All the efforts our friends made to get Milly released had failed. I had reason to believe that if I were sent to Holland, Milly would be allowed to follow me. Some of my friends who had gone to Holland wrote to me that the conditions were much more favourable there. The camp for German civilian prisoners was at Hattem, a small place near Zwolle. Those who could pay for it could stay in private homes. The rest lived in comfortable barracks, and could move about freely in the whole of that area. The food was excellent. After what we had endured in England it must have seemed like paradise.

A second transport was going to Holland in the middle of February. I couldn't decide whether to put my name down for it. It would have been easier if I could have seen Milly and discussed it with her. I couldn't do it in writing. It took three weeks for a letter to reach her, and to get her reply. That would make it too late. I had a talk with my son Rudolf and some of my friends in the camp and they all urged me not to let the chance slip. So on 26th February, the last day for application, I put my name on the list. Dr Dove passed me; he said he was quite sure that the Home Office doctor would pass me too.

When the list of those who would be going to Holland was posted up on 5th March, my name was not there. Then the list appeared of those who were to be sent to Germany in exchange for British civilian prisoners. There my name was right on top, the very first. I was astounded. Why had they done that? They knew my political record of opposition to the Kaiser's regime. I had no doubt that as soon as I reached Germany they would clap me in goal. What should I do? I could of course appeal against my repatriation, ask the Commandant to remove my name from the list. But it went against the grain to have to ask this man for any favour. I consoled myself with the thought that we would be travelling through Holland. I didn't believe that the Dutch would refuse me asylum once I was there. Rudolf and the others thought the same. How could we have known the conditions there?

I delivered my last lecture on 6th March in the theatre. It was my 139th lecture. When I finished and spoke a few words of farewell to the gathering, I saw how genuinely sorry everybody was that I was leaving. The next day Milly's sisters Rose and Polly came with Lazar and Milly Sabelinsky to say goodbye to me. It was not easy to part from such close friends after all these years. Taking leave of my youngster whom I might not see for a long time was especially hard. It was at least a comfort to know he was in good hands.

On 9th March, the camp gave me a send-off. There were tears in many eyes. I spoke and begged them not to lose their courage. When I ended, all rose from their seats and filed past me to press my hand. Late that night when we lay on our plank beds a sound of singing filled the place. It was a farewell serenade by the camp's choral group.

I lay awake thinking. My heart was very heavy. I felt embarrassed when I thought of the affection and gratitude these people had shown me. What had I done to deserve it? For two years I had carried the burden of being their battalion leader, representing their interests, trying to help them as much as I could. But that was my duty. I had accepted the post and only did what I had undertaken. It was gratifying to know that on many occasions I had been able to intervene for them successfully. At times it seemed to me that I was the focus of all the personal tragedies and griefs in the camp. People confided to me things no one else knew. Often it meant nothing more than talking to someone who was sympathetic and understanding. I did all I could. That thought made me feel better.

I didn't close my eyes all that night, my last in the camp. As soon as the morning broke I rose from my plank bed. My son Rudolf also got up, so that he could spend the last few hours with me. He spoke confidently about peace coming soon, and of our meeting again, free men. I didn't want to damp his optimism and tried to hide my fears.

After breakfast I went to say goodbye to those English officers I had got to know and respect. Major Mott was visibly moved when we parted. He said to me: "Don't worry about your son, Rocker. I'll see that he doesn't go to the Isle of Man. I'll give him a job in my office." He kept his word.

When I saw the censor of A Battalion he took me aside and asked me how I was placed for money. He offered me £10, all that I would be permitted to take out of England, He wanted me to consider it as a loan, he said. I would repay it when I could, after the war. I found it hard to control my emotion. I told him that I was most grateful for his offer, but I didn't need the money. I had as much as I would be allowed to take with me. He wasn't satisfied however till I took out my wallet and showed him the money.

When I returned to the battalion, all the men were waiting for me in a crowd to shake hands with me for the last time. Those who were to leave with me were already lined up outside, waiting. All the company captains were also there, with my son Rudolf, to say goodbye again. Major Mott called Rudolf over and told him that he could go with me to the train. Then we marched down the hill under military escort to the station, where our train was waiting.

I shared a compartment with Fritz Poppe, his brother and some friends. I embraced Rudolf. Then the train moved off. All the others were happy and excited; I felt sad. I sat at the window and kept looking out. All my life in England passed before me. I thought of Milly and of all my friends and dear ones, and of the poor people I had left in the camp.

Then I began to wonder what my future would be. What awaited me? Everybody else had some idea of where they were going, what would happen to them. Some were doing back to their homes. Others would remain in Holland. Where was I going?

I was recalled to my surroundings by my friends talking to me. It was spring. The sun shone brightly. My friends were laughing and were happy. Even the soldiers who were coming with us as our escort were in very good humour.

We were on our way to the repatriation camp at Spalding, where we would stay about a week. It was 3pm when we reached Spalding. We still had a fair distance to march from the station to the camp. People in the streets looked at us curiously, but with no hostility. The camp was an old workhouse, packed full of people like ourselves. We were counted and registered. Then I started looking round. Most of the people in this repatriation camp had come from the Isle of Man; many were old friends and acquaintances from Alexandra Palace.

The place was uncomfortable and overcrowded. Luckily we didn't have to stay long there. We were due to leave on 15th March. That morning we proceeded to the port town Boston, which was quite near. We thought that after having had everything we possessed thoroughly searched in Spalding we would be spared all that again. We soon learned better. When we got out of the train we were shepherded into a room in the station building where a young lieutenant, probably only just commissioned, behaved like a wild animal. He and his men went through our belongings as though we were a band of thieves. He swore and stamped and shouted. If one of us didn't produce his key at once he had the lock of his case broken open. Anything that looked new was confiscated. He even took away some of our cases, because he said they were new, and their owners were lucky if they found a discarded coalsack to dump their things in.

The British authorities may not have known about these things. But it was asking for trouble to put a callow young fool like that in charge. He must have imagined that he was on the battlefield giving the Huns what for.

When he was finished with us we boarded the Dutch steamer "Sindora", going to Rotterdam. Suddenly everything changed. The Red Cross sisters on the boat gave us a friendly welcome. Instead of being bullied we were treated with kindness and consideration. I shared a two-bunk cabin with a friend. It was beautifully clean and tidy, and the linen was spotlessly white. It seemed too good to be true. It was like the old days, before the war.

I made my way to the large dining-room. The tables were properly laid, the chairs were comfortable, everything was neat in the Dutch tradition. Fritz Poppe beckoned me to his table, where he sat with a couple of friends over a beer. I looked round. Were these the same people I had known as prisoners in the camp? They looked so happy, they talked freely, they laughed joyfully.

It was late afternoon when the Sindora weighed anchor and slipped away, skirting the English coast. The weather was glorious. The sea was like a mirror. At dusk we anchored again off the English coast. I slept like a log till the morning. The Sindora was then already out at sea, making her way across towards Holland. I looked for the outline of the English coast; it had disappeared completely. I fell into sad thoughts again, wondering if I would ever return to tread the soil of England, which had become my second homeland. I shook off my sentimental thoughts, and began to think how I could possibly remain in Holland when I got there, not be sent on to Germany.

There was a young Dutch steward on board whose looks and manner attracted me. I discovered to my joy that he was a member of the Syndicalist trade union, National Arbeids Secretariat. When I introduced myself as an old friend of Domela Nieuwenhuis he was my man. I told him how I was placed, and asked him if he had any idea what I could do. He said he would try to find out. He was away for about a quarter of an hour, and told me that he had spoken to some of his comrades. There was no chance of getting legal permission to stay in Holland. They thought I ought to talk to the ship's doctor, a man of liberal views, who would do anything possible for me. I went to see the doctor and found him a charming man. He said he would try to think of some way to help me.

By that time it was dusk again, and we anchored off the Dutch coast for the night. In the morning the doctor sent for me. He said there was one man who might be able to help me, the doctor in the Emigration House in

219

Rotterdam. He didn't know if he could really do anything, but I could safely confide in him, and it was worth trying.

The German Consul came on board as soon as we reached Rotterdam. He said that he had come to welcome us. We were taken to the Emigration House, and those who were to go to Germany were separated from the others. We spent the night in a separate room, all the exits guarded by soldiers, so that it was impossible to slip out of the building.

In the morning I had a talk with the doctor. He was very sorry, but there was nothing, he said, that he could do for me. There was an agreement between the British and German governments, and he did not dare as a neutral to do anything that would get his own country into trouble. He did think that there was something I might be able to do for myself though. A few miles out of Rotterdam the train to Germany came to a sharp curve, and had to slow down. I could jump down there. If I got away it would not be difficult to obtain permission to remain in Holland.

I didn't know if I would be able to do it, but I decided to make the attempt. Our train left at 11.30am. I had my seat next to a window. Two or three miles out of Rotterdam the train slowed down. Had it been at night I would have got away. I realised that it would be more difficult in broad daylight. But I opened the door and jumped. I fell heavily. I was bruised, but not badly hurt. I picked myself up and ran. I heard shouting behind me, and the grinding of brakes. The train had been stopped. I ran faster, but my pursuers gained on me. To make things worse, three railway men working on the track barred my way.

I was taken to the Red Cross compartment. Everybody was very kind; someone offered me a glass of wine. They asked me why I had wanted to escape. I told them; it seemed to me that they were sorry for me.

I was disconsolate. I had made my attempt, and I had failed. The hours passed slowly till we reached the first German station, Hassum. A group of German children stood by the bar at the level crossing, piping in their thin voices *Deutschland, Deutschland, ueber alles*. They stretched out their hands to us pleadingly. Things did not look promising here. Half an hour later we were in Goch, the frontier guard post. Our luggage was again examined very carefully; every scrap of paper, printed or written, was taken away from us. We were then brought before the lieutenant in charge of the frontier post. He was a Protestant pastor who during the war had exchanged his clergyman's robe for the Kaiser's uniform. He spoke to us about the war that had been forced on Germany, about unforgiving, relentless Albion, and about the German victory that was sure to come. He prepared us to expect hardships in Germany. Everybody had to make sacrifices to strengthen the Fatherland. He told us of countless regulations that we would have to observe. It was true that we were now free, but freedom had to have a master. And it all ended with cheers for the Kaiser.

When he had finished the lieutenant called me out by name. He looked me up and down, and said: "What have you been up to?" I told him I was too exhausted by the journey to explain now. Couldn't it be left till the morning? He looked me up and down again, and said: "Very well. I'll speak to you in the morning."

Some soldiers took us to a school building outside the town, which was being used for the accommodation of repatriates from England. Supper was served; it was a very frugal meal. A small piece of very bad bread and some cabbage soup, which hadn't seen much fat. The sister who was serving urged us not to leave anything in the bowl. We mustn't waste any food, she said. I could see from the faces of my fellow-repatriates that they were not impressed by what they were seeing of German conditions.

I spent the night with three others in a sort of coach-house, on straw laid on the ground, with one blanket each. We hadn't been spoilt by camp life, and I was glad to stretch my weary limbs. Not that I slept much that night. It was nearly dawn before I dozed off. My friends woke me. We were marched off to the school for breakfast, which consisted of a slice of bread, a smear of so-called marmalade, and some indistinguishable brew called coffee. Then a soldier escorted us back to the railway station, where the office was already hard at work. The procedure was simple. Each repatriate had to say what place he belonged to, and give the name of a relative or friend there. A telegram went off to the local authority and when the reply arrived the repatriate was given a railway ticket, and told to make his own way home.

Lieutenant Merck arrived about 9am. He sat down at his desk and looked through some papers. Then he called out my name. "Now, Mr Rocker," he began, "I'm ready to hear your explanation. Please follow me to my room." He led the way to a poorly furnished little place where he sat down at a small table, and offered me a chair.

I had decided to tell him everything or nothing. He looked at me expectantly. I said: "May I first know whom I am speaking to? I mean, if I am to regard you as a Prussian officer there is no point in my saying anything. But if I could speak to you as one human being to another, then I could talk freely, and tell you everything about myself that you want to know."

He look surprised and said quietly: "Very well, speak to me as one human being to another. I shall try to understand."

I told him everything. I was an anarchist, and I had fled from Germany many years before because of my revolutionary activity. I told him my attitude to the war. As for my attempt to escape, I had wanted to be interned in Holland, not return to Germany.

"I have told you everything," I concluded. "I have nothing more to say. It is now for you to decide what to do with me."

Lieutenant Merck was visibly impressed. He was silent for a moment. Then he said:

"I have never heard things like this from anyone before. You mean to say that you really are an anarchist? But that is terrible! Anarchy is a state of disorder. Surely that is no aim to strive for!"

"People may have different ideas," I answered, "about what is order and disorder. I would say for instance that there can be no greater disorder than we have now. Would you say that this war is a sign of order in the world? Why should it be so terrible to call myself an anarchist? Did you want me to hide the fact, instead of telling you the truth?"

"It is certainly much better that you told me the truth. What I can't understand," the lieutenant said, "is why they interned you in England. They couldn't have said that you were a supporter of our government."

"They didn't," I interposed. "But I wasn't only against your government. I was against the war as such; that was what the British government didn't like."

Lieutenant Merck said that he had heard of me from the other repatriates long before I had arrived. "Some painted you as the devil himself," he said, smiling. "Others couldn't praise you enough, you were the most wonderful person they had ever come across. They told me how you had watched over the interests of our people in the camp. I was told about your lectures, and that you had attacked the Kaiser and the German state. You wouldn't like to tell me anything more about that?" he asked.

"What shall I tell you? You don't expect me to answer everything that this man or the other may have reported about me? I met a lot of people in the years I spent in the internment camps; some of them were men to whom every word I spoke must have sounded like high treason. I didn't intend my lectures to be German propaganda. But neither were they propaganda for any other government. As for the Kaiser, I never mentioned him. I was not concerned with one man, but with a system."

"Suppose we let you go free," he asked. "You know the desperate position of the Fatherland. Would you still, knowing the conditions, go about spreading your ideas?"

I thought for a moment. Then I said with decision: "I can only tell you the truth. Either a man has convictions or he hasn't. If you put the question to me like that I can only answer, 'Yes, I shall always say what I believe, every time I get the opportunity.'"

I could see from the way he took it that he hadn't expected me to answer differently. He stood up, and looked at me. I asked him what he was going to do with me.

"I don't decide these things," he answered. "I can only explain the procedure to you. I shall have to draw up a report about you and send it to Berlin. They will make the decision there. I must await their instructions."

"How long will that take?"

"I can't say, Mr. Rocker. Three weeks, maybe, or three months, perhaps a year."

I didn't like this uncertainty. But what worried me most was that I had no way of communicating with Milly. I might have disappeared from the earth for all that she could know. At the same time I was grateful for the decent way in which Lieutenant Merck spoke to me and treated me. I hadn't expected it of a Prussian officer. But Lieutenant Merck was not a professional soldier.

Difficult days followed. I was quartered in the school building, but I had to appear twice every day at the railway station. The soldiers behaved well.

They knew all about me. Some told me they were social democrats, and tried to talk to me whenever there was a chance. Each week a new batch of repatriates arrived from England. They were a welcome change for me, and there were always some among them whom I had known in the camps in England. They never stayed long. I always remained behind, alone in the big school building, till the next batch of repatriates arrived. Only one soldier who had been assigned to watch me never failed to turn up at night.

I was struck by the way everybody I met, soldiers and civilians, spoke about the war; they were tired of it, and disappointed, praying for peace. At first I thought they said these things deliberately, to trap me into some remark that they could use against me. But I was soon convinced that these were their true feelings.

Three weeks passed in this way. On the evening of 10th April I was alone in the school hall, when the telephone rang. There was no one else there to answer, so I picked up the receiver. It was Lieutenant Merck, asking for me.

"Listen, Mr. Rocker," he said. "I have just received the decision about you. You were out of Germany for more than ten years. As you never reported to a German Consulate abroad you have lost your German nationality. For this reason you will not be admitted to Germany. You must return to Holland. The train leaves at ten o'clock to-morrow morning for the Dutch frontier. I'll arrange it all for you in the morning."

I couldn't believe my ears. But my heart was already drumming out a march of liberty. I could have wished for nothing better. I was already composing in my mind the letter I would write to Milly as soon as I was safe in Holland.

I was up early next morning. I had slept very little during the night. I had felt much too happy thinking that I would soon be out of this, a free man again. Lieutenant Merck was already at the railway station when I came.

"Well, Mr. Rocker, how do you like the decision?" he greeted me.

"I couldn't have wished for anything better."

"I can well believe it," he said. "May I say that I am very happy about it too, for your sake."

He handed me a document that he had already prepared for me to show to the Dutch authorities. It read:

The stateless repatriate from England, Rudolf Rocker is returned to Holland on the instructions of the Deputy General Command VII. He has been refused admission to Germany.

Frontier Guard Post at Goch.
11th April 1918.

(Signed) Merck, Lieutenant.

The lieutenant and all his soldiers shook hands with me when my train drew in, and wished me luck. There were few passengers on the train. At Hassum, the last German frontier station, we all had to get out to be examined. I had just put my foot down on the platform when a man came up and said to me: "You must be Mr. Rocker."

I told him I was; he took me to a small room in the station. Before he could say a word to me the telephone rang. He answered it, then turned to me: "Lieutenant Merck wants to speak to you."

"Listen, Mr Rocker," the lieutenant said. "Just as you left a new batch of repatriates arrived from England, among them a lady who was interned all the time with your wife. She would like to tell you about her. If you take the next train back to Goch you can have a word with her, and go to Holland in the afternoon.

I thought for a moment. Then I remembered that I had heard something in Goch about the frontier between Holland and Germany being closed shortly. I decided not to risk going back to Germany. I asked Lieutenant Merck what the lady had to say about Milly. Was she well? "She says your wife is well and cheerful," he answered.

"Then I shall continue my journey to Holland," I said. "But let me tell you first how grateful I am to you for your kindness in letting me know."

"Thank you," he said. "God be with you! One word more: I hope that some day you will become a Christian again."

My companion was tugging at my sleeve. "Hurry up!" he cried. "The train is leaving."

I picked up my case and ran. I had no sooner got into the train than it moved off. I had gone without being examined. But there was nothing in my case that would have been on the list of prohibited articles.

In half an hour we were at Gennep. A young Dutch lieutenant came and asked for my passport. I said I had no passport. But I had a document which might serve the same purpose. I produced Lieutenant Merck's statement. He read it, and shook his head.

"You mean to say that you are not a German? You were born in Germany, weren't you; your parents were Germans?"

"Yes," I said, "but there is a law in Germany which gives the government the right to withdraw German nationality from anyone born in Germany if it so wishes. That is what has happened to me."

"I have never heard of such a thing," he exclaimed. "If you were born in Germany how can anyone deprive you of your nationality?"

"You see that it has happened to me."

He asked me if he might make a copy of my document. I gave it to him, and he copied it and returned it to me. Then he explained that all foreigners who had no means were interned in Holland.

I said I had been interned in England all through the war. As for means, I had £10 with me, and I had friends in Holland.

"Where do you want to go?"

"To Hilversum."

"Whom do you know there?"

"My old friend Domela Nieuwenhuis."

"Oh, yes, we know him!" said the lieutenant, suddenly very friendly. "Very well, you are free to go."

I had to wait two hours in Gennep for the train to Utrecht. I spent the time writing a letter to Milly. I arrived in Hilversum about 4pm. It was a glorious spring day. I walked to Schoklaan, where Nieuwenhuis lived. He was sitting on the verandah. We hadn't seen each other for ten years. His hair had gone quite white, and he looked old. We embraced, and he gripped my hand without saying a word. His wife came out, and we were soon sitting together, talking.

I was only a lad when I first met Nieuwenhuis in Brussels in 1891. He was then at the height of his powers, and his words at the second congress of the new Socialist International had gone straight to my young heart. I looked at the grand old man with respect and affection.

I thought of the battles that lay ahead, the new struggles that the end of the war would bring. Now I was a free man again. A feeling of happiness came over me. I was ready.

Epilogue

This book ends with Rocker deported from England shortly before the end of the 1914–1918 war, after years of internment as an "enemy alien" — Olympia, Royal Edward and Alexandra Palace.

The general reader who does not know Rocker's years of fruitful work since 1918, till today, should not be left to close this book on the last page under the impression that it was the end of Rocker's life-long struggle. Though Rocker does in his last sentence, as Sir Herbert Read emphasises, speak of "the battles that lay ahead, the new struggles" for which he was ready, one should say a word here about Rocker's later work, the struggles in which he engaged. It was much later than the period of this book, for instance (the manuscript was the one thing he could save from the Nazis when Milly and he fled from Hitler's Germany) that he wrote his great book *Nationalism and Culture*, which Sir Herbert Read calls one of the classics of libertarian socialism.

We leave Rocker in this book a free man again, after so many years of constraint, deprived of his liberty, torn away from Milly and their young son, from his friends and comrades, confined with thousands of other civilian prisoners of war, with most of whom he shared only common birth in Germany against whose Kaiser and regime he had fought, and where he was regarded as an enemy to be clapped in jail if they got hold of him. He was in neutral Holland, with his old friend and comrade Nieuwenhuis.

Before long the German Revolution broke out; the Kaiser and his regime were overthrown. Rocker returned to Germany, and became one of the leaders of the international syndicalist libertarian movement. Unlike England, and America, the scene of Rocker's activities after he left Germany nearly a quarter of a century ago, there was no special Jewish libertarian movement in Germany. Rocker continued of course his interest in the Yiddish-speaking movement and his contacts with his old London Jewish comrades. But his activities, which had never been confined to the Jewish movement, as we know from his London friendships with Kropotkin, Malatesta and other international leaders of the world-wide libertarian movement, his contacts with the English movement, and his positions in the Anarchist International and the Anarchist Red Cross, which he held while he worked with us in the Yiddish movement in London, were now mainly devoted to the general movement.

It is not for me to speak of Rocker's ceaseless work in Germany for the movement, his writings, his lectures, his friendships with leading thinkers in the German socialist movement generally, and with the masses. To me he was still and he has remained my teacher of his London years. I had known him and Milly since I first came to London as an immigrant, a *greener* in 1902 and, largely under the spell of Rocker's oratory and personality joined the movement in which he was for decades the dominating figure among the masses of the Jewish immigrant workers.

In 1929, when I came to Berlin as one of the delegates to the Poale Zion World Conference, one of the first things I did was to go to see Rocker and Milly. He was away lecturing, when I arrived at the house, but a message was sent to him, and as soon as he could he left his meeting to come to see me and to talk to me. We had much to talk about, all about the old days in London that were so dear to him and to me. For I was one of those who had stood at his side in London during the tailors' strikes of 1906 and 1912, in which he had been our guiding spirit, in the formation of the Workers' Circle in 1909, in the affairs of the *Arbeter Fraint* group, and in many other activities of our movement. My visit was a breath of the old Jewish London to whose memory he has remained attached all these years.

In 1932 Rocker and Milly were in London; it was my privilege to welcome them on behalf of the Jewish Workers' Circle, which gave them a public dinner.

The following year Hitler took over in Germany; Rocker and Milly had to flee, leaving behind their home, his big library, most of his manuscripts, practically everything they had.

Since then Rocker's home has been in America. Again, in the New World, he flung himself tirelessly into his propaganda and cultural work. He travelled all over the American continent, lecturing. He wrote and published books. It was in America that he published his magnum opus, *Nationalism and Culture*, which he had written in Germany, the one possession he had saved from the Nazis.

I read in the *Freie Arbeter Shtimme*, and I heard through letters from friends of Rocker's work in America since he had settled there in 1933. I followed his activity with admiring interest. I read and heard of his coast-to-coast lecturing tours. I heard from old London friends who met him on those tours when he came to their towns. I read his articles in the *Freie Arbeter Shtimme*.

In America, Rocker found again many of his former London Jewish comrades and friends, and an active Jewish libertarian movement, with an old-established Yiddish paper, the *Freie Arbeter Shtimme*, and a spirit that reminded him of our old "golden youth" in London.

Rocker exercised an influence in the immensely large Jewish trade union and labour movement in America. I had the opportunity three times to see Rocker and Milly in America, when I was there in 1949, 1952 and 1954. There are many things I treasure in my memory of my American visits; my meetings with Rocker and Milly stand out among them. When I saw them last, two years ago, at their home in Crompond, they were old people, frail and ill; Milly has died since.

This book has its genesis in those American meetings of mine with Rocker and Milly. When I was with them in Crompond in 1949 we spoke about the days of our "golden youth" in London. That is how we came to work out a plan for the publication of that part of his autobiography which concerns his years in London. Together with our comrades in the Argentine we published this book in Yiddish in 1952. It made many of us feel that it would be desirable to have the book published in English. The idea was put forward on a number of public occasions in the Jewish trade unions and the Workers' Circle. When I was again in Crompond in 1954, I submitted a plan to Rocker for the comrades in London to publish the book in English translation. I am proud, on behalf of all the friends who have helped in this work, to present Rocker's book.

Sam Dreen

Ordering Information

AK Press
674-A 23rd Street,
Oakland, CA 94612-1163,
USA

Phone: (510) 208-1700
E-mail: akpress@akpress.org
URL: www.akpress.org
Please send all payments (checks, money orders, or cash at your own risk) in U.S. dollars. Alternatively, we take VISA and MC.

AK Press
PO Box 12766,
Edinburgh, EH8 9YE,
Scotland

Phone: (0131) 555-5165
E-mail: ak@akedin.demon.co.uk
URL: www.akuk.com
Please send all payments (cheques, money orders, or cash at your own risk) in U.K. pounds. Alternatively, we take credit cards.

For a dollar, a pound or a few IRC's, the same addresses would be delighted to provide you with the latest complete AK catalog, featuring several thousand books, pamphlets, zines, audio products and stylish apparel published & distributed by AK Press. Alternatively, check out our websites for the complete catalog, latest news and updates, events, and secure ordering.

Rudolf Rocker
Anarcho-Syndicalism: Theory and Practice
$12.95 • pb • AK Press
ISBN 1 902593 92 8

"The publication of Rudolf Rocker's *Anarcho-Syndicalism* is an event of much importance for people who are concerned with problems of liberty and justice. Rocker expresses throughout his faith in the capacity of ordinary people to construct for themselves a world suited to their inner needs, to create and participate in an advancing culture of liberation in free communities, to discover through their own thought and engagement the institutional arrangements that can best satisfy their deeply rooted striving for freedom, justice, compassion and solidarity, at a particular historical moment. This vision remains as inspiring as when it was written a half century ago, and no less valid as a stimulus to our thinking and our constructive action."—Noam Chomsky

"[Rocker's] exposition of anarcho-syndicalism at the peak of its influence is both a precious document of its time and a valuable reminder in our time of the continuing importance of an essential element in the complex ideology of anarchism."—Nicolas Walter

In 1937, at the behest of Emma Goldman, Rudolf Rocker (1873–1958) penned this political and philosophical masterpiece as an introduction to the ideals fueling the Spanish social revolution and resistance to capitalism the world over. Within, he offers an introduction to anarchist ideas, a history of the international workers movement and an outline of the strategies and tactics embraced at the time (internationalism, federalism, anti-militarism, direct action, sabotage and the General Strike). This new AK edition includes an introduction from Noam Chomsky, and a lengthy historical and biographical preface from Nicolas Walter.

Other Titles from AK Press

Books

MARTHA **ACKELSBERG**—*Free Women of Spain*

KATHY **ACKER**—*Pussycat Fever*

MICHAEL **ALBERT**—*Moving Forward: Program for a Participatory Economy*

JOEL **ANDREAS**—*Addicted to War: Why the U.S. Can't Kick Militarism*

ALEXANDER **BERKMAN**—*What is Anarchism?*

HAKIM **BEY**—*Immediatism*

JANET **BIEHL** & PETER **STAUDENMAIER**—*Ecofascism: Lessons From The German Experience*

BIOTIC BAKING BRIGADE—*Pie Any Means Necessary: The Biotic Baking Brigade Cookbook*

JACK **BLACK**—*You Can't Win*

MURRAY **BOOKCHIN**—*Anarchism, Marxism, and the Future of the Left*

MURRAY **BOOKCHIN**—*Post-Scarcity Anarchism*

MURRAY **BOOKCHIN**—*Social Anarchism or Lifestyle Anarchism: An Unbridgeable Chasm*

MURRAY **BOOKCHIN**—*Spanish Anarchists: The Heroic Years 1868–1936, The*

MURRAY **BOOKCHIN**—*To Remember Spain: The Anarchist and Syndicalist Revolution of 1936*

MURRAY **BOOKCHIN**—*Which Way for the Ecology Movement?*

DANNY **BURNS**—*Poll Tax Rebellion*

CHRIS **CARLSSON**—*Critical Mass: Bicycling's Defiant Celebration*

JAMES **CARR**—*Bad*

NOAM **CHOMSKY**—*At War With Asia*

NOAM **CHOMSKY**—*Language and Politics*

NOAM **CHOMSKY**—*Radical Priorities*

WARD **CHURCHILL**—*On the Justice of Roosting Chickens: Reflections on the Consequences of U.S. Imperial Arrogance and Criminality*

WARD **CHURCHILL**—*Speaking Truth in the Teeth of Power: Lectures on Globalization, Colonialism, and Native North America*

HARRY **CLEAVER**—*Reading Capital Politically*

ALEXANDER **COCKBURN** & JEFFREY **ST. CLAIR** (ed.)—*Dime's Worth of Difference*

ALEXANDER **COCKBURN** & JEFFREY **ST. CLAIR** (ed.)—*The Politics of Anti-Semitism*

ALEXANDER **COCKBURN** & JEFFREY **ST. CLAIR** (ed.)—*Serpents in the Garden*

DANIEL & GABRIEL **COHN-BENDIT**—*Obsolete Communism: The Left-Wing Alternative*

VOLTAIRINE **DE CLEYRE**—*Voltairine de Cleyre Reader, The*

EG SMITH COLLECTIVE—*Animal Ingredients A–Z (3rd edition)*

HOWARD **EHRLICH**—*Reinventing Anarchy, Again*

SIMON **FORD**—*The Realization and Suppression of the Situationist International: An Annotated Bibliography 1972–1992*

YVES **FREMION** & **VOLNY**—*Orgasms of History: 3000 Years of Spontaneous Revolt*

BERNARD **GOLDSTEIN**—*Five Years in the Warsaw Ghetto*

DANIEL **GUERIN**—*No Gods No Masters*

AGUSTIN **GUILLAMON**—*The Friends Of Durruti Group, 1937–1939*

ANN **HANSEN**—*Direct Action: Memoirs Of An Urban Guerilla*

WILLIAM **HERRICK**—*Jumping the Line: The Adventures and Misadventures of an American Radical*

FRED **HO**—*Legacy to Liberation: Politics & Culture of Revolutionary Asian/Pacific America*

STEWART **HOME**—*Assault on Culture*

STEWART **HOME**—*Neoism, Plagiarism & Praxis*

STEWART **HOME**—*Neoist Manifestos / The Art Strike Papers*

STEWART **HOME**—*No Pity*

STEWART **HOME**—*Red London*

STEWART **HOME**—*What Is Situationism? A Reader*

JAMES **KELMAN**—*Some Recent Attacks: Essays Cultural And Political*

KEN **KNABB**—*Complete Cinematic Works of Guy Debord*

KATYA **KOMISARUK**—*Beat the Heat: How to Handle Encounters With Law Enforcement*

NESTOR **MAKHNO**—*The Struggle Against The State & Other Essays*

SUBCOMANDANTE **MARCOS**—*¡Ya Basta!: Ten Years of the Zapatista Uprising*

G.A. **MATIASZ**—*End Time*

CHERIE **MATRIX**—*Tales From the Clit*

ALBERT **MELTZER**—*Anarchism: Arguments For & Against*

ALBERT **MELTZER**—*I Couldn't Paint Golden Angels*

RAY **MURPHY**—*Siege Of Gresham*

NORMAN **NAWROCKI**—*Rebel Moon*

HENRY **NORMAL**—*A Map of Heaven*

HENRY **NORMAL**—*Dream Ticket*

HENRY **NORMAL**—*Fifteenth of February*

HENRY **NORMAL**—*Third Person*

FIONBARRA **O'DOCHARTAIGH**—*Ulster's White Negroes: From Civil Rights To Insurrection*

DAN **O'MAHONY**—*Four Letter World*

CRAIG **O'HARA**—*The Philosophy Of Punk*

ANTON **PANNEKOEK**—*Workers' Councils*

BEN **REITMAN**—*Sister of the Road: the Autobiography of Boxcar Bertha*

PENNY **RIMBAUD**—*The Diamond Signature*

PENNY **RIMBAUD**—*Shibboleth: My Revolting Life*

RUDOLF **ROCKER**—*Anarcho-Syndicalism*

RUDOLF **ROCKER**—*London Years*

RON **SAKOLSKY** & STEPHEN **DUNIFER**—
Seizing the Airwaves: A Free Radio Handbook

ROY **SAN FILIPPO**—*A New World In Our Hearts:
8 Years of Writings from the Love and Rage
Revolutionary Anarchist Federation*

ALEXANDRE **SKIRDA**—*Facing the Enemy: A
History Of Anarchist Organisation From
Proudhon To May 1968*

ALEXANDRE **SKIRDA**—*Nestor Mahkno—
Anarchy's Cossack*

VALERIE **SOLANAS**—*Scum Manifesto*

CJ **STONE**—*Housing Benefit Hill & Other Places*

ANTONIO **TELLEZ**—*Sabate: Guerilla
Extraordinary*

MICHAEL **TOBIAS**—*Rage and Reason*

JIM **TULLY**—*Beggars of Life: A Hobo
Autobiography*

TOM **VAGUE**—*Anarchy in the UK: The Angry
Brigade*

TOM **VAGUE**—*The Great British Mistake*

TOM **VAGUE**—*Televisionaries*

JAN **VALTIN**—*Out of the Night*

RAOUL **VANEIGEM**—*A Cavalier History Of
Surrealism*

FRANCOIS EUGENE **VIDOCQ**—*Memoirs of
Vidocq: Master of Crime*

GEE **VOUCHER**—*Crass Art And Other Pre-
Postmodern Monsters*

MARK J **WHITE**—*An Idol Killing*

JOHN **YATES**—*Controlled Flight Into Terrain*

JOHN **YATES**—*September Commando*

BENJAMIN **ZEPHANIAH**—*Little Book of Vegan
Poems*

BENJAMIN **ZEPHANIAH**—*School's Out*

HELLO—*2/15: The Day The World Said NO To
War*

DARK STAR COLLECTIVE —*Beneath the
Paving Stones: Situationists and the Beach,
May 68*

DARK STAR COLLECTIVE —*Quiet Rumours:
An Anarcha-Feminist Reader*

ANONYMOUS —*Test Card F*

CLASS WAR FEDERATION —*Unfinished
Business: The Politics of Class War*

CDs

THE EX—*1936: The Spanish Revolution*

MUMIA **ABU JAMAL**—*175 Progress Drive*

MUMIA **ABU JAMAL**—*All Things Censored Vol.1*

MUMIA **ABU JAMAL**—*Spoken Word*

FREEDOM ARCHIVES—*Chile: Promise of
Freedom*

FREEDOM ARCHIVES—*Prisons on Fire: George
Jackson, Attica & Black Liberation*

JUDI **BARI**—*Who Bombed Judi Bari?*

JELLO **BIAFRA**—*Become the Media*

JELLO **BIAFRA**—*Beyond The Valley of the Gift
Police*

JELLO **BIAFRA**—*High Priest of Harmful*

JELLO **BIAFRA**—*I Blow Minds For A Living*

JELLO **BIAFRA**—*If Evolution Is Outlawed*

JELLO **BIAFRA**—*Machine Gun In The Clown's
Hand*

JELLO **BIAFRA**—*No More Cocoons*

NOAM **CHOMSKY**—*An American Addiction*

NOAM **CHOMSKY**—*Case Studies in Hypocrisy*

NOAM **CHOMSKY**—*Emerging Framework of
World Power*

NOAM **CHOMSKY**—*Free Market Fantasies*

NOAM **CHOMSKY**—*New War On Terrorism: Fact
And Fiction*

NOAM **CHOMSKY**—*Propaganda and Control of
the Public Mind*

NOAM **CHOMSKY**—*Prospects for Democracy*

NOAM **CHOMSKY/CHUMBAWAMBA**—*For A
Free Humanity: For Anarchy*

WARD **CHURCHILL**—*Doing Time: The Politics of
Imprisonment*

WARD **CHURCHILL**—*In A Pig's Eye: Reflections
on the Police State, Repression, and Native
America*

WARD **CHURCHILL**—*Life in Occupied America*

WARD **CHURCHILL**—*Pacifism and Pathology in
the American Left*

ALEXANDER **COCKBURN**—*Beating the Devil:
The Incendiary Rants of Alexander Cockburn*

ANGELA **DAVIS**—*The Prison Industrial Complex*

JAMES **KELMAN**—*Seven Stories*

TOM **LEONARD**—*Nora's Place and Other Poems
1965–99*

CASEY **NEILL**—*Memory Against Forgetting*

CHRISTIAN **PARENTI**—*Taking Liberties:
Policing, Prisons and Surveillance in an Age
of Crisis*

UTAH **PHILLIPS**—*I've Got To Know*

DAVID **ROVICS**—*Behind the Barricades: Best of
David Rovics*

ARUNDHATI **ROY**—*Come September*

VARIOUS—*Better Read Than Dead*

VARIOUS—*Less Rock, More Talk*

VARIOUS—*Mob Action Against the State:
Collected Speeches from the Bay Area
Anarchist Bookfair*

VARIOUS—*Monkeywrenching the New World
Order*

VARIOUS—*Return of the Read Menace*

HOWARD **ZINN**—*Artists In A Time of War*

HOWARD **ZINN**—*Heroes and Martyrs: Emma
Goldman, Sacco & Vanzetti, and the
Revolutionary Struggle*

HOWARD **ZINN**—*A People's History of the United
States: A Lecture at Reed College*

HOWARD **ZINN**—*People's History Project*

HOWARD **ZINN**—*Stories Hollywood Never Tells*

DVDs

NOAM **CHOMSKY**—*Distorted Morality*

ARUNDHATI **ROY**—*Instant-Mix Imperial
Democracy*